Doing Qualitative Analysis in Psychology

Doing Qualitative Analysis in Psychology

Edited by

Nicky Hayes

Department of Behavioural Sciences,
The University of Huddersfield

Psychology Press
a member of the Taylor & Francis group

Reprinted 1998

Psychology Press Ltd, Publishers
27 Church Road
Hove, East Sussex
BN3 2FA
UK

British Library Cataloguing in Publication Data

A catalogue record for this book is available from the British Library

ISBN 0-86377-740-6 (Hbk)
ISBN 0-86377-741-4 (Pbk)

Typeset by DP Photosetting, Aylesbury, Bucks
Printed and bound in the United Kingdom by Biddles Ltd, Kings Lynn

Contents

PART II: THEORY-DRIVEN APROACHES TO QUALITATIVE RESEARCH

PART III: GROUNDED THEORY AND PHENOMENOLOGY

Acknowledgments

The Editor would like to thank Ros Day, Vina Patel, Christine Sefton, Colin Smith, Mark Simpson, Tanya Sagoo, Rohays Perry, the reviewers, and the contributors for their many different forms of help in the preparation of this text.

Thanks also to Metro Pictures and Blackwell Publishers for allowing us to use material for this book.

This book is dedicated to Amnesty International, and all royalties are being donated to this worthy cause.

Nicky Hayes

1

Qualitative research and research in psychology

Nicky Hayes
Department of Behavioural Sciences, University of Huddersfield

The aim of this book is to provide psychology students, and others, with examples of different ways of going about qualitative research. The idea originally developed during a meeting to discuss issues around qualitative research in psychology, which in turn had arisen from an initiative funded by the British Psychological Society's Scientific Affairs Board. The various psychologists involved in this book all have an interest in, and a commitment to, qualitative research of one form or another. The book's diversity is a testament to the many different forms that such an interest and commitment can take.

QUALITATIVE RESEARCH: SOME BACKGROUND

Qualitative research in psychology is not new. In psychology's early years, it was commonplace: a trawl through the psychological journals of the 1920s and 1930s reveals many papers which discuss personal experience as freely as statistical data. Indeed, the founder of experimental psychology, Wilhelm Wundt, together with other "introspectionists" of the last century, was under no doubt that qualitative methods were as valid a way of developing a scientific understanding of the human being as were quantitative approaches, and more appropriate in many respects (see e.g. Farr, 1996).

This position changed with the advent of the behaviourist revolution, which dominated both American and British psychology for many years. Following a somewhat idealised version of physical science (see Hayes,

1995), behaviourism emphasised a reductionist approach, seeking the basic "elements" of behaviour and rules of combination. Although behaviourism as such was rejected with the advent of the "cognitive revolution" in the 1970s and 1980s, its methodology, and in particular its emphasis on controlled experimentalism, was retained by the psychological community as a whole. Undergraduates were socialised into research paradigms which emphasised the identification of single causes, and in which the ultimate goal of psychological research was portrayed as "pure" data, which was "uncontaminated" by complex, uncontrollable influences from the world outside the research laboratory.

This resulted in a systematic devaluing of qualitative methods (and also, incidentally, of higher-order theory-building) since the idealised model of physical experimentation emphasised reliability, generalisability, and a redefinition of validity. The insistence on reliability of research findings negated the study of unusual or one-off human experiences, while the search for generalisable rules produced an emphasis on normative methods, which in its turn negated the study of human experiences which were unique and personal. Validity became redefined in a self-referential manner, emphasising the comparison of new methods with pre-existing criteria, and de-emphasising relationships between measures of behaviour and the way that people went about their day to day lives. The outcome was a scientific community in which qualitative research was viewed with deep suspicion. Unless, of course, it occurred in a medical context: it is worth noting *en passant* that investigators of brain function or similar areas have always been free to adopt qualitative methods (e.g. Penfield & Rasmussen, 1950). Presumably, the scientific nature of their topic meant that their methods were accepted as "scientific" by association, and were therefore beyond suspicion.

In recent years, however, another paradigm shift has become apparent. Qualitative approaches are becoming increasingly accepted as a valuable part of modern psychology. This change is particularly visible at research levels, where an increasing number of conference papers and research projects are incorporating qualitative analyses to augment and enrich quantitative information, and some have eschewed quantitative techniques altogether. A growing concern about problems of artificiality in research data, together with an equally growing interest in "ecological validity" and research which is relevant to the problems of society, have produced a realisation that qualitative techniques may have a great deal to offer.

A search for factors underlying this gradual paradigm shift produces several sources. One of them is the influence of feminist psychology, with its challenging of positivistic and sterile empirical analyses, and its insistence that psychological research should tackle human meaning and experience as well as behaviour. Another factor can be identified in the growing importance of ethical issues in research, and the development of guidelines and principles for psychological researchers. The conscious rejection of a researcher's entitlement to manipulate the "subject" without their consent led to an awareness of the need to respect the research participant. While some researchers sought more imaginative and considerate experimental techniques, others re-evaluated their research questions, and adopted alternative methodologies such as account analysis, which were more able to express that respect. A third factor may be located in research funding. As more research was commissioned by agencies and commercial bodies, and researchers needed to emphasise the applicability of their research projects, real-world research began to change from a poor relation to a more respected type of psychological. Accompanying this re-orientation was a recognition that qualitative methods were often the most suited to real-world research projects.

Given these factors, and others, it has become apparent that qualitative analysis is not a passing fad on the part of researchers, but something completely different. To some, it is an entire philosophy of research; challenging and replacing outdated positivistic methodologies. To others, it is a much-needed addition to the range of methods available to the research psychologist. Each phase of psychology's history has left its mark on its methodology, ranging from the quantitative surveys and experimental techniques of the behaviourist school, to the clinical interview which was the legacy of Piaget in the 1950s and the ethological methods which evolved in developmental and comparative psychology during the 1960s. It is too soon to label the present period, but the growth of interest in qualitative research is strong, and its growing incorporation into psychology does appear to reflect the present mood.

Further indication of the increasing acceptance of qualitative methods is also apparent in the way that so many undergraduate courses are incorporating an introduction to qualitative analysis into their methodology courses. Virtually all psychology students undertake practical work as part of their courses, and their induction into the research methods of the discipline plays a primary role in their socialisation as psychologists. For the reasons already given, more and more psychology students are seeking to conduct research which is relevant to the real world, and this research is often particularly suited to qualitative forms of analysis. There is, however, relatively little guidance for students on how to set about undertaking such research, although there are a vast number of books on quantitative methods of psychology. Hence this book.

WHAT IS QUALITATIVE RESEARCH?

One of the issues thrown into broad relief by this book is the question of what we mean by qualitative research—or, to be more specific in this particular case, by qualitative analysis. Conventionally speaking, qualitative methodology has tended to be associated with a concern on the part of the researcher with meanings, context, and a holistic approach to the material. It has generally been seen in opposition to quantitative methodology, which, in psychology at least, often produced extremely restricted attempts to measure human behaviour or human cognitive process, which severely lessened their relevance to everyday living.

At first sight, the terms appear straightforward: we use the term "qualitative" in opposition to "quantitative", and this appealing dichotomy appears to represent a clear distinction between the two. When we examine the criteria implicit in that dichotomy, though, the distinction becomes rather less clear. Hammersley (1992) identified seven component meanings of the qualitative/quantitative divide, which are listed in Table 1.1. While each appears on the surface to be a dichotomy, on closer examination they are revealed to refer to a range of values, not a simple either–or distinction. Although Hammersley was discussing these issues in relation to sociological and ethnographic research, and not all of them are entirely appropriate to psychology, there are enough similarities to make them worth exploring briefly.

The first of these component meanings is to do with quantification. For some, this seems straightforward: for example, Strauss and Corbin (1990) insist that qualitative analysis is analysis which does not involve numbers or counting. For others, however, the distinction is more problematic. Quantities can be, and often are, indicated using words: concepts such as "more", "fewer" or "frequent" are not unknown in qualitative research, and these are all about quantification. Hammersley (1992) argued that the real issue here is not about numbers or words, but about establishing an appropriate level of precision for the data. Numbers, too, can be imprecise at times, particularly where they imply an exactness in the data which is not justified. What appears to be a clear dichotomy is really a continuum when we look at

TABLE 1.1
Component Meanings of the
Qualitative/Quantitative Divide

---

1. Qualitative vs quantitative data
2. Natural vs artificial settings
3. Focus on meanings rather than behaviour
4. Adoption or rejection of natural science as a model
5. An inductive vs a deductive approach
6. Identifying cultural patterns vs seeking scientific laws
7. Idealism vs realism

Adapted from: Hammersley, 1992.

it more closely, and that continuum is all to do with the degree of precision which our data expresses.

A second, generally implicit, meaning of the qualitative/quantitative divide has to do with whether the investigation takes place in "natural" or "artificial" (controlled experimental) settings. It is possible, of course, to dismiss the concept of "artificial" settings, on the grounds that a court of law, a shopping centre, or a classroom is no more "natural" than a psychological research laboratory, but this distinction also conceals a more fundamental issue. This is to do with the control which the researcher exerts on the data. Research may take place in "natural" settings yet still be tightly controlled, as both organisational and consumer psychologists are aware. Alternatively, a research project may be located within an "artificial" setting yet still involve a qualitative approach to the material: a classic example here, of course, being Irwin Silverman's investigations of the human subject in the psychological laboratory (Silverman, 1977). The "natural/artificial" distinction thus becomes another range of values, rather than a straightforward dichotomy.

Across the range of values, however, it is certainly possible to argue that qualitative research has become associated with less insistence on control on the part of the researcher, at least at the period of initial data collection. For the most part, psychologists committed to qualitative analysis tend to be interested in listening to and analysing what their research participants can tell them—whether visually or verbally. As a result, they generally seek ways of collecting those data which constrain the research participants as little as possible. This concern is apparent in the various chapters of this book, where it manifests itself in many different ways.

A third meaning of qualitative research which Hammersley identifies is that it focuses on meanings rather than behaviour. Again, this dichotomy reveals itself to be an indicator of a range of values rather than a dualism: some quantitative research is directly concerned with meaning, such as the quantitative analyses of social representations discussed by Doise, Clemence and Lorenzi-Cioldi (1993); whereas there are many examples of qualitative analyses, such as some forms of conversation analysis (e.g. Zimmerman, 1992), where the emphasis is on understanding behaviour rather than meaning. Although, of course, qualitative research sits more happily towards one end of this continuum than the other, it is important to bear in mind that it *is* a continuum and not the simplistic dualism which it might appear to be on the surface.

The rejection of a natural science model of research is another issue that has come to be associated with qualitative research, and in psychology, at least, it ties in very closely with the fifth issue identified by Hammersley, which is concerned with the distinction between inductive or deductive methodologies. There are a number of points to be made here; but the central one is that again, we are dealing with a range of issues rather than *division 2 parts .*

with a straightforward dichotomy. There are many natural sciences, and they adopt a wide range of different approaches to research. Biology, astronomy, and even nuclear physics utilise research methodologies which are very different from the idealised experimentation implicit in some research debates. Whether a researcher uses an inductive or a deductive methodology is again less of a dichotomy than it may seem, and the distinction is also less tightly linked with the use of qualitative methods than some have implied. The chapters in this book provide a range of examples of qualitative analysis in this respect: from inductive, grounded-theory approaches to an explicitly hypothetico-deductive approach.

The sixth meaning which Hammersley attributes to the qualitative/ quantitative distinction may have more relevance for sociology and anthropology than for psychologists; although if it is reformulated into an issue about description as opposed to prediction it has relevance in psychology too. Many of the contributors to this book aim to cultivate understanding through description. Others, though, use qualitative analysis as a way of investigating predictive laws or principles; while for many, the iterative processes involved in description lead on to the development of more general laws. Yet again, the apparent dichotomy disguises a range of possibilities.

The final issue in Table 1.1 is that of idealism vs realism. Some theorists (e.g. Smith, 1989) have associated quantitative research with a realist epistemology, and qualitative research with idealism. This raises the philosophical question of whether there is a necessary connection between qualitative method and a particular epistemological position. Some of these issues are explored in the final chapter of this book, while others are scattered throughout the other chapters, but the range of approaches manifest here implies that a simple one-to-one connection is elusive, to say the least. While qualitative research may sometimes lean towards idealism and quantitative research towards realism, neither is irretrievably associated with one or the other.

The overall message, then, is that any attempt to produce simplistic distinctions between qualitative and quantitative research is liable to fall apart on closer inspection. Absolute pronouncements about qualitative research, or even just about qualitative analysis, are unlikely to hold true in all circumstances. Our aim for this book, therefore, is that it should reflect some of the diverse forms and richness of qualitative analysis in psychology. It does not aim for homogeneity, or consensus.

ABOUT THIS BOOK

This book aims to provide the student with something which is a little more than a "cook-book" of techniques. Of course, it can be used in this way, and a student or researcher who wishes to is welcome to do so. On the other hand, adopting a qualitative methodology can involve a fundamental change in the way that the individual regards psychological research. To this end, the book's contributors have each outlined the methodological and theoretical features of their approach to qualitative research, in order that the reader can become familiar with some of the assumptions which they are making. They have also described their particular techniques for undertaking qualitative analysis and where possible illustrated them with a practical example drawn from their own research. By combining theory and methodology with practical examples, we hope that the book can also be used to provide an insight into some of the issues and debates which qualitative research can generate.

There are three main sections to the book, although it must be admitted that they are somewhat arbitrary distinctions. Other ways of grouping the chapters were possible, and were also considered. But the end result is that, roughly speaking, Chapters 2–5 are primarily concerned with the analysis of accounts and discourse; Chapters 6–8 are examples of theory-driven approaches to qualitative research; and Chapters 9–12 deal with grounded theory and its ramifications. A brief introduction is provided for each section.

As even a brief glance will reveal, the book adopts a pluralistic orientation towards the question of qualitative analysis, which reflects the many different orientations adopted by its authors. The diversity of the chapters and their content raises a number of issues, and spans several different continua. The contributors to the book have not attempted to adopt a single view of qualitative analysis, nor have they even confined themselves to an agreed meaning of the word "qualitative".

Labelling all of the various issues raised by this book would be an impractical task. But some are worth mentioning explicitly. For example, a continuum could be drawn which had hypothetico-deductive models at one end and the rhetorical frames of discourse analysis at the other. Another continuum deals with a range of approaches to theory. Some chapters use a research framework in which all data is interpreted in terms of a prior theory; while others adopt a grounded theory approach, in which theoretical insights develop through an iterative analytical process. These are, of course, surface manifestations of massive philosophical debates about the nature of science and enquiry; and each, as we can see, provides us with different types of research insight.

Another set of issues is concerned with the data. The chapters in the book reflect a variety of forms of data, ranging from verbal data in the form of accounts, interviews, and spontaneous discourse, to visual images in the form of murals or self-portraiture. They also reflect a range of treatments of the data, particularly in terms of the amount of processing which they receive prior to interpretation. Some deal with their data "neat", as it were, while others deal with it by applying rhetorical frames, by extracting attributions, or even applying complex coding procedures. The value of each of these approaches is apparent from the chapters themselves.

Research questions are also diverse, ranging from something as straightforward as an airline company wanting to know how to increase passenger satisfaction, to an appraisal of political messages in murals; from an attempt to understand the social processes of memory construction, to an appraisal of the social as well as the artistic dimensions of self-portraiture. While many of the topics of the book lie within the vague classification known as "social psychology", the range of these topics carries its own message about their potential for application in other fields.

Psychology is itself a pluralistic discipline, and there are many ways that qualitative analysis can contribute to that pluralism. As we have seen, research psychologists make widely differing assumptions: about their data; about the nature and importance of theory; about the process of analytical enquiry; and about the relevance or value of particular research questions. That pluralism is a strength, giving a flexibility and dynamism in the way that we approach the study of human experience. Some of that strength, we hope, has been reflected in this book.

ACCOUNT ANALYSIS AND ITS RELATIVES

INTRODUCTION TO PART I

Rom Harré

This first group of chapters is concerned with account analysis of various forms, and begins with a discussion of approaches to the study of accounts from Rom Harré. Chapter 2 is set within Harré's ethogenic perspective for the understanding of social life. Put very simply, ethogenics involves the argument that the appropriate unit of study for social psychologists is not the act or action, but the episode. Life is lived as a series of episodes, not as a series of disconnected acts, and it is these which give structure and meaning to our experience.

In studying episodes, we need to look at the whole context of what is happening including the people concerned, the ways in which they express themselves, the background to what is going on, the setting in which events are taking place, and so on. So instead of just looking at individual utterances in conversations, for instance, we need to look at the whole conversation in terms of its social meaning. In that context, the accounts which we give of our experiences form an important part of what gives social life its meaning: through accounts, we define ourselves and the nature of our experience, and in so doing re-structure and organise our reality. The giving of an account is, of course, a social episode in its own right, and in that sense it is primary data; but it is also a second-order appraisal of prior episodes and their social implications. Account analysis is therefore a major focus for research within the ethogenic approach.

In this chapter, Rom Harré discusses some of the methodological and theoretical requirements for a qualitative approach to social psychology. As a second-order source, the account is capable of revealing something of its underlying "psychologic", and the chapter is concerned with outlining methods by which that goal may be achieved. There are three main phases in this process. The first is to do with exploring the resources which are available for the discursive production of an aspect of social reality. The second is to do with understanding how those resources are put to use in the production of social life; and the third with the development of models which may integrate this information into an understanding of social reality.

Within the first of these three phases, Harré discusses conceptual analysis and repertory grid analysis. Conceptual analysis may have several techniques associated with it, and Harré describes two: language analysis, and "psychologic". Both the language that people use, and the nature of their second-order expressions or appraisals, are structured elements in their accounts which can provide considerable information about underlying concepts. Repertory grid analysis, when combined with the first method, can extend the depth of the analysis even further. Using this method, the researcher is able to develop a map, or display, of the internal structure of a semantic field by eliciting personal constructs and exploring their applicability to other elements. Combining the two methods, therefore, allows the researcher to gain a rich idea of the discursive resources available within the production of the account. Harré explores this with an illustration drawn from research aimed at identifying a psychologic of embarrassment.

The second phase, of understanding how resources are utilised in the production of social life, also has two methods described in the chapter. The first of these is that of discourse analysis, which in Harré's approach has two aims: firstly, to reveal the act/action structure of a particular episode of human interaction, and secondly, to identify and understand the construction of the various psychological phenomena which are brought into being as the episode unfolds. Using the three concepts of position (or voice), act-force (or social significance) and conventions (or story-lines), Harré demonstrates how this form of analysis can be applied in the analysis of conversation. The second method described in this part of the chapter is concerned with account analysis. This approach takes the stance that an account is a secondary text, and consists of looking for the roles, conventions, meanings and norms which are contained within the account. The three concepts of position, act-force and convention have their relevance here as well.

Finally, Harré explores issues of model-making, and the construction of a social psychological understanding of the episode. At one level, episodes may be viewed as consisting of layers of problem-solving procedures. At another level, there are a range of social questions about power and the discursive strategies which are used to maintain it; while at yet another level, episodes may be analysed in terms of the use of standard forms of accounting, such as ritualised patterns or the application of typologies.

Mick Billig

In Chapter 3, Mick Billig describes the use of discourse analysis for exploring conversations. The research uses conversations about the royal family, taken in the context of family discussions. These were drawn from a larger research project into discourse about the British royal family, which was designed to investigate ideological and socially significant themes emerging from the way that families discussed the topic.

The form of discourse analysis discussed in this chapter has its roots in the discursive approach to psychology: an approach which is far more than simply a method of analysis or a research technique. Rather, it comprises an entire theoretical approach to psychology, with philosophical roots in the work of Wittgenstein and Austin. This approach emphasises the primacy of language, seeing discourse as an end in itself, and not as a tool for identifying some hidden underlying psychological condition. Discourse analysis, therefore, looks at the patterns of language use in everyday conversation, and at the social functions and implications of speech acts.

What this means, of course, is that it is meaningless in discourse analysis to attempt to study a conversation outside of its social context. The analyst needs to develop an understanding of the role of the speech act, and of what people are doing (consciously or unconsciously) through their discourse. The study of conversations inevitably takes place within the context of shared notions about "common-sense", including a number of maxims and clichés, which rhetorical analysts refer to as "common-places", and which often contradict one another. These common-places are part of the context of the discourse which is being studied, contradictions and all. They are not problematic, because of the way that people adopt different "voices" in different social situations, which reflect equally valid realities. Indeed, the study of apparent contradictions in discourse can be one of the most revealing sources for a discourse analyst.

Discourse analysts may become concerned with a number of different areas of investigation, chief among which are: the analysis of explanations and the social functions which they serve; explorations of "memory talk" and the way that memories are jointly agreed and constructed through social interaction; and analyses of the discursive repertoires and rhetorical stances which people adopt in varying situations, and which in the discourse model have come to supersede the study of attitudes. Mick Billig illustrates something of each of these types of investigation, focusing particularly on the social construction of memories.

Mick Billig also provides both guidance and discussion about collecting the material and transcribing it. From the point of view of discourse analysis, there are advantages to collecting data through group discussions rather than individual interviews, and these are theoretical in nature as well as practical. As has been mentioned above, an understanding of the social context within which the discourse takes place is essential for discourse analysis, and the discussion group itself provides part of that social context. In the case of family group discussions, the context provided by the group is particularly rich.

The chapter also encompasses a brief introduction to some of the most useful transcription conventions, and some indication of the likely nature of choices for indexing, such as the distinction between topic-based indexes, and those concerned with conversational actions. Billig discusses theoretical hunches, the goals of developing a composite picture or an in-depth analysis of examples, and the cyclical nature of drafting and re-drafting the report. The analysis of a single brief extract reveals how ideological themes demonstrate their associated contradictions, and explores how memories are both recalled and re-created as specific incidents are discussed. What emerges throughout this account is a thoughtful and articulate explanation of the dynamic and continuous interactions between researcher and material which characterises discourse analysis.

Halla Beloff

The approach to qualitative analysis illustrated by Halla Beloff, in Chapter 4 reveals intriguing contrasts and similarities to Mick Billig's work. The most dramatic contrast, of course, lies in the fact that Beloff uses visual imagery rather than the written word, and in terms of the epistemological and philosophical basis of Billig's analysis, this difference alone might be expected to render an uncrossable gulf between the two approaches. Yet, in Beloff's model, the visual image itself is treated as a rhetorical stance: Beloff uses the techniques of rhetorical or discursive analysis to discuss the various types and levels of message encapsulated in the image, in much the same way as the discursive analysis of a conversation explores the various types and levels of message encapsulated in the conversation and its context.

The chapter is concerned with the series of self-portraits produced by Cindy Sherman, in 1987—or rather, with a selection of them. At regular intervals, ever since 1977, Sherman has presented an exhibition consisting of images of women—all of them self-portraits, but the images so very different from one another that the self portraiture is by no means apparent. Beloff explores the questions this raises about definitions of identity, together with the nature of self-portraiture.

So far so good. But other rhetorical themes are also present in Cindy Sherman's work, which become apparent as Beloff discusses a series of self-portraits which explore the cultural icons and images encapsulated in movie characters and settings. These portraits show how the images move beyond accounts of self, to bring social, and even archetypal, concepts forward into our awareness, or near-awareness. Another series explores grotesqueries of one form or another, challenging many of the accepted conventions of portraiture and exploring a range of themes, from death to gender role.

Beloff's analysis of the data shows us how the methods and approaches of discourse analysis can be adopted when exploring the visual image as well as for the written the spoken word. Beloff identifies a number of themes which emerge from Sherman's data, using a number of different categories. There are general themes to be extracted, as well as specific messages demonstrated particularly graphically by certain images. Beloff explores five of these themes, and discusses their broader implications, and the ways in which they become integrated into one's overall experience of the art-work.

Like other chapters in this book, this chapter ends with a "how to do it" guide for the particular approach to qualitative analysis under discussion. Reading visual rhetoric is inevitably to some extent a non-verbal process, and part of its challenging nature derives from the way that the process imposes a requirement that the non-verbal experience must be recognised and analysed verbally. For many years, Halla Beloff has been a virtuoso model for other psychologists in this field, eschewing simplistic or mechanistic techniques which negate the personal and social meanings of the experience, and advocating a personal involvement in the process of analysis which can only enrich our psychological understanding.

Carol Sherrard

In Chapter 5, Carol Sherrard explores the potential for discourse analysis to investigate the kinds of topics which more mechanistic forms of psychology refer to as "attitudes". While traditional social psychology has regarded an attitude as a relatively stable, enduring trait, the discourse approach regards them as dynamic, unstable phenomena, which are continually being created and re-created through conversation. Discourse analysis focuses on the way that attitudes shift, and their functions also alter, during discourse, and emphasises that attitudinal observations or statements are essentially a form of persuasion, shaping and shaped by the conversation which the individual is participating in at that particular moment, and in that particular context.

For this reason, discourse analysts are particularly interested in the forms of language expression which reveal attitudes, in the way that attitudes shift during conversation, and also in any attitudinal inconsistencies which are revealed as the discourse proceeds. These inconsistencies have traditionally been problematic for attitude theorists operating on a model of attitudes as stable, internal traits; but they are far less so for those who examine them adopting the discourse approach. Indeed, in this approach, it is the inconsistencies which can provide the most valuable data, revealing as they do the interactive and persuasive nature of the communication.

The interest in language expression means that discourse analysis will often focus on the particular word or phrase which is used in the discussion, and will explore the implications of the choice of that particular word or phrase rather than any other. Language—whether written or spoken—is not seen as objective or impartial, nor is it regarded as a transparent medium. Words are used in everyday discourse as much for their effect on the other person as for their expression of an internal state, so the forms of expression adopted during a particular communication need to be explored in their own right, as both persuasive and defensive contributions to the social interaction which is taking place. For this reason, controversial or challenging topics lend themselves particularly well to discourse analysis.

Sherrard uses a step-by-step approach to illustrate how this sort of discourse analysis might be carried out. She begins by outlining the stages which such an analysis might involve and subsequently goes through each step again using a particular example: a section of an interview about class and aesthetic taste, conducted as part of a wider field of research. Both of these step-by-step analyses provide a great deal of useful detail, and also contain several "pointers" which are directly helpful to students attempting to conduct discourse analysis.

Sherrard also indicates a selection of questions which researchers can use to focus their interpretation of the discourse, and which will help to structure that interpretation by indicating a specific level of analysis. The worked example of the interpretation provides examples of how these questions operate in practice, and shows how they can come together to reveal a number of different rhetorical devices, which together encapsulate the ways that various attitudinal statements or positions have been used during the course of the conversation.

2 An outline of the main methods for social psychology

Rom Harré
Department of Psychology, Georgetown University

INTRODUCTION

It has sometimes been said that the qualitative approach to the study of psychology is "unscientific". It is not always clear just what is meant by such a criticism. The natural sciences are notable for the precision with which they characterise their data and the generality of the theories that are constructed to account for what has been discovered. Some "old paradigm" psychologists think that qualitative methods must lack precision and generality. In this chapter I shall describe some of the methods that have been developed by critics of the old paradigm. There can be no doubt that, though they do not lead to numerical results, they are nevertheless of great precision. The question of generality is more difficult to address, since it seems that there are some features of human psychology that are found among all human beings, of whatever culture, and others that are not.

There are many kinds of precision to be found in the natural sciences; some can be transferred to psychology and some cannot. Numerical measurement against a fixed standard has no place in most branches of psychology. However, exacting and careful working out of the relationships between concepts is necessary whatever aspect of human life we are study-

Part of this chapter has been extracted from the book *Social Being* (2nd ed.), by Rom Harré, published by Blackwell 1993. Reproduced with permission.

17

ing. Some of the methods to be described in this chapter are aimed at establishing very precise analyses of meaning, as a major feature of human action.

Generality is another matter. It may be that in some cases generality can only be achieved by reaching for higher and higher levels of abstraction. For example in studying human emotions we find that there are great differences between the repertoires displayed by people from different cultures. By talking of "affect", a term invented by psychologists for all forms of bodily feeling at a very high level of abstraction, a kind of generality is achieved, but almost all the psychologically relevant features of our emotional lives are lost. For example the all-important distinction between moods and emotions is lost if both are described as "affecting states". We must be more modest in our work. We should start with detailed studies of local ways of thinking, feeling, acting, deciding and so on, without presuming that the same patterns will be found amongst other tribes. If similarities do show up, well and good. If they do not that too is important.

There are still deeper matters to consider in trying to devise a systematic method of studying human life. The natural sciences make wide use of causal concepts. Explanations of physical, chemical and biological phenomena are built around the idea that what we observe or bring about experimentally are effects of causes, and that there are unobservable causal mechanisms which produce these effects. In many episodes of human engagement the cause-effect pattern seems wholly out of place. For example it would be difficult to account for a tennis match in cause-effect terms. Tennis is an activity played according to rules and conventions, while the players make use of strategy and tactics in their efforts to win. Of course the racquet–ball relationship is causal, but it would be a gross distortion of psychological reality to offer a causal explanation of a victory that depended on controlling the centre of the court. Ceremonials are much like tennis, though rarely competitive. In cases like these explanations must be given in terms of roles and rules. A psychological explanation of much that goes on in a courtroom must make reference to the diverse roles of the actors and the rules and conventions that govern what they can say and do.

The question that we need to answer is this: for all those many human phenomena such as making decisions, forming friendships, liking and disliking people, bringing up children and so on, should we adopt the cause-effect analytical and explanatory format or should we go for the role-rule way of understanding what is going on?

There are two main reasons for developing a methodology on the basis of the role-rule point of view. One has to do with our general picture of how human beings act. If we are thinking in cause-effect terms we must presume that the individual human actor is a passive spectator of the working of some causal mechanism. Friendship would not be something we work at but an automatic response to the obtaining of such conditions as frequency of meeting, shared interests and so on. If we are thinking in role-rule terms we shall take people to be active agents, using their knowledge of the local rules and conventions to bring various projects to fruition. Friendship is something we work at creating, marking its stages in various ceremonial ways and so on. There is another reason for adopting the role-rule approach. It comes from attention to how infants and children become competent members of their societies. Instead of thinking of human development as a matter of maturing individuals, each new stage triggered by some external event, but predestined in the way development proceeds, we see development as a process of gradual acquisition and privatisation rule and practice from a public world. What was once explicit becomes implicit and habitual.

Why is there any debate? Is it not obvious that only the role-rule principle makes any sense in investigating most human behaviour? The problem is this: In most of our social and cognitive activity we do not consciously access rules and we are rarely aware moment by moment of the roles we are filling. In these circumstances are we driven by the workings of causal mechanisms, or are we carrying out the injunctions of implicit and tacit rule-systems? The methods of research to be described in this chapter are based on the assumption of the second of these alternatives. It is the job of the psychologist to make implicit rules and meanings explicit, to make the tacit overt. The job of the psychologist is to bring back the tacit to conscious awareness.

Finally, the fact that human beings are above all *talkers* should be at the forefront of our attention. So much of our lives are managed in public discussion, in conversations of all kinds. So much of our private thoughts are patterned on public conversational conventions. Language initiates, controls and repairs our interactions. It is the medium by which most of what we want to accomplish is achieved, both privately and publicly. Language proper is surrounded by a penumbra of language-like activities, to which the same combinations of methods that are appropriate for purely linguistic studies can be usefully put to work.

We shall need to recruit the services of analytical philosophers for the first phase. Philosophical analysis will reveal the interrelations and conceptual structure of the vocabularies with which the members of a loosely bounded community act and with which they repair and comment upon action. The fine grain of local conceptual resources, down to individual versions of these, can be revealed by the use of repertory grids. Neither of these interlocking methods will reveal how people put these resources to work in the moment-by-moment joint production of social episodes.

To reveal the normative constraints on the discursive processes of the public production of social reality we shall need to draw on the techniques of discourse analysis, pioneered by the ethnomethodologists and communication theorists. We shall also need to use account analysis, since it is only in accounts that we see the explicit formulation of a version of some of the local norms of correct action.

The final step will be to sketch the method of dramaturgical replication, in which the knowledge made explicit in the studies reported above can be put to work in a simulation of the social world which can be created by its explicit use as a script for action.

METHOD I: CONCEPTUAL ANALYSIS

Outline of the Procedures

Conceptual analysis is directed towards the discovery of those structures of ordinary language that are at work in the way that people manage those of their activities that are roughly comprehended under the rubric "psychological". By that I mean such activities as "deciding on a course of action", "displaying hurt at having been humiliated", "manifesting an attitude towards some topic", "remembering" and so on. The method is identical with that practised by Wittgenstein and by the philosophers of the classical "Oxford" tradition, namely a description of how this or that word is used. The aim, of course, is different. In using this method in psychology we are not trying to resolve intellectual puzzlements or dispel illusions, though that may from time to time be a bonus.

Conceptual analysis is also directed towards setting out the normative principles of the relevant discourses; what are the correct and incorrect ways of using the appropriate vocabulary. This aspect of analytical methodology has been called "psychologic" by Smedslund (1988), and is the basis of the technique Stearns and Stearns (1987) have called "emotionology". In these studies we are partly concerned with the local conditions under which people make use of the conceptual connections embedded in their linguistic resources.

The Technique of Language Analysis

The first step is to assemble the vocabulary with which we ordinarily create some psychological phenomenon, such as deciding or remembering. This vocabulary will involve both first and second order expressions. By that I mean that it will include expressions such as "the other day I . . ." and the expressions by which we comment upon and repair the uses of the first order expressions, for instance words and phrases involving the word "remember". An "emotionology", as Stearns and Stearns have defined it, is the second order conceptual system by which people manage the first order system. Compare the way we use such an expression as "you clumsy oaf" with the way we use expressions like "angry". The first is a way of creating an anger display, the second for commenting upon it. Only the second belongs to an emotionology.

As Wittgenstein so often warns us, we must suspend any preconceptions or theories we may have picked up about a certain vocabulary. His own supremely elegant and powerful investigations of concepts like "reading" and "thinking" are wonderfully free of preconceived ideas about what the structured use of these concepts might be. Above all we are to be beware of picking on one use and trying to make all the others conform to its. This leads to the second phase of the method: the assembly of instances of the use of the vocabulary in question, from which one makes various attempts to formulate a "grammar", that is an account of the norms which these examples exemplify. One must also look for counter-examples to the norms one has proposed. This is not for the purpose of applying a falsificationist methodology, but to map out the boundaries of the use of a word. If "deciding' is conceptually related to "thinking" what are we to make of the use of a phrase like "McEnroe decided to play a drop shot" when the situation seems to be such as to preclude an interval of reflection?

The Technique of 'Psychologic'

The method through which a psychologic is displayed involves two main principles.

First, the internal structure of the system of a fragment of psychologic, say that around the concept of "action", will manifest itself in necessary or conceptual truths. A working sign of a conceptual truth is that everyone, in the local language community, will assent to it. This is, of course, only a necessary and not a sufficient condition for that logical status. Further analytical work must be done (Parrott & Harré, 1992). For example everyone might assent to the proposition that "an action is what someone intends". Only as embedded in a whole network of such propositions could it be shown conclusively that this is not an empirical generalisation. The point is an important one. In a recent controversy around this very pair of concepts Coulter (1992) shows Bilmes to be wrong in taking "intending" to be a mental state, just correlating with acting. But to do so Coulter assembles a range of uses.

The second principle ties conceptual structures to what people do. People organise their cognitive activities, their actions and their emotions in accordance with these conceptual truths. They are not only operative in the organisation of accounts, but also—tacitly for the most part—they are at work in the organised production of the action and of other psychological phenomena.

The methodology involves two steps. People will assent both to conceptual truths and to broad empirical generalisations. Participants are asked to identify which statements, from a repertoire, they think are always true, sometimes true and never true. This is the test of *universal assent*. But only some of those statements universally assented to will be conceptual truths and so be part of the network of concepts that constitutes a psychologic. The investigators must work with the candidate generalisations to try to construct an organised system. That is the second step. Factual truths will lie outside such a system. This is the *test of logical coherence*.

Only if both these are passed do we have grounds for announcing the outlines for a fragment of a psychologic.

Illustration: Towards a Psychologic of Embarrassment

I shall draw on the work of several psychologists in sketching the method of psychologic at work in this example. However I shall mainly be using my own investigation, carried out with J. Parrott and published in our paper of 1992. We can begin with an informal or rough analysis of the concept of "embarrassment", before we turn to the fine details of a psychologic exploration.

There are several other emotions of social control; prominent among them are chagrin and shame. Chagrin is displayed, for instance, when we realise that we have failed in the execution of a project to the success of which we have publicly committed ourselves. It is a kind of disappointment, but one which involves our public reputation. Shame is akin to embarrassment, in that it is both "cognitive", we show we know what we did was morally wrong; and "expressive", it serves as a public act of contrition. Embarrassment is appropriate in moments of public action but the failure is not a moral fault. In many cases embarrassment serves to display our realisation that we have broken or ignored a social convention or rule of good manners.

It seems that there are two main ways we can fail in an embarrassing way. Our conduct can be improper or unconventional, with respect either to social action or to bodily presentation. Or our conduct can be inept or incompetent, with respect to social action or bodily presentation. So far as I know (and I am indebted to Dan Robinson for the observation) only the latter form of failure was distinguished in classical Greece, by the name *amechania*.

Young Americans assent to a number of statements involving the concept of embarrassment that they take to be generally true; for instance both "Realising one's public behaviour is offensive can be an occasion for embarrassment" and "Receiving public praise can be embarrassing". Behind these lies the deeper principle that occasions for embarrassment arise when one believes one's behaviour, appearance etc. is the subject of appraisal by others. Is this an empirical generalisation or an axiom or theorem of a psychologic? Again the informants in our study assented without exception to the following pairs of statements. "If one believes that others are aware that one has committed a moral fault one would be ashamed" and "If one believes that others are aware that one has behaved ineptly one would be embarrassed". Are these empirical generalisations, axioms, or theorems of a psychologic?

The answer to these questions can come only from the result of an attempt to construct a psychologic. We believe that we have succeeded in organising some of the inner conceptual structure of at least part of the field of the emotions of ineptitude and moral fault in the following:

Axiom 1:   P can react with signs of confusion if, on any occasion, P believes that P or P's conduct is properly an object of comment by others, Q, R, and so forth with whom P is socially interacting.

Axiom 2:   P can react with signs of confusion if, for any reason, P believes that P or P's conduct is a proper subject of moral disapproval by others, Q, R, and so forth with whom P is socially interacting.

Definition 1:   (a) P is socially interacting with some Q, if P believes that Q is aware of P; (b) P is socially interacting with some Q, if P and Q share some standards of correct conduct (including the presentation of bodily appearances).

Definition 2:   (a) Being disapproved of is a mode of personal assessment; (b) Being approved of is a mode of personal assessment.

(Note: Definitions 1a and 1b express two of the necessary conditions for an interaction to be counted as a social interaction.)

Axioms 1 and 2 express the most general conditions in which embarrassment and shame are to be expected. Yet they seem to miss the core psychological content of the concept. What is it about how we believe we look that occasions embarrassment rather than any other possible emotion? We need an axiom that ties our reactions to real or imagined comments on how we look or what we have done to an implicit valuation of persons.

Axiom 3:   P is said to be embarrassed when P displays signs of confusion in reaction to real or imagined comments on P's appearance or conduct that would imply that P is inept, ignorant, or foolish.

Axiom 4:   P is said to be ashamed when P displays signs of confusion in reaction to real or imagined comments on P's appearance or conduct that imply that P is evil, indisposed, or otherwise morally defective.

Axiom 5:   Some offensive conduct is an occasion for disapproval.

Axiom 6:   Some praiseworthy conduct is an occasion for approval.

(Note: Axioms 5 and 6 express necessary truths about the concepts of conduct and its assessment, not about the concept of embarrassment. They are drawn from another fragment of PL.)

Theorem 1:   Some offensive conduct is an occasion for embarrassment.

(This theorem follows from Axioms 1, 2, and 5 together with the relevant definitions.)

Theorem 2:   Some praiseworthy conduct is an occasion for embarrassment.

(This theorem follows from Axioms 1, 2, and 6 together with the relevant definitions.)

Further theorems developing the 'shame' concept can easily be proved.

It follows that the generally accepted statements of the paragraph above are conceptual truths, and so serve to display the inner structure of the concept of embarrassment, in relation to other similar concepts. Of course there are also a number of statements which attract general assent that tell us what kinds of conduct and what situations and predicaments our informants found embarrassing. These we take to be empirical generalisations.

In relation to the larger project of founding a social psychology on the principles of the discursive approach, what have we found out in these investigations? Linguistic analysis and psychologic explorations begin to reveal the discursive resources or conceptual repertoires with which competent social actors jointly create evolving social realities. The work of analysis is essentially static. It reveals a system which is locally and momentarily stable, and on the joint use of which the possibility of managing a social episode depends.

METHOD II: REPERTORY GRID ANALYSIS

Outline of the Procedure

There are many excellent manuals explaining the details of the techniques of repertory grid analysis, for instance Fransella and Bannister (1977). Computer programs are available for ready and rapid analysis of the data. I shall give only a sketch of the procedures without going into detail—just enough,

I hope, to make clear why this is an essential tool for a psychology based on the discursive idea. The literature of personality psychology is rich in "instruments", that is scales and checklists for ascertaining the effect of certain "treatments" on the subjects of an experimental procedure. Leaving aside the objections to the cause-effect metaphysics on which this kind of procedure is based, there is a pair of insurmountable problems in taking any of the answers seriously.

What guarantee is there that the participants understand the vocabulary of the checklists in the same manner as the experimenter does, and in the same manner as each other? Consistency is no guarantee either! The Milgram experiment is a startling example of a conceptual gap between the understandings of the participants and that of the experimenter. For Milgram the leading concept of his psychologic was "obedience", but it is easy to show that the psychologic shared by most of the participants in their understanding of what was said by the experimenters was "trust".

The second insurmountable problem concerns the question of whether the participants in an investigation would have used the vocabulary of the "instrument" were they free to comment "in their own words". So called "pretesting" of an instrument is no guarantee! In my judgement these problems render a huge proportion of the published studies in social and personality psychology worthless. These "instruments" are works of the Devil.

Kelly (1955) invented the repertory grid technique partly to overcome this set of problems. He had the idea that people make their way into the material and social world much as scientists do in their studies. They develop concepts for tackling the particular job in hand. "Man the scientist" joins the repertoire of images of humanity alongside *homo sapiens*, *homo ludens*, and many others. While I find Kelly's slogan unconvincing, his technique has proved to be remarkably powerful.

A Sketch of Repertory Grid Technique

The components of a grid are a set of elements, predetermined by the investigator, such as people or situations, and a set of constructs, created by the participants, each for his or her own grid. A construct is a pair of polarised concepts, such as "rich ... poor". Each construct can be taken as a scale, with absolute or relative intermediate values, that is as a representation of a rating or of a ranking of elements. In the most sophisticated development of this kind of analysis constructs themselves can become elements in further grids. Analysis of each grid reveals the structure of the resources used by its creator for the classificatory task in hand. Comparison between grids reveals changes over time, if the grids are made by the same person at intervals; or similarities and differences between the conceptual resources of participants, if some assumptions about common meanings of key terms can be justified by the application of the analytical techniques of Method I.

Construct elicitation can be achieved in a wide variety of ways. The handiest is simply to take the elements proposed for a study in threes. As a participant, one asks oneself "in what way are the first and second alike and different from the third?" Then one takes the first and third against the second and the second and third against the first; and so on through the whole set of elements. Schematically a grid will begin to look like Fig. 2.1.

Once the grid is complete the participant ranks all the elements with respect to all the constructs, using whatever numerical scaling system is appropriate.

Analysis is aimed at finding out which concept-pairs or constructs are consistently used for the same sets of elements and which are more widely deployed; and which elements are taken to be alike and in what ways. A fully analysed repertory grid could be interpreted as a display of the internal structure of a semantic field.

The question remains as to why some sets of constructs are consistently used for the same element or set of elements. Are the constructs merely lexical variants of the same concept-pair, or are they internally related as they would be in a psychologic? Method II, repertory grid analysis, needs to be combined with Method I, linguistic analysis and psychologic, to give a fully detailed and methodologically adequate answer to the question originally posed: what are the resources available to someone for the discursive production (with others) of a strip, fragment or aspect of local social reality? The next stage of an investigation will require somewhat different techniques, since we need to have a way of understanding how the resources available are put to use in the production of social life.

METHOD III: DISCOURSE ANALYSIS

Functions and Structures of Discourse

The research programme of new paradigm social psychology is built around a very general notion of "discourse". Almost any intentional use of language is to be counted as a part of discourse. Since the analytic methods now to be described are aimed at the understanding of the dynamics of

Elements   e1   e2   e3   etc.

Constructs

C1a ... C1n
C2a ... C2n
etc.

FIG. 2.1.   The form of a repertory grid.

social life they must be extended to cover not only linguistic ɛ
also the use of any mode of communicative exchange, inclu
dress and so on that plays a part in the discursive constructi
logical phenomena.

A discourse, in the special sense given to this rather loosely used term in
new paradigm social psychology, is a sequence of jointly produced acts. The
object of discourse analysis is two-fold:

1. The analysis is aimed at revealing the act-action structure of a
   sequence of actions constitutive of an episode human interaction. This
   includes the special case of reflexive interactions when the other is
   oneself.
2. The analysis is also aimed at identifying the psychological phenomena
   which are brought into being in the course of the unfolding episode
   and understanding how they are discursively constructed.

These will include emotions, cognitions of various sorts such as inferences
and decisions, personas, selves, memories, genders, health and illness and
many, many more. It must be emphasised that it does not mean to say there
are no material conditions, such as the shapes and functions of bodily parts,
the state of the nervous system, bacterial and viral infections and so on, on
which the discursive edifices that we experience as psychological states and
processes are built.

In discourse analysis we are interested in revealing the structures of such
edifices and how they are built. How do we decide what actions to include
within a discourse? The criterion must be based on an assessment of function. A simple version could be whether the actions under scrutiny are taken
to have illocutionary force, that is whether they are involved in the joint
accomplishment of social acts. The research topic, so to say, of discourse
analysis is how the structures and the functions of discursive exchanges are
related. The active uses of discourse include not only the creation of psychological entities and states, but also certain classes of social relations. For
instance there are discursive practices by which people are assigned certain
speaking parts and roles ("voices") in the development of an episode. Such
"positions" can be defined in terms of one's rights, duties and obligations as
a speaker. For example, in some recent studies of the joint construction of
memories, Middleton and Edwards (1990) showed that the women members
of the group were positioned differently from the men, in that their rights to
correct tentative memory proposals were weaker than those of the men.

The functions of discourse are manifold. It is in and through discourse
that we construct the forms of personal experience, sometimes called
"subjectivity", for instance by Hollway (1984). This includes such structures
as that centred organisation of experience we call "the self". But it is also in

and through discourse that we construct our social being and the episodes in which it is made manifest. This aspect of human life is the topic of this chapter.

Discourse Analysis and Account Analysis

An account is a discourse in which the intelligibility and propriety of some other discourse is made clear, challenged or repaired. Potter and Wetherell (1987) include account analysis under the general umbrella of discourse analysis. Of course the giving of accounts is a discursive activity. But I think it important to distinguish two kinds of discourse. There is that with which social acts are accomplished and there is that with which we comment upon and theorise about those social acts. Accounts are discourses of the second kind. It is true and important that we realise that in giving accounts, we are, *inter alia* performing social acts. So any study of accounts must involve consideration of the account as a first order performance. Methodologically we will find it essential to distinguish between discursive activities which are wholly first order and those which are both first and second order. Some of the norms of social action are made explicit in accounts, though for all sorts of reasons. In first order discourse the norms of action are implicit. I shall treat the analysis of first and second order discourses as distinct analytical tasks.

The Structure and Elements of a Discourse

Episodes can be arranged in a spectrum with respect to the degree to which the sequence of act-actions constitutive of the episode is controlled by a pre-existing structured template, such as a formal protocol for the carrying through of a ceremony. To understand the formal episodes we need concepts like role and rule. To understand the less formal we can make use of the three interrelated concepts of position (or voice), illocutionary or act-force (or social significance), already introduced above, together with the idea of local narrative conventions (or story-lines). In analysing a record of some social interaction as discourse, a record obtained through video or audio technology or even by the old fashioned medium of note taking, the analysis can be initiated by trying to identify these three features: "position", "act-force", and "story-line". These are the discursive concepts by means of which we hope to reveal the dynamics of social episodes.

As an episode unfolds it is possible that some of the action will include acts of repositioning. Once the actors are repositioned the significance of their actions as social acts may change, while the story-line that is being lived out can modulate into a different set of narrative conventions.

When analysing records of discursive interactions it is vital to bear in mind that a person's actions, their intended behaviour, may be seen by other interlocutors in many different ways. It is not unusual for the public act-force of what someone is taken to have done not to be what they intended. From the point of view of social psychology it is the force that an action has in the public sphere that matters. A remark may be meant as a piece of advice by a speaker but is taken by another participant in the conversation as an act of condescension, while another takes it up as the speaker intended. It follows that a discourse analysis of an interactional episode may reveal more than one conversation occurring simultaneously on the basis of a single flow of utterances. From the point of view of the social psychologist, it is the conversations that are or should be the focus of study, since it is through them that social status is created, attitudes displayed, memories authenticated and so on. How can we tell how many and what conversations are occurring? Only by attending to the subsequent actions of the participants, and the act-forces we take them to display. Each act constitutes a social psychological reality.

The concept of position or voice brings out the important qualification that "speaker" or "actor" ought not to be identified with the named or indexed person. The unit of analysis is "actor" not "person". The analysis of an episode from the discursive point of view is quite likely to disclose that the match between "actor" or "speaker" and "person" is complex, with some people appearing as more than one actor and others as less than one. There are very interesting cases in which a person's contributions to conversation are always supplemented (and sometimes corrected) by one of the others. So the illocutionary or act-force of the first person's utterances is created by the contributions of the second person.

The act-actions created by mutual intention and uptake among the participants in social interactions form structures, usually strongly sequential, though there may be other forms of order too. What does discourse analysis reveal about these structures? There are three main structural forms, which I shall distinguish as the formal, the narratological and the minimal.

In a formal structure positions are roles, and there are well-defined "accomplishment points" in the sequence of act-actions. In the course of a trial there is the moment of giving the verdict, and then there is the moment of pronouncing sentence and so on. Story-lines give way to ceremonial protocols. However formal episodes, such as judicial trials, include other classes of episodes within their role-rule structure. There are nested informal and minimal episodes embedded within the formal framework.

There are any number of questions which discourse analysis can answer. For instance, how is order maintained in a court of law or in a parliament? In these institutions recourse is had to the protocol in which the proper order of act-action types is laid down. There are formal devices for ensuring its hegemony (Atkinson, 1985), and these two are structured by recourse to further protocols. How are people able to participate in such episodes? In general they are knowledgeable about where to find a script or some other representation of the protocol constitutive of the episode in question as being of a certain kind, or they are reminded of their next moves by someone to whom that role is assigned. This too is generally bound by protocol into a further formal episode. More often than not yet another formal step is undertaken through which the actors are committed publicly to respect the protocols. This may take all sorts of forms.

I distinguish episodes as "minimal" if they serve to accomplish a bare acknowledgement of personhood, and at the same time, a minimal structure of rights, a primitive moral order. For instance the simple discursive exchanges between motorist and pedestrian at a stop sign establish a personal relation between the protagonists, and assign differential rights to proceed. In a discursive analysis of these brief encounters, we should be able to identify a local lexicon of actions whose act-force is mutually understood, some conventions of sequence defining a minimal structure (a zero-level story-line) and two or more simple positions, one with the right to go, the other with the obligation to give way. The exchanges with beggars and their "clients" form another class of minimal episodes whose position/act-action/ story-line structure would be worth serious study. It is often the case that a discursive analysis of a more complex episode reveals that it opens with a minimal episode in which a bare acknowledgement of the personhood of the other is accomplished.

To illustrate the use of discourse analysis at its most subtle, namely in the analysis of the structures of informal episodes in which psychological phenomena are routinely brought into existence, I shall use the position/act-action/story-line triad to uncover the structure of an episode transcribed by Deborah Tannen (1986, p. 82). The conversation ran as follows:

(9) *Deborah:* 'Yeah?'
(10) *Peter:*   Before that ... I read The French Lieutenant's Woman? Have you {read that?}
(11) *Deborah:* {Oh yeah?} No. Whó wrote that?
(12) *Peter:*   John Fowles.
(13) *Deborah:* Yeah I've heard that he's good.
(14) *Peter:*   'He's a gréat writer. I think he's one of the bést writers.
     Deborah: hm.
(15) *Deborah:* /?/
(16) *Peter:*   'He's really, good.
(17) *Deborah:* /?/
(18) *Peter:*   But I get very busy ... {Y'now?
                 {Yeah. I-hardly ever
(19) *Deborah:* reàd.

(20) *Peter:*   What I've been doing is cutting down on my sleep.
(21) *Deborah:* Oy![{sighs}
(22) *Peter:*   [And I've been [Steve laughs]. . . .
               and I[s
(23) *Deborah:* I do that too
               [but it's painful.]
(24) *Peter:*   ] Yeah. Five, six hours a 'night,
               and]
(25) *Deborah:* [Oh Gód, hò can you dò it. You survìve?
(26) *Peter:*   Yeah làte afternoon mèetings are hàrd. . . . But outside
     Deborah: mmm
               of thàt I can keep going [pretty well
(27) *Deborah:* [not sleeping is
               terrible . . . I'd múch rather not eát than not sleep
               P
               [Sally *laughs*]
(28) *Peter:*   I pròbably should not eàt so much, it would . . . it would
               uh . . . sáve a lot of time.

From (9) to (17) there is one story-line being followed, while from (18) to (28) there is another. The shift in positions takes place at (18) in the remark ascribed to Peter. The first episode displays Deborah and Peter positioned as the complementary pair, "teacher" and "learner". The story-line is "instruction" and the speech-actions of the positioned interlocutors accomplish the relevant acts. But at (18) Peter repositions himself as "martyr" and this move is confirmed by Deborah who herself takes up the complementary position of "friend". A new story-line unfolds in which Peter tells a strip of his life with the narrative conventions of "hard times". Again the speech-acts shift to create the story. There are a sequence of statements, overtly describing a way of life, which have the performative force of complaints. But these complaints are also displays of personhood, as one who continues despite difficulties, a supervenient story-line 'hero triumphing over the odds', in which the 'hard times' story-line becomes a sustaining element. Deborah's remarks are a continuous stream of confirmations of the double line—how hard your life is and how heroically you overcome it.

This is a mere sketch. Much more would be required to complete an analysis. The choice of vocabulary, pronouns and so on are crucial elements in the way the effect is achieved. I need only enough detail to point out two significant features of the example. Neither story-line nor positions are freely constructed. The conversation has a *familiar* air. It reflects narrative forms already existing in the culture, which are part of the repertoire of competent members, who, like Peter and Deborah, can jointly construct a sequence of position/act-action/story-line triads. What psychological phenomena are these two jointly creating? At least Peter's personality—or rather, one should say, the one on show in this conversation. They are also creating a relationship, maybe a friendship, for the accomplishment of which this kind of joint work is a necessary ritual part. And so on.

METHOD IV: ACCOUNT ANALYSIS

Accounts as Texts

Accounts have a key role in both social action and social psychology. Social psychological texts are accounts and must be analysed as such. All accounts are texts, since accounting is a discursive practice, almost always accomplished directly with words. (Sometimes there are gestural accounts, but I shall concentrate in this discussion only on those which are spoken or written.) But what are accounts directed towards? The answer is to other texts, those of which discourse analyses in the manner of Method III can be given. This use of the term "text" is a common contemporary extension of the usual meaning, of a written or printed discourse. A conversation, indeed any episode to which the concept of "meaning" can be usefully applied, is in this extended sense, a text.

What does accounting accomplish? In general it is the act by which a text is made relatively determinate with respect to its *intelligibility* and its *warrantability*. Let us call the texts to which accounts are directed "primary" and the accounts "secondary". It should be clear by now that it is always possible for accounts to be taken as primary texts and further accounts to be constructed as secondary texts relative to them. To undertake accounting at all, the intelligibility and warrantability of the last level of account must be taken for granted. As Wittgenstein reminded us, the giving of rules must end somewhere—at a certain point he says "my spade is turned". There is rock bottom. Accounts at that level are constitutive of a form of life.

Searching Accounts

An account is a secondary text. As such it can be subjected to three methods of analysis which I have outlined, namely conceptual analysis, repertory grid analysis and discourse analysis. But the point of distinguishing account analysis from the other three analytical methods, is the task to which this kind of analysis is directed. At each level accounts describe norms and conventions. The principle upon which account analysis works is simple to state but not so easy to establish. It is this: the norms described (that is, made explicit) in an account as a secondary text are among the norms implicit in the primary text. The secondary text, as an account, is directed to displaying the intelligibility and warrantability of the primary text. Methodologically account analysis could hardly be simpler—

just search the account for explicit statements of rules and conventions, meanings and norms. These can be assembled according to a variety of schemes. One of the most fruitful is to classify the rule/convention material relevant to defining what is meaningful and proper action by reference to the distinctive kinds of episodes in which action of that kind would be appropriate. Along with this goes material describing the norms of self-presentation, to accord with the unfolding act-action structure.

Occasions for Accounting

How and when to elicit accounts? There are four main kinds of occasion in which people tend to provide accounts. Von Cranach (1981) and others have shown that accounts are routinely offered when the smooth flow of co-ordinated joint action breaks down. To the implicit question "What shall we do next?" the answer is often on account. We could call this, following Goffman, the "repair function". Then there are breakdowns in intelligibility of what is being done. It may be that the action is clear enough but the act is indeterminate. "I meant to..." followed by an explicit performative verb such as "congratulate", is the kind of opening that signals an account the function of which is to make an act determinate. But there may also be breakdowns with respect to the action level—is the actor doing whatever it is intentionally? Thirdly there are breakdowns in the warrantability of what is being done. Accounts here function to show that what was done, as act-action, is correct, proper and so on or not correct etc. Here norms of structure are made explicit. "In these circumstances I would have [meaning "you should have"] done so and so....". An account may look like advice. This raises the issue of accounts of accounts, and the analysis of the accounts within the framework of Methods I to III. For instance we may need to invoke the position/act-action/story-line triad to understand the illocutionary force of a statement as an account. Finally there is the situation of social instruction, in which a knowledgeable member of a cultural group gives overt instruction in the norms of intelligibility and warrantability to an untutored or ignorant novice. It is worth remarking that much of the instructional activity through which new members are incorporated into a culture, psychologically, is by psychological symbiosis, in which inadequate contributions offered by junior members are routinely supplemented by the senior to complete proper performances. By far the commonest occasions for accounting are breakdowns in the intelligibility and warrantability of actions.

What does account analysis contribute to the analytical task? We must remember that the psychological theory underlying the whole of the discursive programme is that human action is a skilled performance by active agents realising projects according to local norms. Account analysis enables us to add yet more material to our description of the resources that must be available to the competent and skilled actor. We must, however, beware of falling into the trap that has ensnared so many would-be scientific psychologists, the error of putting these resources into the heads of the individual actors. Most of the norms of those forms of human action in which psychological phenomena are created are immanent in the routine social practices of a culture, rather than available for discursive presentation. It can hardly be emphasised enough that the discursive presentation of the norms of a culture is a second order activity, the work of psychologists, grammarians, sociologists and the like. Of course people do give and receive accounts. But most are indirect and many are embedded in higher order account givings. That is why we cannot rely on Method IV alone but must *progressively* develop our understanding through the systematic and sequential use of the four methods of analysis of discourse.

CONCLUDING REMARKS

An enormous advantage of the discursive methodology over other ways of trying to elicit the norms of human action is that it can reveal (disclose) the constructive aspects of other forms of life. Unlike the experimental method or the main devices of so-called cross-cultural psychology, it is morally and metaphysically neutral. The traditional methods of academic psychology embody specific ontologies and local moral orders. A beautiful example of the use of the methods described in this chapter can be found in Lutz's (1988) marvellous study of the emotions of the Italuk. So far we have said nothing about the way to analyse, classify and explain the story-lines and formal "scripts" that are our way of expressing the orderliness of social interactions.

For that step we need to turn to the physical sciences for guidance—to the methodology of models. This is a problem for psychologists because of their idiosyncratic use of the word "model".

The Uses of Models: Social Action as a Problem Solving

I shall try to show that social episodes are made up of multiple "layers" of problem solving procedures. In performing the rituals for the introduction of a stranger to a social group we must establish that the being in question is a person to whom and by whom general duties of the maintenance of sociality are owed. In the same episode there are other, more specific problems to be solved, such as the question of the relative social status of the stranger once he or she is admitted to our group. The way problems of this kind are solved has important psychological consequences, for instance in how the constructive processes of memory formation will turn out in any actual case.

But there is a second dimension of generic problems, a dimension which is ever present in social interactions. At any moment we may need to solve the problem of whether and how what is going on is intelligible and warrantable as social action at all. Generally speaking this class of problem is solved by the giving and receiving of accounts.

However there is still the issue of the ultimate boundaries of sociality. Even in social psychology the question of "power" cannot be avoided (Parker, 1991). I address that issue in two ways. "Power" as "force" delineates the boundary of "the social", that is a solution to an everyday interpersonal problem achieved by physical coercion is an asocial solution. But what of the threat of physical coercion? Doesn't the social status, assumed character and so on of the one who threatens, relative to the one who is threatened, enter into the episode? It seems to me that threats of force are indeed part of a certain class of social solutions, so that for me they do not lie outside the boundary of the social. They are proper material for social psychological investigations.

The main question with regard to the kind of "power" that is exercised within the bounds of sociality, becomes "How is power of one person over another established and maintained discursively?", I shall call instances of this phenomenon the "Rasputin effect". The role of "power" as a sociological concept in describing how one group can have hegemony over another raises other kinds of questions, not to be addressed here. Power in this sense is not to be explicated as the summation of myriad instances of the Rasputin effect.

Act/Action Sequences as ritualised Solution Techniques

The great Japanese novelist Mishima once pointed out that we have to show both to ourselves and to others that we "willed" our actions. There seem to be two aspects to such an achievement. For one, social actors have to achieve recognition by the others around them that they are indeed social actors. Some categories of people, for example children, can find this recognition hard to achieve. Then, too, an actor has also to make what he or she says and does intelligible and meaningful to the others present, those whom the actions and speech affect and who realise that the person was the author of them. Each of these aspects supports the other. To recognise someone as actor is to see their actions as informed by their intentions and that person as an actor, realising them in actions. The recognition of speech and movements as meaningful, that is, as actions, is to see them as informed by intentions.

In accordance with the theory of the meaning of social actions, the problems of intelligibility are solved as a continuous day-to-day achievement by the use of two main techniques. We attain intelligibility most easily if we draw upon standardised solutions to the specific social problems our social and physical environment presents us. These solutions involve a standardised, integrated personal style appropriate to each type of problem-situation. There is a local typology of personas available to draw upon. We recognise, by reference to cues not yet fully investigated, stylistic unities of action and the appropriate heraldic regalia of such as policeman, nurse, bank clerk, leftish ecologically-oriented mother of two, and so on. A detailed study of these organised styles, aetiology and the processes by which they come to be widely enough known to be a social resource for the achievement of intelligibility would be a useful contribution. Style, and regalia associated with specific roleplaces in football fan groups, have been closely studied by Marsh, Rosser, and Harré (1977).

The solutions to standard problem situations that are available under each persona are, it seems, learned in a standardised form in each socially distinct locality. The use of ritual and ceremonial forms for the production of an action-sequence appropriate to some recognised social task guarantees the intelligibility and effectiveness of what has been done. The ritualisation of apology, for example, allows each of us to maintain our dignity as actors when one of us inadvertently bursts into the other's space or time.

Wide though the scope of these ritualised ceremonies may be in solving socially problematic situations, there is a penumbra of uncertainty remaining. Empirical studies are beginning to show that improvisation of solutions draws upon the same repertoire of actions which serve as components, that is as parts of the "vocabulary" of standardised solutions available in a local culture (Williams, 1976).

Human beings have a further resource for achieving the intelligibility required of their actions, namely accounting. Accounting is speech which precedes, accompanies and follows action. Actors give accounts to ensure the twin goals of intelligibility and warrantability, that is, the meaningfulness and propriety of their actions. Empirical studies have shown that accounts involve, among other items, statements of rules, implicit or explicit exposition of meanings, and stories and anecdotes, the social meaning of which may need some interpretation. Accounts may draw on the rhetoric of causality but are not to be taken as unproblematic, introspective causal explanations. Rather, accounts reveal the sources of the structural properties of action in the resources of individuals, and allow us to develop hypotheses of ideal social competence for a given society against which the actual resources of any individual can be matched. Whatever one may think of the merits of introspective investigations of alleged cognitive causal processes is quite irrelevant to account analysis since it is not aimed at the goal. The study of the efficient causes of human action may not be possible, at least in the immediate future, because the stimulating causes of the socially identical actions of different people may be quite idiosyncratic. The commonalties of social life are structures which pre-exit action and speech and it is to the study of these that accounting theory is directed.

If we regard the day-to-day social world as a co-operative achievement, what sort of achievement is it? From the standpoint of this model we can view it as the successful and continuous attainment of solutions to a myriad of problems of action and understanding, modulating from one set of conventions to another. Clear cut gaps seldom develop in the flow of interaction. We modulate smoothly through sequences: attending a meeting, breaking up, walking down the corridor, and having a drink in the bar. In the course of these sequences the very same topics may be under discussion but action proceeds according to distinctly different conventions of behaviour and self-presentation, but maintaining a socially coherent and continuously interacting group. To keep each stage going and to make smooth transitions from one to the next, all kinds of small problems must be solved.

Theoretically, we can draw a distinction between problems which have socially constructive solutions which bring people together into a fragment of the orderly, meaningful action sequences which constitute social life, and problems which have socially maintaining solutions where threats to existing orderliness are dealt with in a ritual fashion. In detailing the importance of socially maintaining solutions, I am not claiming that existing forms of order should be maintained; only that as a matter of fact they are preserved. Those who wish to change the social order had best know how it is achieved.

3 Rhetorical and discursive analysis: How families talk about the royal family

Michael Billig
Department of Social Science, University of Loughborough

In this chapter, the approach to psychology based on discourse analysis will be discussed. It will be illustrated by examining a piece of research which investigated the ways in which British families talk about the royal family. This research uses some of the techniques of discourse analysis, especially those which examine the rhetorical aspects of giving opinions. One point, however, must be stressed right at the outset. Discourse analysis is not a methodology as such. It is not a set of technical procedures, which can be learnt in themselves and then applied to topics, regardless of the analyst's theoretical orientation. Discourse analysis, as used in social psychology, is much more than a methodology, or set of procedures for conducting research: it is a wider, theoretical approach towards psychology. Unless the general approach is understood, then one should not attempt to conduct discourse analytic research.

BACKGROUND TO DISCOURSE ANALYSIS

The theoretical background for discourse analysis, as practised by social psychologists, is derived from what is being called "discursive psychology" or "rhetorical psychology". The outlines of this approach are to be found in Potter and Wetherell's important book *Discourse and Social Psychology* (1987), which provides a very useful introduction to the ideas and methods of the discursive approach. There is now a growing body of publications outlining the discursive approach (see, for instance, Antaki, 1994; Billig,

1987 and 1991; Edwards & Potter, 1993a and 1993b; Parker 1992; Potter & Wetherell 1993). In fact, the discursive approach is now being adopted by an increasing number of social psychologists, particularly in Britain.

Discursive psychologists share a basic assumption, which emphasises the importance of language. They claim that many of the phenomena which psychologists have traditionally called "internal states" are, in fact, constituted in social activity, especially through discourse. Thus, by studying how people talk and how they use language in practice, we can study many of the things which psychologists have previously thought to occur "within the heads" of participants.

The discursive position is derived philosophically from the works of Ludwig Wittgenstein and John Austin. In his later writings, Wittgenstein argued that emotions, feelings or thoughts are not inner events, which occur only within the head of the person who is said to have the emotion, feeling of thought. The proof of this is that we have words to talk about feelings and emotions. If we pay attention to the way people use such words, Wittgenstein suggested, we will see that emotion-words, such as "happy", "sad", or "depressed", are related to social activities. In *Philosophical Investigations* (1953), Wittgenstein stressed repeatedly that people have to learn how to use phrases such as "I am happy" or "he is happy". We do not learn to do so by labelling in internal state, which no-one else knows about. Instead, we see how other people use the word, by noting the conditions in which the term "happiness" is conventionally used. In short, we learn the conventionally accepted criteria, or signs, for "being happy". These criteria will include social activities and outward behaviour, such as smiling, laughing, or speaking in an animated tone. By learning the criteria for what is meant by the term "happy", we can confidently apply emotion words to others, in order to say conventional phrases such as "you're very happy this morning".

Discourse analysis attempts to translate these philosophical ideas into an empirical project (Harré, 1986; Shotter, 1993a and 1993b). As applied to psychology, discourse analysis examines how psychological discourses are used by people in their ordinary conversations. Discourse analysts pay particular attention to studying what people are doing when they make claims about emotions or thoughts. For instance, if discourse analysts wished to study happiness, they would observe how and when people conventionally make claims about being happy and what is socially involved in making such claims. The discourse analyst, on hearing someone declare "I am happy now", would not take these words to be an indicator of some internal state which constitutes the "real happiness", as if the person, in using the words, were merely describing a private state. Instead, the discourse analyst would note when the words are used and what replies are made by the recipient of the words. As such, the discourse analyst would put the words into their discursive context, and analyse what the person is doing by performing the "speech act" of declaring "I am happy now".

Discourse analysts have found that our speech acts, especially those using psychological words, are much more complicated than traditional psychologists have assumed. A hypothetical example, involving the utterance "I am happy now" can be considered. What the person is doing and claiming by making such an utterance depends on the context. One might imagine a woman saying it to a husband whom she had previously left. The phrase, then, would have a particular set of meanings to be understood in that context. In such a case, the woman would not be neutrally claiming to describe some inner state, which is momentarily occurring within her brain, while she is talking. She might be justifying her previous actions and arguing why she no longer wishes to return to her ex-husband. There may also be an accusation—I was not happy when I was with you.

The layers of meaning can only be uncovered by examining the utterance in its context. For instance, if the ex-husband replies "But you were happy when we were together", the analyst will know how the woman's remark is being understood: the ex-husband is displaying that he takes her remark to refer, not merely "now" but also to the past, and that she was comparing "now" to the time which they shared together. If the woman were then to reply "But I wasn't really happy then", we would know that she has accepted the way he took her first remark: she does not dispute that a reference to the past is an appropriate response to her remark. In this respect, she accepts his understanding of what she was doing when uttering "I am happy now". Thus, the dialogue shows that the remark in this context does not merely refer to present feelings. The remark is understood as part of a dispute about past and present, and about what can be claimed about past and present. Although the participants might disagree about so much else, they would be agreeing on this.

Discourse analysts would claim that to understand "happiness", we must look in detail at the ways in which people use the concept of "happiness" and what they understand by claims about "happiness". This can involve analysis of written texts, such as letters or even novels (Parker, 1992). Most importantly, it also involves the detailed analysis of actual conversations. For this purpose, discourse analysts have adapted some of the techniques of "conversational analysis", which micro-sociologists have developed for examining the intricacy of daily interactions (Atkinson & Heritage, 1984; Edwards & Potter, 1993a; Heritage, 1984; Potter & Wetherell, 1987). By tape-recording conversations, and then analysing in detail the transcripts of such conversations, analysts have found that even the most trivial exchanges are rich in meaning and involve skilful interactions between participants.

As regards psychological issues, discourse analysts have been investigating a number of topics. For instance, one line of work has been investigating how people offer explanations (Antaki, 1994; Edwards & Potter, 1993a and 1993b). By and large, the offering of explanations is not socially neutral, but is a rhetorical act, in the sense that it involves justification and criticism and the attempt by the speaker to persuade hearers of their interpretation. Thus, "I am happy now" might be offered as an explanation to the question "Why don't you come back?". However, it is not a simple explanation. In this case there might be an element of justification of the self, and, as such, a rejection of potential criticism. Also, there might be implied criticism of a claimed unhappy past, for which the other is being implicitly held responsible. In this way, the explanation is itself a rhetorical act, whose meanings are to be understood by examining the context and by exploring how the participants understood that context. A wealth of interaction, including shared and disputed meanings, can be unpacked by paying close attention to conversational data and its rhetorical implications.

Another issue, to which discursive psychologists have paid particular attention, is memory-talk (Billig, 1990; Edwards & Middleton, 1988; Edwards, Middleton & Potter, 1992; Edwards & Potter, 1993a). The emphasis is upon examining what people are doing when they make memory claims and how, in the course of conversations, people can, through their joint talk construct stories about past events. In this sense, memory can be a joint, social activity. Indeed, the social aspects of memory are particularly important for humans. Because we have language, our memories are not confined to our own personal experience. We learn about the memories of others, which are embedded in our culture. Thus, we can talk about the experiences of previous generations, or about people we have never met. In this way, we can claim to remember things which we have never experienced. There can be social rituals for such joint remembrance, or commemoration. Future generations can jointly remember past war-heroes, as a society collectively creates and remembers its history. No other species can do this, because no other species has language and can engage in "memory talk".

In mainstream social psychology, much research has been devoted to the topic of attitudes. Some investigators have claimed that the topic of attitudes is *the* central subject matter of social psychology. Traditionally, social psychologists have considered attitudes to be the feelings which people have about various issues or figures. For example, one's attitude towards the prime minister is presumed to be the feeling— either positive or negative—that one experiences whenever one sees or hears about the prime minister. In this sense, attitudes are often presumed to be stable internal states.

Discursive and rhetorical psychologists, however, take a very different view of attitudes (Billig 1991; Potter & Wetherell, 1987). In fact, discursive psychologists dispute that attitudes, in the conventional sense, exist at all. They claim that one should not assume that people have stable responses towards attitudinal issues. Instead, one should pay close attention to what people are saying and doing when they give their opinions. Discursive psychologists have suggested that people rarely have straightforward views in the way suggested by attitudinal theory. Instead, people typically have a variety of ways of speaking—discursive repertoires—at their disposal. The same person can talk in a conciliatory or an uncompromising way, depending on who they are talking to and what they are doing within their conversation.

In this respect, discursive psychologists insist upon the rhetorical aspects of "giving views". Attitudes are rhetorical stances in matters of controversy, and, as rhetorical stances, the act of giving attitudes involves criticism and justification. When one gives one's opinion on a matter of controversy—for instance, one's view on capital punishment—one is not only making a claim about one's own stance, or claiming to represent an internal feeling, one is also taking a critical stance against the counter-view. As such, there is an inherently argumentative dimension to the giving of views, and, thus, to what traditional psychologists have called "attitudes" (Billig, 1987). What this means is that there is often a lot going on in discussions when people are engaged in giving their views: they may be wanting to appear reasonable and consistent, while arguing against the views of others and while seeking to persuade their hearers. Discourse analysts, then, seek to uncover the complex richness of the social business of "giving opinions". This is done by attending to the details of what is said and how it is said.

That, then, is the basic theoretical background to the discursive or rhetorical approach to psychology. One very important principle should be borne in mind: discourse analysts study discourse because they are interested in discourse. *They do not treat discourse as a sign of psychological phenomena which are presumed to lie behind the talk.* Thus, discourse analysts do not study discourse because internal states are unobservable and discourse offers some sort of second-best alternative. Indeed, one can go further and claim that discourse analysts positively reject the idea of using discourse as a sign of an underlying attitude or emotion. Thus, if one is trying to study discourse in the hope of discovering what are the *real* attitudes behind attitude-talk, the *real* memories behind memory-talk, or the *real* emotions behind emotion talk, one might be doing interesting qualitative research—but one is not doing discourse analysis.

Discourse analysis is more than following procedures for collecting and categorising discursive data; it involves a theoretical way of understanding the nature of discourse and the nature of psychological phenomena. As a result, discourse analysis must always be more than a methodology.

THE DILEMMATIC NATURE OF COMMON-SENSE

As was mentioned, one topic which has been much studied by discourse analysis has been the variability of "attitude-talk". People, each time they give their views, do not just repeat themselves word for word. Sometimes they might express themselves forcefully; at other times they adopt a more temperate tone. Each person has a variety of "voices". For instance, a teenage girl, when talking about social issues, might speak differently to her mother than to her father; and she might speak differently when talking amongst her own female friends. If her friends start expressing a nihilist view—that nothing matters in this world—she might find herself echoing some of the tones of her parents, because she feels that the nihilist view cannot stand unqualified. On the other hand, as her father lectures her on the responsibilities of life, she might start countering with the nihilist tones of her friends. It is fruitless to ask which is her *real* view, except that her *real* view involves different, even contrary, tones. Unless she is being deliberately deceitful, all such tones can be equally *real*. Their meaning will depend upon what is being done in the various conversations.

For such switching to occur regularly, common-sense must contain contrary themes. In talking about social issues, people usually draw upon phrases, maxims, even clichés, which are commonly shared within the particular community. To use the old rhetorical term, these are *commonplaces*. Rhetorical psychologists stress that, if people are to use common-sense in their discussions and in their thoughts, then common-sense must be 'dilemmatic'. Common-sense is not a unitary schema, but will contain contrary themes, which, if rhetorically pitted against each other, give rise to dilemmas (Billig, Condor, Edwards, Gane, Middleton & Radley, 1988). For example, in contemporary society there are common-sense dilemmas about crime and punishment. Our common-sense, or ideology, contains contrary themes about the desirability of both justice and mercy. Members of contemporary society tend not to be divided between those who will only argue for strict justice, believing that mercy is in principle undesirable, and those who will only argue for the merciful treatment of offenders. In talking of issues of crime and punishment, especially when talking of specific instances, people will often oscillate between justice and mercy. And if, in discussion, people feel their fellow speakers are tending too much towards one end of the dilemma, they will be likely to add to the conversation a sharp, rhetorical blast of the contrary value. In this regard, people express themselves within a rhetorical context, and their so-called "attitudes" must be understood in relation to this context.

Studying Common-Sense Discourse

The dilemmatic nature of common-sense can be illustrated with examples from a project which investigated the way that English families talk about the British monarchy. A fuller report on this project is presented in *Talking of the Royal Family* (Billig, 1992). Although the topic of modern monarchy has tended to be ignored by social scientists, it is ideologically significant, especially for understanding the contemporary ideology of British nationalism (Nairn, 1988). Monarchy, as a symbol of inequality, fulfils an ideological function: acceptance of monarchy implies an acceptance of social inequality in a highly visible form. However, if ideology is dilemmatic, then the discourses about such ideological themes should not be straightforward.

The research project was based upon tape-recorded discussions of sixty-three families talking about royalty. All the families lived in the East Midlands of England. They were recruited to represent a cross-section of people, so as to include working and middle class, urban and rural families. There was an interviewer who visited the families in their homes and tape recorded the discussions. The interviewer raised topics in order to provoke discussion between family members. There was no set schedule for the discussions, but the interviewer encouraged the family members to talk among themselves as much as possible.

From a rhetorical perspective there are a number of advantages in studying discussion groups rather than responses to formal, or even semi-structured, individual interviews. In groups it is possible to observe the patterns of argumentation, and thereby witness the processes of thinking in practice, as respondents engage in the cut-and-thrust of discussion. As they do so, it is possible to listen to the variety of themes which speakers use to express their views.

If there are theoretical reasons for using discussion groups in preference to individual interviews, then for the project of investigating how people talk about the royal family there were particular reasons for using family discussions. In the first place, family discussions tend to be more relaxed than discussions based upon artificial groups of strangers. In family discussions, it is possible to catch glimpses of "naturalistic" conversation as family remembers relax in their own homes and talk spontaneously among themselves. In so talking, they would be continuing to act out their established relationships. In the royal family project, the best interviews, in this respect, were those in which the interviewer needed to intervene the least.

There was an additional reason for using families to talk about the royal family. In speaking about royalty, it was expected that people would be talking about family matters—such as the raising of children or being a wife and husband—in relation to royalty. They would be speaking about matters which were not remote, or confined to the richest family in the land. These would be matters which, quite literally, were close to home. Speakers would be talking about themselves as they talked about royalty. Moreover, in talking about families in their own family home, they would, of course, be acting as family members and conducting their own bits of family business. Exploring these parallels was very much part of the project.

The first stage for analysis involved transcribing the material. The interviews lasted a variable amount of time. Some went on for over two hours and some about an hour. Clearly, this volume of recorded discussion involves a vast amount of material. In making transcripts, one should aim to be as accurate as possible both in transcribing the spoken words and also in identifying the speakers. It is important to listen at length to the recordings before starting the transcriptions, in order to recognize the voices. There will be passages in any discussion which are difficult to transcribe either because people were speaking at once, or a speaker was unclear, or because it is difficult to determine the identity of the speaker. In such cases, it is always better to indicate in the transcript that a passage was unclear or that the speaker's identity was problematic. It is not a good idea to make a "guess". If one does guess, it is possible to end up making detailed analyses from transcripts whose accuracy cannot be adequately trusted.

In making transcripts, one should use conventional symbols indicating interruptions, speakers talking at the same time, pauses, raised voices etc. A useful summary of such symbols is contained in the appendix of Potter and Wetherell (1987). A few examples can be given here. All are taken from the detailed transcript reproduced later.

... Interruption; the second speaker interrupts the first

Daughter: You did ...
Mother: I didn't
[Overlap, or speakers talking at the same time; the bracket is used to indicate which words are spoken at the same time
Daughter: Kiki Dee [isn't an opera singer
Son: [It wasn't Elaine Paige
(.) brief pause
Daughter: No (.) Elaine Paige, yeah
... unclear passage, which could not be transcribed
Mother: No. ...

More details are contained in Potter and Wetherell (1987). By and large, the transcripts should contain as much accurate information as possible about the talk. Care should always be taken over the transcripts, because, for most practical purposes, the transcripts provide the material for the analysis.

Analysis of Discussions   Billig's Method of analysis.

The discussions on the royal family yielded immensely rich, densely textured discourse, revealing that the British public can talk at length about its royal family. There were over three thousand pages of transcript. Faced with this volume of discussion data, one should not ask how one could ever analyse *all* the material. It is not possible ever to exhaust the material nor to produce a *complete* analysis. At best one can only skim the surface; however hard one studies transcripts there is always more than can be done. Indeed, this is true also of discourse projects in general, not just those which generate vast amounts of transcripts.

With this caveat in mind, there are guide-lines which can be offered for analysis. In the first place, the analyst must read, re-read and re-read again the transcripts—and, if possible, also go back to listening to the original tapes. There can be no set rules about how many times each transcript should be read, except to say that the more familiar analysts are with the material, the more they will extract from it. As analysts read the material, they will start looking for regularities or discursive features which take their attention. In so doing that should start developing "hunches", or intuitive understandings of what is going on. Any such "hunches" or intuitive understandings, of course, do not arise from thin air, but are developed out of more general reading and theoretical understanding. And, most importantly, the "hunches" should lead to close observations and analyses, to discover whether they are, in fact, supported by the detail of the data.

At this stage, analysts should begin indexing their material. As regards the indexing of the royal family data, there were basically two sorts of index category used. First, there were categories based upon topics of conversation—such as "criticism of princesses" or "blaming the media". Such indexing is necessary, in order to compare how different speakers, from different families, talk about similar topics. The second type of indexing referred to details of conversational action—for instance, indexing different forms of interruptions or ways of expressing agreement. It is inevitable that the analyst will develop the indexing categories whilst in the process of doing the indexing. It is unrealistic to expect that all necessary categories can be determined in advance. As one reads the transcripts, one should start noticing more features, and one may wish to index these. Sometimes this will entail going back and re-reading previous read transcripts, in order to index them for the new category.

Some discourse projects will pay more attention to the discursive details and others will concentrate more upon the "topics". The choice of level for analysis will depend upon the theoretical questions which are being asked. The royal family project tended to pay more attention to the topics. However, it was also borne in mind that any expression of a topic would involve the speaker engaging in finely detailed conversational and interactional dynamics. In this regard, the topic cannot be split from the conversational dynamics, for in any actual utterance the two are welded together.

In handling data of this sort, the analyst has a choice to make: whether to attempt a composite picture or to focus on in-depth analysis of examples. As regards creating a composite picture, the analyst can try to piece together extracts from different conversations in order to try to construct patterns of thinking. This composite picture would depend greatly on examining material which speakers recognise as "common-sense". These can be commonplace accounts, which appear so commonly sensible that they are rarely challenged by speakers. Or, they could be the sort of common maxims or bits of common-sense which are often used in argument to bolster contested positions, and which are treated by speakers and hearers as being sensible, reasonable or beyond direct challenge.

On the other hand, some discourse analysts prefer to select particular extracts from their corpus of material, and then subject these extracts to detailed analysis. In doing this, analysts can show how complex and interactively rich seemingly straightforward interchanges can be.

The royal family project tended to use both tactics, although in *Talking of the Royal Family* more emphasis was on the composite picture technique (see Billig, 1989, however, for a case study, devoted to showing the complexity of giving "strong views"). There can be no detailed description of procedures, which can be followed precisely in order for analysts to build up a composite picture. So much depends upon the details of the material collected and the theoretical hunches of the analyst. However, one point can be stressed: the analysis is achieved through writing. One does not do the analysis, and *then* write-up the results. Instead, one begins writing, and tries to arrange the material through writing. One should not underestimate the difficulty of this task. Nor should one offer the comfort that it becomes easier with experience. There is no substitute for drafting and re-drafting, trying out ways of analysis, and then abandoning them. In short, progress can be judged by the volume of unsatisfactory drafts in the waste-paper basket.

By painful trial and error, the analyst works towards the "final draft". However, one should never believe that the "final draft" is final in any absolute sense of providing a final, or complete, understanding of the material. The final draft is only final in the sense that the analyst feels that, for reasons of deadlines, exhaustion or boredom, no further improvements are likely to be made and that the current draft contains analyses which might be of interest to readers. In this respect, all analyses—including those which are finally published—can only be provisional.

Results and Discussion

From the recorded discussions in the royal family interviews, it was possible to observe ideological thinking in practice. The talk about the royal family involved more than merely talk about royalty. The discussants also explored argumentatively the moral order of society: in arguing about royal controversies, people were talking about key moral, ideological issues. For instance, there was much debate about how royals should behave. Common-sense, which was commonly accepted and commonly repeated, dictated that royals should neither be too "ordinary", nor too "royal" (or too "high and mighty"). For each common-place, or generally accepted social value, there was an alternative and opposite common-place. The common-place statement "they're just human, after all" might be counterposed by "they're quite different, really/they have to set standards". The same was true for general truisms about the institution: monarchy was often said to represent the "priceless" heritage of the nation and monarchy was said to be a good money-making enterprise which attracts the tourists. The tensions between common-place themes reproduce royalty as an object of interest and as a topic to be debated endlessly.

A further example of contrary themes is provided by the historical tales which were commonly told. As respondents talked about the royal family and about nationhood, they frequently gave common-sense accounts of history (Billig, 1990). Two different accounts, in particular, were given and these could be, and often were, brought into argumentative opposition. There was the story of decline and the contrasting story of progress:

History as National Decline. This account depicted the present as a decay from past standards, and thus, the nation was imagined to be in decline. It was said that people were less respectful towards the royals today than had been the case in the past. In particular, the newspapers published too much scandal and were intruding upon the royal way of life. The royals themselves, especially the younger royals, were not behaving with the sort of dignity which royalty used to display in the past. This way of talking compared present times, which were said to be marked by disrespect and disorder, unfavourably with a past age of respect and good behaviour. Such talk tells a story of decline from better days.

History as National Progress. A second narration imagined a story of national progress. Old aristocrats and regal tyrants had been defeated. The British today, so it was said, lead freer and materially better lives than their ancestors had in past times. The past was barbaric, whereas the present is civilised. One would not wish to go back to the old days of superstition, when ordinary people bowed down before their social superiors. In this account, there was a feeling that people today are more in control of their lives and are more socially equal than previously. Now, people could talk of themselves as being on a par with kings and queens, where previously a mute acceptance of authority was said to be required. The present was depicted as the climax of the past: old-fashioned evils and barbarism had been overcome. Modernity was celebrated in what was essentially a liberal account of national progress.

Both narrations of history—the conservative and the liberal— were part of common-sense and are to be used by the same people. At one point a speaker might use the liberal, or populist, theme, particularly to qualify the conservative account which might have been produced by another speaker. On other occasions, even within the same conversation, the same persons might switch to the conservative account (for examples, see Billig, 1990). Rhetorically, each theme seems to call forth its opposite. In this way, the two histories exemplify the dilemmatic nature of common-sense.

Example of Collective Memory

The composite picture of the two histories illustrates a further theme in the discursive approach to social psychology. The speakers, in talking of the nation's past, were recalling and recreating "collective memories". As was said earlier, human memory, unlike that of any other species, is not linked to personal experience. Through language and culture, we can share the memory of our group. In this case, a national memory was being retold. In the talk about royalty, national and family memories were often inter-twined, as respondents spoke about their memories of the great, memorable royal events. However, the retelling of personal memories about royal events is not a simple business. It, too, is full of rhetorical interplay, and the memory itself can be collectively recalled and recreated.

This can be illustrated by a detailed example. Not all the analyses of the royal family discussions were based upon the reconstruction of composite pictures. There were also extracts which were selected for particular, detailed analyses, in order to illustrate general points of theory. The following extract can be used to highlight how complex interactions can be involved in the re-telling of memory-stories.

The interview in question was conducted with a working-class family, comprising the mother and father (aged thirty-nine and forty respectively) and their twenty-two year old son and twenty-one year old daughter-in-law. The father had just been saying that men were not interested in royal weddings. His daughter-in-law had agreed and then had gone on to say how she would always remember Charles and Diana's wedding. "I will never forget that," she declared. Her father-in-law then displayed his own lack of interest—and lack of memories—in the royal wedding. In so talking, he was displaying that he remembered other things about the memorable day.

(D: Daughter-in-law; F: Father; I: Interviewer; M: Mother; S: Son and husband of Daughter-in-law)

F: I can remember when Charles and Di got married I did an extra 4 hours that afternoon at work and I got 12 hours double time for that {*D laughs*} oh and a day off in lieu

I: So you made the most of it

F: Well certainly yeah I mean I'd got to work anyway I was on early shift and at that time we did 4 hours extra in the afternoon so it was my turn to do it so I made the extra 4 hours at double time you see as well and a day off because it was a bank holiday sort of thing that sticks out in my mind

D: Elaine er Elaine Paige sang at er Charles and Diana's wedding

S: Ssh (*to baby*)

F: I remember Charles and Di as regards Princess Anne's wedding and even Princess Margaret's wedding erm I mean there may be a vague recollection but I don't there's nothing that sticks in me mind to say Ah I know what happened when they go wed sort of thing you know and the same with Princess Alexandra er (.) I recall them getting wed you know er but as regards anything that's [stuck in me mind

M: [It weren't her name's Kiki

      [whatever her name is

D: [No Elaine [Elaine Paige

S: [No it wasn't

M: It weren't it was [Kik it weren't it were an opera singer

D: [No (.) Elaine Paige yeah Elaine Paige Kik Dee [isn't an opera singer

S: [It wasn't Elaine Paige it was

M: I didn't say Kiki Dee…

D: You did…

M: I didn't Kiki la er er ever such a foreign name

D: Elaine Paige sang in the Church

M: She didn't {*laughs*}

D: She did I'll never forget it

M: No.…

D: [She did

M: [It was she was an opera singer [who who sang for Princess Charles Prince Charles and…

D: Elaine Paige sang as well   [cos she'd got an invite

M: [Elaine [Paige {*laughs*}

```
S:                                              [ She didn't
F:   No it was this Tiki Te Kawana or [ whatever her name is
M:                                     [ That's it Tiki Te Kawana
                                     that's it an opera singer =
F:   I don't think that's [ her name but it sounds like that
D:                        [ Elaine Paige went {M laughs} she did
M:   She might have been there but she didn't sing {laughs}
F:   No she sang when Andrew Lloyd Webber got married
D:   Oh {everyone laughs partly at baby singing}
```

Several points can be made about this extract of the family recalling the royal wedding: As people are engaged in the business of recalling the past, so they are doing more than that. In the extract, the family members are also interacting together, and in so doing, they are continuing to conduct family business. The father, in telling how little he remembers of the royal wedding itself, is displaying masculinity, for he has claimed weddings to be female business. Thus, his claim not to remember the wedding and the detailed story about his work routines on that day are also accounts about his self, his masculinity and his relationship within the family. Similarly, his wife and daughter-in-law in telling their wedding stories are doing female business, for they have agreed that women, not men, are interested in these matters.

The claim to recall the past is itself rhetorical and is to be understood as such. The daughter-in-law has said that she will always remember the wedding of Charles and Diana. A part of the details which she claims to remember is the singing of the popular singer, Elaine Paige. The other members of the family dispute the memory, claiming that Elaine Paige did not sing in the church. The mother suggests that it was Kiki Dee who had done the singing. The daughter-in-law argues her case repeating that she will "never forget it". This claim is used to justify her argument that it was Elaine Paige. The other members of the family do not accept the warrant as convincing. They dispute the identity of the singer. Thus, the claim to "never forget something" or "always remember it" is not taken literally as proof of a perfect memory. It is part of the story, which is under discussion.

In the discussion, the family argues about the identity of the singer: she didn't, she did, no, she did ... and so on. The transcript reveals the pattern of the argumentation. During the dispute, there is much interruption. In arguing, the participants are not merely contradicting one another: they are reconstructing the memory of the memorable day, working out the detail of the mystery singer. This remembering is not an individual task, but is collectively achieved through the discussion. Significantly the deadlock between the mother and daughter-in-law is broken by the father. He supplies the suggestion "Tiki Te Kawana or whatever her name is". This name—or the deliberately offered approximation of a name—is accepted by the others: "That's it," declares the mother. And the debate moves on, with the daughter offering the compromise the Elaine Paige might have attended as well. The point is that the father is accepted as providing the missing memory, even though he claims not to have watched the television broadcast of the event. He is also accepted as knowing about Andrew Lloyd Webber's wedding, despite having denied an interest in weddings. This illustrates something crucial about human collective memory. General social knowledge can sometimes be accepted as more convincing than the claim to personal remembrance ("I'll never forget..."). In this way, the non-participant can contribute to the joint construction of the past, and can be held to remember what the declared observers have forgotten. All this is possible because human remembering is a social and discursive activity, which is not necessarily tied to the recall of personally experienced sensations.

There is a final point to be made and this relates to what was said right at the beginning of this chapter. The discourse analyst does not use the transcripts to discover what *really* occurred: whether the father *really* did work the hours which he claimed to; whether Elaine Paige *really* sang at Andrew Lloyd Webber's wedding; or whether the young woman *really* will never forget the royal wedding. What counts, for the discourse analyst, are the claims being made and disputed by the participants.

In this respect, the discourse analyst will not conclude from this extract that women *really* are more interested than men in royal weddings, but will say that it seems to be common-sensically accepted that women are more interested: none of the participants disputed this, and they oriented their comments to such beliefs. Indeed, as the composite picture in *Talking of the Royal Family* illustrated, this claim was often made and was rarely disputed.

However, there is something more that the discourse analyst can do on the basis of the quoted extract. The analyst can point out that men, despite their outward display of uninterest in royal weddings, can sometimes supply the missing memory of the royal wedding. This illustrates how widely diffused royal details are amongst the British population: even those, who wish to disclaim knowledge, share the cultural knowledge of royalty.

If it seems ironic that the father recalls the wedding details, despite his professed lack of interest, and if the debate about the singer's identity seems to have its comic side, then, perhaps, this illustrates the most important guide-line in discourse analysis. In going through pages of transcripts some passages seem to leap out; they might be filled with humour, irony and surprise; they might make the analyst smile. This is the sort of passage, which you, the analyst, might wish to tell your friends, for it makes a good story. And this is precisely the sort of passage to include in the analysis. If your theories are encouraging you to include the dull passages, and to omit the "good stories", then get some better theories. After all, analysts, at all stages of qualitative research, have to back their own judgement. And can there be a better guide than the feeling that there is a good story to tell?

NOTE

The research reported in this chapter was supported by the Economic and Social Research Council on the project "Socio-psychological analysis of family discourse" (Grant Number R000231228). *Procedural Guide For Discourse Analysis*

PROCEDURAL GUIDE FOR DISCOURSE ANALYSIS

(Intended as a rough guide and not as an inflexible procedure: at all stages you must exercise judgement)

1. Read background material about discursive psychology and about the topic you want to study;
2. Read some more;
3. Decide on the type of data you wish to study;
4. Collect data. If the data are printed materials, proceed to 9);
5. If you are collecting speech data, then collect your tape-recordings;
6. Listen to tape-recordings;
7. Transcribe the recordings;
8. Check the transcriptions against the tapes;
9. Read the transcriptions/data;
10. Keep reading them; start looking for interesting features and developing "intuitive hunches";
11. Start indexing for themes and discursive features;
12. Read, read and read, especially to check out "intuitive hunches" against the data; always try to look for counter-examples;
13. Start writing preliminary analyses, testing your "hunches" against the details of the data; always be critical;
14. Keep drafting and re-drafting analyses, comparing different extracts, looking in detail at extracts and being aware of counter-examples;
15. Keep writing, reading, thinking and analysing until you produce a version with which you are not totally dissatisfied;
16. Be prepared to return to Stage 1.

4 Making and un-making identities: A psychologist looks at art-work

Halla Beloff

International Social Science Institute, University of Edinburgh

The subject matter of psychologists' work is wide. Increasingly we have been told enough to consider topics and questions which do not allow the application of the traditionally respectable methods. Recently study in domains which are fascinating in their own right has come into academic psychology. After all, some of us can resist everything except temptation...

One of the questions, then, has been, can psychologists contribute something specific to the understanding of art work and of visual images in particular? The first answer seems to be no, in the sense that our usual base of theory and even our conceptual vocabulary does not apply to the domain of aesthetics. This is a consideration before we can come to the matter of objectivity and replicability. All these problems arise, while the fallibility of our argument and conclusions looms all too large. Yet, if we are in the business of understanding the texture of everyday life, do we not have an obligation to accept the challenge of one of the significant dimensions of civilised activity—the making of objects which are the product of scholarly craft, which provoke intellectual pleasure, emotions such as joy or hostility, and on occasion rapture?

There are, in fact, a number of ways in which a psychologist might approach the task (Beloff, 1994a, 1994b). One could consider images as plain examples of cultural products, like advertisements or popular movies, and try to "read" out of them the themes which the power hierarchies put in place to control the populace—if that were our ideological assumption.[1] Alternatively, within the same domain, one could hope to find themes of

55

leisure, luxury and diversion, not to say opium, which the masses and/or the elite need for their diversion.

Experimental aesthetics is not at issue, but the analysis and interpretation of a series of visual images, in this case a study of photographs. This chapter will outline one enterprise which might be considered another form of rhetorical and discursive analysis (cf. Billig, Chapter 3) using the broad basis of discourse analysis on visual rather than verbal texts.

One might also remember here that contemporary artists, working after the innovation of conceptual art, are themselves not naïve to the ideas, or cognitive context, of their imagination and of their resulting work. They may be partners in our own enterprises which want to dissect the concept of identity and to unmask the idea of self behind the 'face' as Goffman (1967) uses the term.

PORTRAITS AND SELF-PORTRAITS

I have been thinking about what it means when someone makes art works which present a series, a long series, of portraits which show a set of young and not so young women, all openly facing us— showing us their identity and the props of their very different lives, temperaments and states of mind, and where the subject of that series is in fact *one* young woman, the artist *herself.*

The trick is that there *seems* to be no mask. But clearly there is one. And I will attempt to argue that it is a mirror one; that is, that other women can see their selves there.

Cindy Sherman (1987), from her first exhibition in 1977 when she was a postgraduate art student in Buffalo (she is now 38 years old and has been described as aggressively ordinary (Dorment, 1992[2]), has presented at regular intervals a "gallery" of women in, and as, works of art. There have been some 227 of them to date, every one labelled 'Untitled', for which she happens to have posed herself (see Fig. 4.1 and Fig. 4.2).

Sherman's face and body are the raw materials she works with. She has been called the world's first *female* female impersonator (Dorment, 1992). However, they are not ordinary self portraits. They are tableaux in which a woman has dressed up, in an assortment of outfits, 'pretending'— in some atmospheric setting.

These are a kind of costume drama. It is like a childhood game played in front of a camera. They started off spontaneous-seeming. As if she were doing things for herself. Free. But there is sophistication in the conceptions.

While photographically they are rather simple. Anyone can press the button, and her father used to do so—once she had set up the scene, the scenario. When I studied her original exhibition in London, I went round

FIG. 4.1. Untitled #21.

FIG. 4.2. Untitled #119. Reproduction in black and white.

fascinated by the cast of people playing the roles of women that I knew about. It wasn't till later that I realised she had posed for the entire cast herself. I then experienced a mixture of sensations, feeling foolish, admiration for her smile, puzzlement about 'what it was all for'.

One Cindy Sherman or Many?

So there are two things at issue here. One—the fact there appear to be different people. Two—our response when we realise it is always the same person.

She made a career in transformations. The results are magnetic. That is what the art critics and theorists say. She's 'fixing', in the American sense of the word, identities. She chooses. She invents herself in public. She's always in charge. Why would anyone want to do that—to give such performances? What does it mean? Can psychologists learn anything from the enterprise? Can we use it for our own work on identity?

Traditional self-portraiture by artists can be seen in various ways. It is a kind of *charming joke*. Michelangelo's own image is on the Sistine Ceiling. It is *convenient*. Rembrandt van Rijn painted himself at least 70 times in various costumes and posts—most like Sherman therefore—but with specific external purposes i.e. as a set of promotions to show customers how they might appear themselves (Beloff, 1990).

Obviously I don't know Sherman's reasons, but she seems to see herself as a *performance artist* who is then photographed, to record the event. I put this forward because there is no hint of narcissism in the images. And in the same way that autobiography need not be self-justifying, auto-portraits need not be narcissistic.

Performances implies that she was indeed just 'showing' us the repertoire of roles that a segment of woman was involved in: young, white, middle class, Jewish women in the North East United States. It would perhaps have been presumptuous for her to do otherwise. But there is another special point, these pictures speak to us directly in and of themselves. They are not illustrations.

They are, however, psychological arguments. The deeper implication was simply that as *she* does, *we* could all play those roles. It was chance that put us into any one category and only into that one. She has demonstrated the power of the social variance in women's gender identity (see Fig. 4.3).

At this stage her admirers said, this is a remarkable visual demonstration and conceptual argument but what can such an artist do next? She has had no difficulty in developing her 'argument'. In the further series called Film Stills (although each particular image was still Untitled) she showed us how the movies of Hollywood, including, significantly, B pictures, influenced our visions, not only of western women in general, but our visions of our selves.

FIG. 4.3.   Untitled #15. Reproduction in black and white.

It is important to note here that not only 'stills' from movies but photo-graphs of film stars at their supposed *off moments* are a vivid part of our mental set of possibilities (see Fig. 4.4).

These pictures present the 'outward show' of characters. We decode them from their setting, their costumes and their stance, gesture, facial expression. These have all been in black and white. Initially because in the '70s' serious photographs were in 'literary' black and white and as film stills, because those *films noirs* were in black & white.

Now in Gallery II we start in colour, but also with a critical concentra-tion on expression and the making external of internal states. The back-grounds become obvious back-projections of out-of-focus slides and the women attend to some internal scenario (see Fig. 4.5 and Fig. 4.6).

They are pre-occupied with alarming concerns, sad solitudes. However, it must not be thought that these women subjects remain simply powerless playthings of gods or men. They come to loom larger. They are wary. They play a more athletic role. They lift their heads. They are angry (see Fig. 4.7).

Within the compass of the normal, there comes now a whiff of danger. "Yawningly ordinary and reeking with nasty possibilities" (Dorment, 1992).

FIG. 4.4. Untitled #54.

FIG. 4.5. Untitled #112. Reproduction in black and white.

FIG. 4.6. Untitled #133. Reproduction in black and white.

60

FIG. 4.7. Untitled #122. Reproduction in   FIG. 4.8. Untitled # 153. Reproduction in
black and white.   black and white.

They represent, to us in Europe at least, United States life. (Cf. David
Lynch's film **Blue Velvet**). It is here that there appears 'the victim' to join the
virgin figures (see Fig. 4.8).

When her audience asked again, what next?—and remember that in
modern art there must always be a next—Sherman took us into another
world— Gallery III—of the brazen but the eerie, to the edge of madness and
to freaks and monsters wearing actual masks and prostheses (see Fig. 4.9).

Here are catastrophes, grotesqueries, bigger, more powerful, no longer
amusing. Undigested nightmares rising from the fairy tales of the Brothers
Grimm enter the stage (see Fig. 4.10).

And here come bits of bodies, inspired it has been suggested, by the
battlefields of the American Civil War. Is there another internal war
going on? "I call this my disgusting period" (Dorment, 1992). She has
said that she wants to make her work more challenging. How can the col-
lectors want to hang that over the couch? On the other hand, even art
critics have noted here the psychopathological context or rather *content* of
the 'banquets'. They could represent bulimia and other aspects of the sha-
mefulness of women's lives. Hence perhaps her near-disappearance from
the 'act' (see Fig. 4.11).

FIG. 4.9. Untitled #138. Reproduction in   FIG. 4.10. Untitled #158. Reproduction in
black and white.   black and white.

Gallery IV shows us rough charades, i.e. "humorous, repellent and just plain dumb". She has said that she wanted to show the crude distortions which the Old Masters used—"better" (see Fig. 4.12).

For us the high interest here is undoubtedly the transvestite images. They are more than a novelty. Surely they have an inevitability in terms of her progress. They had to come. They comment on both gender roles. They certainly call them into question–deconstruct them, to use the fashionable term (Garber, 1993). Here are questions about how far gender roles are based on essential biological factors and how far they are arbitrary cultural traditions. If they are just socially constructed, we could dismantle them and build them up in other styles.

Sherman may even be presenting dreams of prophecy and power. If there is simply a lot of historical convenience involved, could there come a time when the dominance and power of the male will fade away? If it is hard to believe that, we can still dream... (see Fig. 4.13).

Yet, how different are the men and women here? She does not seem to try very hard. Does she ever stop being a woman? I would again say, a plain interpretation could be that even here—we feel we could be all of them. The argument might be that the social construction of gender is more superficial than some of us would have thought it to be.

FIG. 4.11.   Untitled #172. Reproduction in   FIG. 4.12.   Untitled #216. Reproduction in
black and white.   black and white.

The Critique, or is it the Interpretation?

So to return to the beginning: how are we to understand this enterprise and
what could a psychologist contribute to the interpretation? What concepts
and qualitative methods would we need? In USA-speak, "How is one to
critique this?" For this author, it is a feminist set of identity works and needs
to be approached as such. This is clear not just because it is a woman
portrayed—after all, images of women are all around us—but because
particular 'statements' are made. Let us consider the statements under
several headings.

The *subversion* of the concept of stable 'essential' identity. This men like
to hold (because it justifies their traditional power and hold on positive
attributions for themselves) but which women consider worthy of discussion. Stable femininity and masculinity must imply that the tradition of male
dominance is not only natural but here to stay. If, however, identities can be
so easily, and elegantly, interchanged then the biological foundation cracks
and all kind of social changes become thinkable. The power imbalance
could be righted.

In 1984 when Sherman produced some work for the Paris fashion house,
Dorothee Bis, she said about her images in general (Harrison, 1991, p. 273):

FIG. 4.13.   Untitled #224. Reproduction in black and white.

"A lot of it is a reaction to growing up bombarded by stereotypes of what a woman is supposed to look and act like—beauty and civilised ways of behaviour. I preferred anything that was different from that—going against what the fashion magazines said."

Most images show a good-looking woman who has taken care in her self presentation. We are shown not only the social construction of appearance but *beauty*. In my understanding of the meaning of the concept of beauty, I follow Efrat Tseelon's (1992) fine argument in which she acknowledges that "... 'looks' are a defining feature of a woman both in terms of how others respond to her, and how she experiences her own self."

Then a woman is doubly stigmatised. Firstly because she is evaluated against an idealised criterion, which she is virtually bound to transgress. And secondly because her natural bare face and body, being unacceptable, must be disguised, improved, controlled. Hence the psycho-analytic notion of femininity as a masquerade.

If we further follow the Goffman (1964) division between discredited and discreditable stigma, that in the normal/deviant drama "every individual participates in both roles", Sherman personifies that argument.

The fact that she uses *parody* as a means, as a style, is relevant within feminism. "Parody inscribes disaffection" (Spurling, 1988). And the parody exists in the 'ordinary' women images, not only in the History of Art ones. Sherman's images, in showing stereotypes, challenges them. The very enactment of that long, long series must be a satire. The status quo depends on a certain degree of solemnity in the social discourse, about its agenda. Any levity—jokes, exaggeration, ribald commentary, mean that the instigators and we consider alternatives with an open mind. Feminists who certainly work for change in relations between the sexes must welcome the metaphorical space that Sherman puts between herself and the rules of worthy womanhood, as she shows how superficial the rules can be.

She shows *difference*. She has appropriated and extended the genres that she as a woman has inherited. Using herself is a fine way of rejecting the false detachment of masculine formality.[3]

The work is critically of our time. Sherman is the ideal *post-modernist*—because in the critical mode, she has appropriated images in the world. She has re-done them to show another true meaning. As Jean Baird's analysis succinctly states it, we have "... an ideal figuration for the critique of representation, given that she appeared to dissemble any notion of the true woman behind the vacant lot of the feminine facade" (Baird, 1991). This is the technical language of fine art criticism, simply saying that in the Sherman re-presentations of the representation of 'woman' she shows the emptiness behind the facade of feminine clothes, make-up, and body language. The narratives in the images, and there are always stories, are not only 'the front' of the heroine, but that is all there is, ever.

The End of the Identity Romance

Here is the Nemesis of Identity. The appropriated selves are interchangeable and loseable. This is a series of fakes. If the Sherman images are not her self, they are *signs*. She has de-constructed images of woman through her 'silly' dressing-up. One person being all those different persons surely demonstrates that any one self is similarly built up from props and gestures. There is less of an essential essence and more of an act all the time.

She and we, are by definition in the post-modernist mode. And then we have to think again about issues of self presentation, the dramaturgical model and the fraught issue of sincerity. Briefly, within the impression management approach, any conscious attention to one's own performance is a form of insincerity. Anything that is not wholly spontaneous, impulsive, thoughtless, is.

This is part of the culture not only of Protestantism, but of modernity. However, if we hold with the drama model (again of Goffman), then our social life is simply a concern of our *style* and honesty is not relevant. I would like to say that Sherman has demonstrated elegantly the claims of Goffman's theatre.

The Woman Angle

So what about the *dressing-up and the woman angle* It is generally agreed that dressing-up has more 'meaning' for a woman. The world of appearance is where women have been placed. Women's bodies in western civilisation have been used as a cipher on which masculine psycho-dramas have been projected (Pointon, 1990; Saunders, 1989). But in her images, this is not the case. She is not exposed. She is not the subject of the discussion. She has always said that she is very ordinary. (That is not to say that men do not in fact dress-up, do not create their identity. But that is yet another paper.)

Sherman has played the serious game of unpacking identity work, while giving virtuoso displays of identity construction. She provokes ideas among psychologists, art historians and students of the culture of post-modernism.

She has worked motivated by pleasure and desire, and that is the aim of each of us as a civilised person. In her elusive, indeed invisible identity, she demonstrates both self-assertion and cultural revelation. Showing *her* pleasure and desire in the work. *We* experience it when we read the images.

There is a rich pleasure in looking at the work. This is not to be ignored. And the pleasure comes from recognition, identification, engagement. Quite apart from the shock when we think *they* are all *she*. But it must not be forgotten that we still don't know *Sherman*'s face. I want to say again, this is not about the woman Cindy Sherman's psyche.

This kind of analysis of visual discourse has been used here to consider identity work in a new way and yet to me it demonstrates one fundamental point which puts psychologists in their lower place. Words are pedestrian, they provide closure. It is presumptuous to provide closure to Sherman's own elegant communication in which she confounds culture while celebrating the politics and the myths from which western 'face' is made.

Some Guidance for Reading Visual Rhetoric

The evidence that we are interested in can range far from fine art pictures. Any images may be of interest: advertisements, newspaper reportage, greeting cards and birth announcements, funny postcards, magazine feature illustrations and children's books.

1. It is good to read general texts on the field, for example, John Berger's *Ways of Seeing* (Penguin, 1972), Erving Goffman's *Gender Advertisements* (Macmillan, 1979), Jo Spence's *Cultural Sniping* (Routledge, 1995) or Judith Williamson's *Decoding Advertisements*

4. MAKING AND UN-MAKING IDENTITIES

(Boyars, 1978). Finding specific references for your project can start here, although you will want to come back to these several times.

2. Pin up the pictures that you are working with (or photocopies of them) round your room. Live with them for a while.

3. Study/examine each image studiously and meticulously. That is, pay serious attention to *all* the content. Leave nothing out, background as well as foreground. Write down what is there.

4. If there are people in a picture, imitate/reproduce their stance, gesture, expression. What does it feel like standing or sitting or walking like that? Is it comfortable? What kind of feelings seem to be induced? This is one kind of "naturalistic" information that you can elicit. Ask some others to try to do this and tell you what they feel.

5. Go back to 3. What does it all *mean*? Is it plain, mundane kind of evidence involved? Or are metaphors in play? Are there symbols here? Could it all mean the opposite?

6. Why were the pictures made? Who for? What are the motives of the maker/s of the images? What needs were supposed to be satisfied?

7. Start writing a neat plain description. Then straight away try making some interpretations that go beyond the surface. Try these out on friends. When they don't agree or add information, don't necessarily accept these at their face value, but think about them...

8. Go more deeply into psychological writing on the issue involved, identity, gender construction, the meaning of childhood or whatever.

9. Re-evaluate your descriptions, both plain and interpretative. Rewrite.

10. And as usual, you may want to/need to have another go at the cycle.

11. You should end with something that is not the last word, but that you will be able to defend with spirit and pleasure.

NOTES

1. The establishment does not have absolute control, of course, and in Chapter 8 Finn shows how do-it-yourself political images are used to fine effect by "the people" to communicate specific alternate messages.

2. Grateful acknowledgement is made to the insights of Richard Dorment and to the interview which Sherman gave him.

3. That detachment is perhaps further demonstrated by the fact that this chapter was mooted by the editor and then accepted for this book.

5 Repertoires in discourse: Social identification and aesthetic taste

Carol Sherrard
Department of Psychology, University of Leeds

INTRODUCTION

Discourse analysis is a new approach to social psychology, focusing on how people deploy language and other forms of communication over the course of real social interactions. These interactions are viewed as the site where human beings are in process of constructing each other, and themselves, as social beings. Potter and Wetherell (1987) is a key text for this new approach. Other key readings are given at the end of this chapter.

Previously, social psychology has conducted laboratory experiments or used questionnaires, rather than observe natural interactions. This is because it wished to confine observation to highly specified phenomena in controlled conditions. Such an approach is necessary for the hypothesis-testing method which underlies traditional social psychology. Discourse analysts, and other qualitative researchers, reject this method, and the theory of knowledge and science it is derived from, as inappropriate to the study of humans as *social* beings. The rejection of traditional psychological method is justified by the narrow focus and artificiality this method induces. It not only discourages study of real social interactions, but it also, by elevating method over content, has had the effect of removing the really interesting content from large areas of social psychology. Traditional social psychology, even in its applied variety, is an arid terrain, dotted with abstract structures such as "attribution", "health belief model", "theory of reasoned action", "attitude", all carefully constructed but without attention to how they might operate in people's everyday experience and interaction. The result has been that such structures have been viewed as static systems, lodged somewhere inside individuals' heads, ultimately to be linked to the even more abstract and permanent basic cognitive processes. (Compare Billig's account of how discourse analysts use Wittgenstein's insights about the actual usage of emotion words to critique this individualist view: Chapter 3, this volume.) This traditional view, while not in principle denying the part of social interactions in these structures, simply ignores their social aspect because it is too difficult to conceptualise and control experimentally: it is vague and messy.

In complete contrast to this view, discourse analysis is based on the conviction that many important psychological phenomena can only be analysed within a framework of social interactions, because that is where and how they are constructed. The challenge of vagueness and messiness must be met by developing new methods, not simply by avoidance.

Interaction as seen from this new, naturalistic standpoint is called "discourse". The new term "discourse" is needed, because it includes all, and more than, the separate terms such as "language", "non-verbal communication", and "interpersonal interaction" are usually understood to include. The fragmentation of interaction into separate topics of study is a good example of how previous approaches have destroyed the integrity of what people generate and experience globally. "Discourse analysis" includes not only structures, but also content and meanings as they are generated in interaction (Potter and Wetherell, 1995). It can include dress, and other manipulated aspects of the physical environment when these manipulations have symbolic value (Harré, Chapter 2 this volume).

It is possible to think of "discourse" as the site where beliefs are constructed and continuously negotiated and renegotiated, with people deploying their language, argument, rhetoric, body movements, physical appearance (in so far as they can control it) and social status in a single, integral stream of action. In contrast, if we think separately of "language", "non-verbal communication" and "attitudes", we are liable to be drawn into the old view of communication as a transparent medium transmitting something separate which lies behind it, and be tempted for example to look at language structures as *essentially* separate from their content. While the traditional approach intends to separate meaning and content only as an analytical convenience, the practical outcome is that we are led to leave meaning out of our psychological account altogether. This disastrously distorts the picture of social interaction as it is actually understood by human beings as they engage in it.

Of course focus is necessary in any research, and it is possible to look at one aspect of discourse without needing to have a complete analysis of everything that is happening at the same time. The difference between such an approach and the traditional, atomistic one is that systematic links across domains are integral to the discourse-analytical approach, rather than seen as crossing discipline boundaries.

The piece of research to be described in this chapter focuses on language and content in talk. It is based on the discourse-analytical view that beliefs are created in interaction with other people. Beliefs are therefore dynamic and flexible, undergoing shifts and variations as conversation develops. They are not simply a property or product of the individual; they are jointly produced by people interacting with each other.

By focusing on the shifts and variations in beliefs, discourse analysts emphasise the ways in which beliefs are far from stable entities, but are continuously created, negotiated and renegotiated as people talk to each other. The two-way nature of conversation is taken seriously. In conversation, people are both constructing beliefs and adapting them as they orient to other people, try to influence them, and are influenced by them. Rhetoric, value-laden choices of words and syntactic structures, are therefore of special interest to discourse analysts.

Writing, which at first sight appears more static and individual, can also be seen primarily as a form of implicit dialogue or rhetorical audience address (Banister, Burman, Parker, Taylor, & Tindall, 1994; Sherrard, 1988). Questionnaire responses, the traditional form of attitude study, can also be seen as participation in a form of dialogue with the researcher, rather than, as originally intended, a form of response uncontaminated with the researcher's and the respondents' social positions in relation to each other.

Because of its emphasis on everyday rhetoric, discourse analysis is most revealing in dealing with interactions about controversial topics such as politics, race and gender. The stances people take on these issues are not seamlessly coherent. Speakers contradict themselves as they orient now to one, and now to another question or assertion (or expected reaction) from their conversation partners.

Discourse analysis is also a *critical* approach to social psychology, taking the view that it is impossible for the analyst to be objective and neutral about social issues which are inherently controversial. Very often the political views of discourse analysts themselves are quite evident from their writings. The critical stance means that the approach to people being interviewed, for example for their political beliefs, may be quite the opposite to that adopted in, for example, counselling. The discourse-analytical approach is the very opposite of non-judgemental: it may even be challenging and confronting, since the aim is to lay bare the varying rhetorical, persuasive and defensive stances of the person interviewed (Potter & Wetherell, 1995).

The discourse analyst ideally begins from a knowledgeable stance of their own about the issues raised in the discourse to be analysed. The analyst also needs sensitivity to the evaluative and connotative dimension of language. That is, an appreciation that language is not, as it is often presented, simply a transparent medium for the transmission of stable facts and ideas. It may be difficult at first to shift away from this "transparent medium" view of language, simply because it is so pervasive, especially in science. It is also important to see, though, that the evaluative aspect of everyday words is also highly consensual, and can therefore supply a firm basis for argument (Osgood, Saporta & Nunnally, 1956). For example, there is no need for a questionnaire study to establish that the word "nag" has a more negative connotation than "horse": this judgement is made instantly and unani-mously by all speakers of English. The use of such linguistic judgements in analysis is intuitive, but these intuitions are not vague. They form part of the linguistic competence we share with other speakers of our language, and indeed must share with them, for language to be possible. (Roger Fowler's book *Linguistic Criticism* is an excellent introduction to the evaluative aspects of both literary and everyday language.)

Discourse analysis is *interpretive*. Although word meanings, and even evaluative word meanings, are consensual, the *implications* of utterances have to be interpreted. Most utterances imply more than their literal words assert (see Billig's drawing out of the different possible implications of the assertion "I am happy now", said by a divorced wife to her former husband; Chapter 3, this volume). This need for interpretation means that the dis-course analysis procedure cannot be reduced to a series of mechanically applied steps with a single "correct" outcome. Nevertheless, it is possible to specify a set of guidelines which will enable the reader to carry out an analysis. The final interpretation and conclusion are relatively more difficult because they call for synthesis and judgement. However, this is true of all branches of psychology. In the more traditional branches, the effort to present the discipline as a scientific procedure (highly specified steps with "correct" outcomes) leads to underemphasis of the need for synthesis and judgement.

THE STUDY

The interview to be analysed here is from a set of interviews with people about their views on how aesthetic taste are related to social class (Sherrard, 1995; Sherrard & Bousfield, 1991). There is already some evidence that aesthetic taste is related to self-image, to social class identity, and to the social judgements that people make about each other (Bourdieu, 1984).

Bourdieu's theory sees social classes as relating to each other through multiple dimensions of power and status. They engage in reciprocal com-parison and distancing on these dimensions, but recognise the hegemony (if not the legitimacy) of a dominant class. The implications of this for aesthetic taste are that tastes are used as one of the markers of social class, and the classes engage in comparisons and evaluations of each others' tastes. There is a standard or canon of taste (seen to emanate from a dominant social class) which is recognised, even if not accepted, by everyone. Non-dominant classes may attempt to gain status by either accommodating to, or alternatively contesting, the dominant class's standard of taste. Shakespeare and Mozart, for example, are names universally recognised as belonging to the canon in Britain. People not appreciating their works may either defer to "superior tastes", or assert a different standard of taste.

For Bourdieu, then, aesthetic taste is a social class marker of power/ status dimensions. It structures individual preferences, self-image, and the perception of others' social identity. It is also very deeply, even bodily felt. Bourdieu points out the biological origin of the "taste" metaphor, from which "disgust" (from the Latin *gustare*, to taste) is an extention: "When they have to be justified, tastes are asserted negatively—by the refusal of other tastes. They are foremost DIStastes, disgust provoked by the horror of the tastes of others. Each taste feels itself to be natural... This amounts to rejecting others as unnatural. Aesthetic intolerance can be terribly violent. Aversion to different life-styles is one of the strongest barriers between classes" (Bourdieu, 1984, p. 56).

Although Bourdieu's theory treats taste per se as a relatively stable feature of the relations between classes, the *content* of tastes is seen as continually shifting through social interactions (through the media, as well as face-to-face). Tastes are continually manifested in everyday choices and actions such as dressing, grooming, eating, decor, and use of leisure time. The point of the study described here was to try to observe the related discourse processes of self-image construction, and social-judgement-making, as they take place in *talk* about aesthetic taste and social class. Because it involves a person's deeply-felt valuation of themselves and others, aesthetic taste is a sensitive and contentious issue, so it was expected that there would be plenty of shifts and contradictions in the talk about it. Even more so, as the people interviewed were Access students taking a course in Comparative Arts. Seeking entry to higher education through an Access qualification, these students had (self-ascribed) working-class origins, but were aware that higher education would move them toward a middle-class identification. The Comparative Arts course had served to increase their sensitivity to, and fluency in talk about, issues of aesthetic taste in "the arts".

Steps in Analysis

Before proceeding to the study itself, it may be helpful to set out an overview of the steps we will need to carry out the analysis.

Step One: Select a Topic and the Respondent(s)

The best way to appreciate the essentially dynamic and flexible nature of discourse is to listen carefully to some conversation on a controversial topic. Choose a topic on which you have some knowledge and opinion of your own, and which also has some social importance (do not restrict yourself to personally or locally relevant issues, since your interpretations and conclusions should be relevant to society-wide issues).

Recruit one or two other people who will agree to talk to you, or to each other, about it. Make sure you have their permission to record and analyse the conversation. Undertake to keep the recording confidential, and your analysis, when written up, anonymous. (These points about permission and confidentiality arise from the ethical code of the British Psychological Society, 1993). Use a good quality but simple cassette-recorder, such as the Sony TCM-818. Although more complex recorders may produce better recordings, their separate microphones can be intrusive, they require more attention from you, and are more error-prone in operation. The quality of recording from a simpler machine is quite adequate for discourse analysis purposes.

Step Two: Listen to the tape

Once you have made your recording, listen carefully to it. If you have not done this before, you will be surprised at how "untidy" spontaneous speech is at all levels. Sentences are often not finished, because the speakers change what they were about to say in mid-flow, or they make errors, or are interrupted. There will be many disfluencies, such as slips of the tongue, incomplete words, inaudible words and stutters. When you come to transcribe the tape, you will find that you have to interpret even at this level: that is, you have to make a decision about what the speaker actually said. You will also have to edit, leaving out the disfluencies and inessential matter. (Compare what Billig says about transcription, in Chapter 3 of this volume. Discourse analysts do not all follow identical transcription practices, but an apparent contradiction between Billig's recommendations and mine can be resolved. Billig advises that it is not a good idea to make a guess, when a passage is unclear (meaning inaudible), since one will then be making interpretations on a base which is not necessarily accurate. Of course one should not supply words which were not uttered, or totally inaudible. My point is rather that a totally accurate transcription in some objective sense is not possible, since spoken language is highly fragmented and indeterminate. Words are frequently mispronounced or incomplete: nevertheless the context makes it obvious what the intended word was. The smooth flow of normal interaction depends precisely on conversation partners being able to supply these "repairs" for each other. Too pedantic an approach to transcription would lead to discouragement, since large parts of the recording would have to be disregarded, and this is distorting in itself.)

Step Three: Transcribe the Tape

Having heard the tape through at least once, you will be in a better position to transcribe it, since knowledge of the overall conversation helps you to better understand individual stretches of discourse. Transcription should preferably be onto a word processor. This will make your analysis much quicker and easier with its "search" facility, and the facility to number lines of the transcript.

As you go along, look for points where a speaker contradicts a previous assertion of their own. This will help you to begin to distinguish the different stances (called "repertoires" in discourse analysis) which the speakers move between.

Step Four: Identify Repertoires and Resolutions

A repertoire is a recognisable, relatively self-contained point of view. Speakers draw on different repertoires as they talk and shift their stance, so there will be at least two repertoires in one speaker's talk on a controversial topic. (Repertoires are similar to the "contrary themes" of common-sense which Billig discusses in Chapter 3, this volume.) A repertoire will be characterised by discourse devices. These are evaluative words and phrases, possibly a single overall metaphor, and possibly syntactically distinct phrase types. The more a phrase departs from the standard phrase syntax (simple, active and declarative—as opposed to complex, passive, question or negative) the more likely it is to be imbued with some evaluative meaning (Brown and Yule, 1983). For example, in contrast to the simple, active, declarative "Mary told John", the phrase "What Mary did was tell John" may appear sarcastic. However, the specific evaluation conveyed will depend very much on the context. It is important in discourse analysis always to bear in mind the context of the whole discourse being analysed, both at the level of the "text" itself, and at the level of the interaction. The researcher should also bear in mind the context of the interview (who is being interviewed and why: what is the relationship, e.g. of class, power and authority between interviewee and interviewer?).

Beyond the devices of linguistic form, you will discover more openly rhetorical devices such as appeals to fact, appeals to authority, appeals to common sense. Beyond the "repertoire" devices, there are likely to be some *resolutions*, that is attempts by the speaker to resolve contradictions when they become apparent.

Step Five: Interpretation

To some extent, you have already started doing this in Step Four, since it is impossible to notice specific forms of language without forming some ideas as to what their functions are. What you need to do now is to draw these ideas altogether into an overall characterisation and critique of the speaker's deployment of discourse devices. *What* are they saying, *how* are they saying it, and most importantly *why* are they saying it?

Trying to answer the *"why?"* will take you into the highest level of analysis. This will involve trying to understand the speaker's particular social position and worldview: the values they are promoting, and how these tie in with their interests. This is the least straightforward, though most important, aspect of discourse analysis. It depends on full use of your own general and academic knowledge, and a skill in analysis and critique which is much like the skill of literary criticism. This skill can be acquired, through practice and reading, in the same way that literary criticism is acquired. There are no "right" answers, only more or less convincing analyses. Obviously you need to avoid selectivity and bias, that is, avoid selecting only those portions of the transcript which "fit" a preconceived idea you may have had about the speaker's worldview and values. Although a completely objective appraisal and interpretation of another person's values is impossible, particularly if you hold strong opinions yourself, you can avoid crude selectivity by following the principle of including the whole transcript in at least your first attempt at analysis. This principle will ensure that you pay attention to everything that is said.

WORKED EXAMPLE

Step One: Select a Topic and the Respondent(s)

The interview is one of a series on how people see social class as affecting aesthetic taste. The respondent is a twenty-three year old student taking an Access course (one year of post-school education leading to a qualification equivalent to 'A' level GCEs). Like most Access course students, he is seeking the qualification for entry into higher education. The interview took place at his college, and lasted for roughly an hour. The interviewer, visiting for the purpose of interviewing, but also clearly as an academic and colleague of one of his lectures, was likely to be seen first and foremost as having a status and relationship to him similar to that of his lecturers. He may orient to this by feeling a pressure to endorse academic values; conversely to try to subvert them, or to oscillate between these stances.

Step Two: Listen to the Tape

Listening to the tape after the interview confirmed that it was mostly audible, and could be used for analysis. Listening also increased my familiarity with the respondent's discourse, by giving me an overview of how the interview developed.

Step Three: Transcribe the Tape

The interview was transcribed, using square brackets [] to indicate unclearly audible segments, or incomplete segments which have been repaired. For simplicity and ease of reading, disfluencies were left out and replaced with (...) (although some discourse analysts might be interested in disfluencies because they can indicate points of uncertainty). The transcript was arranged in numbered lines so that they could be easily referred to in the analysis and interpretation.

Step Four: Identify Repertoires and Resolutions

Two conflicting repertoires appeared when the respondent was talking about social class. Sometimes he spoke as if class was a definite, external reality. I have labelled this the "Class" repertoire. At other times, he implied that class labels were only words, and that people could choose to apply them to themselves, or not. This repertoire included strong assertions about the possibilities of moving out of the working class, so I have labelled it the "Social Mobility" repertoire. Examples from each repertoire are given below. The line numbers give an indication of their position in the interview.

Class Repertoire

"I know the reality of classes"

(48) I know the reality of *classes*, you know, er social
(49) structure and everything, I'm certainly are of *that*

(103) I must be from the borderline middle class/working class

(137) They say there *is* a bigger gap, but perhaps there is between
(138) middle class and upper class, but I think there's smaller gap
(139) between working class and middle class, you know, down there.

Social Mobility Repertoire

"You've got to get out"

(61) It's— depends if you want to use the word 'working class'
(62) any more, anyway, really, if there's somebody who you still

(63) think is *the* working class, I mean the working class now
(64) compared to the working class twenty years ago, it's not the
(65) same, is it?

(131) Stick to their own, working class supposedly stick to their
(132) own but (...) I don't think they all do. I think you've got
(133) to get out of this working class—saying, using that word,
(134) quite honest. I don't think that holds much any more. I
(135) mean I think it's dying out, I mean there's a lot of new
(136) words, and I think that's a bit old, and especially now,
(137) like sex equality, what's that to do with class?

Notice how, even inside the Social Mobility repertoire, the language of
"Class" is still sometimes used (repertoires can overlap and interleave):

(77) I think even working class, especially now
(78) there's more for working class to go and get things. Yeah,
(79) I think they have the opportunities. I'd like to think it was
(80) down to the individual, but wherever you are you're gonna get—
(81) say if you're working class—people who (...) don't want to
(82) move on or explore things new, you know?

The Social Mobility repertoire is mixed, in both referring to social class
yet denying its reality. There are two distinct vocabularies, associated with
(1) class as reality, and (2) class as a mere word. Class-as-Reality uses
words such as "stick" (lines 131–2 "roots" (line 116), "down", indicating
an underlying metaphor of (self)-stunted growth, while Class-as-Word
talks about "if you want to use the word "working class" (61) and goes
on to use phrases such as "go and get" (178), "go on" (120 below) "move
on, explore" (82), using the overall metaphor of forward movement and
progress:—

(107) *Interviewer:* So, you don't think that your taste is
(108) affected in any way by background?
(109) *Student:* No, not at all.
(110) *Interviewer:* Not at all, your taste is completely free, you
(111) think?
(112) *Student:* Yeah, yeah, I wouldn't say—yeah.
(113) *Interviewer:* Not even influenced?
(114) *Student:* By working class, you mean? No, I (laugh) no—oh,
(115) I won't say it, but—I wouldn't say "I like this because it's
(116) working-class", or "stick to your roots" and all that (...)
(120) No, think you learn as you go on. Er what you see, what
(121) you like (...) personally
(122) speaking I think that some people it might work like that,

(123) I think it does. Not so much for working class but for the
(124) middle, upper class it is like that.

The Social Mobility repertoire is marked by phrases which include quotation clauses. That is, some clauses are spoken as though they have quotation
marks around them, and this serves to distance the speaker himself from
them. These are clauses which quote what the speaker considers to be the
out-moded language of class:

(17) I think it's out of date. Yeah, there's (...) "the great working
(18) class", and "the classes divided" and all this (...) you hear it
(21) to some extent but I think it's overplayed quite honestly.

Resolution Device:

"Ten years from now, you won't be able to be working class any more."
We have seen that this speaker is putting forward two conflicting views of
what social class is: on the one hand talking about it as if it were a real
feature of the world, and on the other dismissing it as an out-dated way of
talking. He resolves this conflict by resorting to an assertion that society is
changing rapidly; that the social classes are disappearing as such:

(144) there's chances for people. And I don't think, you know, if
(145) it goes on like everybody'll be middle class—great, I don't
(146) think, you know, there's not going to *be* class, either.

(205) I think, ten years from now, you won't be able to be working
(206) class any more.

Step Five: Interpretation

The metaphor of progress underlying this respondent's Social Mobility
repertoire comes to its full fruition in his resolution: he decides to view
society as progressing ever more rapidly. This is an appeal to the doctrine of
'Progressivism'. Progressivism is a widespread belief in western societies,
often simply assumed, without reflection, to be an obvious truth. Lakoff and
Johnson in their book *Metaphors We Live By* (1980) argue that the belief is
pervasive, since it appears not only in the form of explicit metaphor of the
type our respondent uses, but also in implicit metaphor. Words which use
the implicit spatial metaphor of "up" vs "down" almost always use the "up"
pole for positive evaluation, and the "down" pole for negative evaluation:
compare "peak of fitness" with "declining condition"; "high-minded" with
"base thoughts"; "have control over" with "struggling under". These
metaphors are implicit, in the sense that the expressions are so frequently
used that they are not thought of as metaphors. Similarly, the word "future"
is more likely to be implicitly associated with the positive poles "upward"

and "forward" rather than with "downward", showing that Progressivism has become embedded in our way of thinking about the future.

The optimism required for this student's belief in the disappearance of social class within ten years can be gauged against Anderson's (1992) statistics on class differences in access to higher education. Since the first expansion of higher education in the 1960s, the difference of participation in higher education between middle and working-class children has hardly changed from about 5:1, while for class 1 the participation rate is 60%. Regional variation still favours the south-east of England (not the north, where this student lives).

For comparison, the opposite view of history as *regression* is held among some groups in society, who look back to the past as a better time, and make use of "Golden Age" imagery (Goodwin, 1982). This can be a feature of conservative thinking, and is also seen in some older people's worldviews (McCulloch, 1992).

The comments of Abrams and Hogg (1990) on belief in social mobility are also useful here. They point out its link with another widespread doctrine, individualism "exemplified by the proverbial tea boy who works his way up to company director" (p. 5). Individualism includes the belief that any achievement is possible through the unaided efforts and merit of the individual: it is well represented in our respondent's discourse:

(84) (...) I think it has to be down to the individual—'cos my
(85) brother he was working class and he's a lecturer in psychology
(86) like you (...)
(88) But he only—and my dad were a builder, you know I don't think
(89) that's exactly a middle-class job (...)
(91) And yet (...) he went out and did it and he were no different to
(92) anyone else so (...) from that point of view I have to say it has
(93) to be the individual.

Abrams and Hogg (1990) point out that "working one's way up" "involves disidentification with, or possibly non-recognition of the subordinate category", that is, the social group from which the individual is seeking to move upward. These features are also apparent in our respondent's discourse. He is disparaging about the "stuckness" of identifying with the working class, and its tastes. Yet, we have seen that, in espousing individualism, he sees himself (by identification with his brother) as working class. The second identification allows him to claim some of his brother's merit in succeeding through individual effort. This conflict is immediately resolved by the dual move of bringing in the notion of "choice", and shifting his class location to the borderline between middle class and working class:

(95) The choices are there. Maybe there are some people [who]
(96) struggle but it—yeah I think it can—can be done. I think
(97) there is too much (...) emphasis on the poor working class and
(98) how hard done to (...)
(100) I think that's overplayed, I really do (...)
(102) And you know (...) if I thought I were working class
(103) it wouldn't be fair saying that, would it? I must be from
(104) the—borderline middle class/working class.

Overall, the student's view of social class, and its relation to aesthetic taste, can be seen to reflect his own social position. He denies that there is any influence of social class on taste in his individual case. Yet he believes the link exists for other people, especially for the middle and upper classes (lines 121–124), and he implies the existence of a group who express solidarity with the working class by sharing its tastes (lines 110–117). As an Access student, sometimes thinking of himself as working class (and sometimes as borderline middle class/working class) and aspiring to higher eduction, it is more supportive of his self-image for him to believe that he is not subject to class influence.

The question of social class and aesthetic taste was interpreted by this student as challenging the personal autonomy of himself and of (most) working-class people. He was much more concerned with the question of class as exerting *any* sort of influence on him, than with the question of taste. Nevertheless, he was willing to assert that middle-and upper-class people's taste *is* influenced by their class background. This is a dimension of inter-class comparison not considered by Bourdieu, and, interestingly, it is one that attributes greater *individual* power (individual autonomy) to people in the subordinate class. The opportunity to express the bodily-felt *dis*tastes mentioned by Bourdieu was not taken, though this may have needed an interview more focused on concrete tastes, than on the abstract question of how social class relates to taste. The student, instead, bent this question to his own concerns about personal autonomy and stability to move out of the working class.

The other stances he takes up also appear to flow from his personal aspirations, although they are stances which have been observed before (Abrams & Hogg, 1990) in people in the same social position as himself (upwardly mobile). So, while on the one hand it is hard for him to deny that class exists (since he has to put to himself the proposition that he is moving out of the working class), the reality of class can be diminished in three ways. Firstly, by seeing it as a mere way of speaking; secondly, by seeing it as a reality (again), but one which is disappearing very fast; thirdly, by dissociating himself from class through the meritorious doctrine of individual effort.

By the end of the interview, he has deployed the rhetorical devices of *respecting fact:* "I know the reality of classes", *redefinition:* "you've got to get out of (...) using the word", *appeal to Progressivism:* social class is rapidly disappearing, and *appeal to individualism:* personal achievement and merit. All of these devices are used in support of aspirations which appear personal to him, but the views encapsulated in these devices are systematically related to both his social position (upwardly mobile) and to his self-image (upwardly mobile, and not influenced by class)

FINAL REMARKS

Having tried to show how discourse can "work", it is now time to face some difficulties of the approach (some real, some imagined). First, there is the relationship with the respondent(s). Many researchers nowadays feel that the respondents should benefit in some way from the research. After all, they have given up their time and revealed personal information to the interviewer. Probably they will have revealed more to the interviewer than the interviewer has to them, and this makes them vulnerable. On the other hand, the discourse analyst is interested in the respondent from a critical standpoint. This really is an ethical dilemma, and as such it has no simple "correct" solution. Each case can only be weighed carefully for its costs and benefits to both parties. Clearly the respondent must not be harmed, but here we can appeal to one of the ethical principles of the British Psychological Society: that respondents should not be exposed to risks greater than they would ordinarily encounter in everyday life. Meeting a discourse analyst, even a confronting one, seems to fall within this category. The benefits of such an encounter seem to lie most obviously with the researcher, but ultimately the research should benefit, if not the respondent directly, then society as a whole in contributing to the increased understanding of social psychology. These problems of the personal encounter do not apply when analysing (published) texts, since these are already in the public domain.

Another difficulty is met when trying to synthesise many interviews into a single interpretation. It will be obvious that discourse analysis is very time-consuming, even for a single interview, yet usually analysts will want to interview several people, to be sure of accessing the characteristic responses of a social group, rather than of one, possibly odd, individual. There are really two problems here. One is that of sheer time and difficulty in synthesising. There is no solution, other than willingness to commit the time and effort required, although a speedy word-processing programme with good facilities is a great help. The other problem is worry about the "representativeness" of the "sample" of people interviewed. The solution here is not to think of "representativeness" in statistical terms. Discourse analysis is a qualitative method. Not depending on numbers for the persuasiveness of its arguments, it does not need to meet the sample-size requirements of "representativeness" as defined statistically. The method is, instead, to demonstrate to a convincing degree the existence of some categories of human responses. This is the logic of "case studies" (Bromley, 1986): generalisation to *all* members of some statistically pre-defined population is not the intention.

The reader may now ask "what is a 'convincing degree'?". In reporting a study, there is not enough space to reproduce every stretch of speech which supports a repertoire the analyst claims to have found. Nor would this be helpful, as points must be made succinctly if they are to be understandable. The analyst must report evidence selectively, but sufficiently to make the case. Discourse analysis incorporates safeguards against distorting selectivity, by requiring the analyst to keep in mind the whole transcript. An ideal solution would be to include complete transcripts as an appendix. There is not enough space for this in academic journals, although authors can make their transcripts available separately on request (as I hereby do here). It is possible for students to append full interview transcripts to their projects and extended essays, and this should ideally be done.

KEY READINGS ON DISCOURSE ANALYSIS

Gilbert, G.N. & Mulkay, M. (1984). *Opening Pandora's Box: A Sociological Analysis of Scientists' Discourse*. Cambridge: Cambridge University Press.

Potter, J. & Reicher, S. (1987). Discourses of community and conflict: The organization of social categories in accounts of a "riot". *British Journal of Social Psychology*, 26, 25–40.

Potter, J. & Wetherell, M. (1987). *Discourse and Social Psychology*. London: Sage.

Potter, J. & Wetherell, M. (1995). Discourse analysis. In J.A. Smith, R. Harre and L.Van Langenhove (Eds.), *Rethinking Methods in Psychology*. London: Sage, 80–92.

Potter, J. & Edwards, D. (1990). Nigel Lawson's tent: Discourse analysis, attribution theory and the social psychology of fact. *European Journal of Social Psychology*, 20, 24–40.

Wetherell, M., Stiven, H., & Potter, J. (1987). Unequal egalitarianism: A preliminary study of discourses concerning gender and employment opportunities. *British Journal of Social Psychology*, 26, 59–71.

Wooffitt, R. (1992). *Telling Tales of the Unexpected: The Organization of Factual Discourse*. Hemel Hempstead: Harvester Wheatsheaf.

II | THEORY-DRIVEN APPROACHES TO QUALITATIVE RESEARCH

INTRODUCTION TO PART II

An important aim of this book is to present students and others with a variety of different forms of qualitative analysis, and a variety of ways that qualitative research can be undertaken. The following three chapters take an approach to qualitative analysis which is very different from that of the discourse analysts. Where the discourse approach eschews prior theory, at least to the extent of regarding it as important that the outcomes are entirely data-driven, the following three examples of qualitative analysis are theory-led, drawing on existing concepts and models to inform their analysis.

Nicky Hayes

One problem which often worries those unused to qualitative methods of analysis is the way in which a researcher goes about extracting relevant information for the study, from the mass of data available. There is some anxiety that, as a result of the human tendency to develop perceptual sets, the selection of material will be subject to unconscious bias and therefore almost inevitably support the researcher's point of view. Consciously or otherwise, researchers may ignore, or simply not notice, information which runs counter to their own point of view.

One possible half-way point between limited, qualitative research techniques which are designed to preclude the possibility of experimenter influence of this nature, and more reflexive research methods involving qualitative analysis, is to use theory to provide a prior direction for thematic analysis. Using this approach, the themes of the analysis are established beforehand, as a result of definite predictions which emerge from the theoretical framework which is being explored. This is the approach adopted in Nicky Hayes' chapter.

The research described in Chapter 6 relates to an investigation of social identification at work, arguing that the working group represents an important, if not essential, feature of organisational life for most people. Three aspects of social identity theory were operationalised into practical areas of application for working life, and used as the basis for interpreting staff experience in a longitudinal, action-research-based investigation of two small companies.

In view of the close theoretical connections between social identification and social representation theory, and also between social representations and attributional analysis, the analysis of the data focused on the attributions provided by employees during their interviews. These were extracted from interview transcripts, and those attributional statements relevant to the three themes of the consultancy were selected for analysis. The thematic analysis was thus entirely theory-driven. Changes within the two companies over time, and differences between the companies, were highlighted in the resulting descriptions.

It can be seen, then, that this approach is much more closely related to the hypothetico-deductive model of scientific investigation than most of the other studies in this book. Prior theory provides the themes, which then structure the way that the data is explored. The strength of qualitative data, however, is that it allows the researcher to develop unpredicted insights, and to learn from the research participants' contributions. For that reason, the analysis was not strictly about confirming or disconfirming explicit hypotheses. Rather, in keeping with the more open approach to data offered by qualitative analysis, it was concerned with exploring what the data had to offer, but in a manner which had some prior structure, which offered the opportunity for direct and systematic comparisons between and within groups, as well as exploring specific meanings for particular individuals.

Peter Stratton

According to some definitions, such as that maintained by Strauss and Corbin (1990), qualitative analysis is simply analysis which does note involve numbers or counting. If this book were adhering rigidly to that model, then Chapter 7, by Peter Stratton, would not have been included. There is, however, a broader definition of qualitative analysis which has been equally often applied by psychologists, which is concerned with the depth and richness of the data which is being analysed. Effectively, the idea is that quality is located in the material itself, and the challenge is to the simplistic and superficial nature of traditional quantitative analysis.

Peter Stratton's chapter follows this approach to qualitative analysis. It does, ultimately, involve some numbers; but the qualitative nature of the analysis lies in the richness of the material from which those numbers have been derived, and how well those numbers are able to handle and describe that richness. For the purist, adhering rigidly to the Strauss and Corbin view of qualitative analysis, this reasoning may seem specious; but the aim of this book is to present some of the diversity of qualitative analyses as they are applied by psychologists, including approaches, like this one, which lie at the interface between qualitative and quantitative approaches.

Like Chapters 6 and 8, this form of qualitative analysis is theory-driven, with its roots firmly in attribution theory. Peter Stratton uses the Leeds Attributional Coding System (LACS) to identify some of the fundamental assumptions and beliefs revealed by conversational data. The system is based around the idea that, as people talk, they ascribe causes or reasons for occurrences and events, and these causal attributions can reveal far more about that person's underlying concerns and world-view than can be identified using conventional questionnaire or structured interview techniques.

Unlike traditional marketing research, in which participants' responses are strictly constrained, Stratton's research method involves the use of systemic interviewing techniques, aimed to encourage respondents to talk freely and at length about their views, ideas, opinions and beliefs. This produces a rich source of data, which can range far beyond the immediate topic under investigation, but which nonetheless contributes a great deal to our understanding of that person's concerns.

The analysis, then involves exploring a rich supply of conversational data for the underlying assumptions, values, beliefs and world-views which are both explicit and implicit in what the person is saying. The exploration takes the form of a search for causal attributions—statements which indicate some form of causal belief on the part of the speaker. The way that these attributions can be extracted from the data is outlined in the chapter in a simplified form.

Once the attributions have been extracted, the task is to identify their distinctive characteristics. A great deal of psychological research has explored the nature of attributions, and in particular such attributional dimensions as whether the causes are perceived as long-lasting, controllable, and so on. The Leeds Attributional Coding System was developed on the basis of this research, and involves identifying five significant attributional dimensions: stable/unstable (likely to continue in the future or not), global/specific (affecting a range of outcomes or just that particular thing), internal/external (originating with the person concerned, or with external agents), personal/universal (specifically affecting that individual or affecting everyone else as well), and controllable/uncontrollable (whether the person could have exerted a significant influence over the outcome or not).

Each of the attributions extracted from the original interview material is coded, in binary form, which is where the numbers come in. But it is important to remember that this type of numerical data is entirely different from simply categorising content and counting its occurrence: in this technique, the numbers appear only at a very late stage, and represent a theoretically-developed and rich level of analysis. The method's claim to be regarded as a form of qualitative analysis lies in the meaningful nature of the data which it is dealing with, and the meaningful way that the outcome is presented.

The remainder of the analysis involves exploring the patterns of attributions which are connected with topics of interest which have emerged from the research data. The rich data provided by even a single interview can provide insights which would be entirely missed by a more superficial research technique, and yet which can be crucial to understanding the essential underlying issues. Attributional patterns can emerge repeatedly even in apparently unconnected contexts, and these can be useful indicators of more general issues. For example, the link between lack of control and perceptions of vulnerability which emerged from this particular research project was able to give the airline, as well as the researchers, a valuable pointer when seeking ways of improving their customer service.

Although Stratton's chapter differs from others in this book in several respects, this approach to qualitative analysis has its place when we are looking at the range of options and possibilities offered by the new orientation. In the same way as the previous chapter is able to connect thematic qualitative analysis with theory-driven hypothesis-testing, so this chapter can show how bridges can also be built between meaningful data and the use of numbers: how there may be connections between qualitative and quantitative analysis rather than an arbitrary and uncrossable barrier between the two.

Gerry Finn

Like Chapters 6 and 7, Gerry Finn's Chapter 8 adopts a theory-led approach to qualitative analysis. In this instance, the theory concerned is that of social representation theory: the approach to social understanding developed by the French psychologist Serge Moscovici, which emphasises the nature of collective social understandings and their relationships with individual beliefs and belief systems.

Social representations are intimately linked with social identification, and the qualitative analysis presented in this chapter is directly concerned with the social representations which emerged in the protestant and catholic communities of Northern Ireland during recent conflicts. Such representations and such identifications are strongly historical in nature, which means that any attempt at a psychological understanding of them must take into account both historical events and perceived history. For this reason, Finn begins the chapter with a very brief summary of the salient history. As can be seen later in the chapter, the perceived history emerges through the qualitative analysis itself.

The chapter, then, begins with a brief overview of the salient history, and goes on to discuss the relevant theoretical background in terms of social identification and in particular social representations. However, social representations are not always verbal in nature, and nor are they always expressed—even indirectly—through verbal media. In this chapter, Gerry Finn has opted to explore the social representations of different political issues and factions in Northern Ireland through an analysis of the vivid and carefully constructed wall paintings in Northern Ireland. Both groups have used murals to express political/historical messages and perceptions, and the themes and images apparent in these murals are fascinating indicators of the social representations held by the different communities.

Although dealing with visual image rather than the spoken word, Gerry Finn uses a rhetorical analysis to explore the ways that social representations are revealed through themes and images. The analysis is of necessity incomplete—it has not been possible, for example, to reproduce the murals in full colour, and colour themes are another dimension which carry their own implications for this material—Finn explores a number of issues which emerge from the murals, both in terms of their historical context, and the rhetorical stance which they adopt in the context of the conflict within which they were painted.

As Finn points out, wall paintings by their very nature are located within a specific time and context, and may remain for variable time periods. An analysis of this nature, therefore, encapsulates the social and historical perceptions of the period when the mural was created. So it is through the exploration of a variety of murals, created at different times and representing the views of different groupings in the community, that social representations become evident. The sample of murals discussed here is far from being all-inclusive, but represents a selection illustrating how a variety of issues may be drawn out of visual material, using the techniques of rhetorical analysis and the theoretical framework offered by social representations. The separate discussions of loyalist and republican murals allows the researcher to identify similarities, but most importantly to use the contrasts between the two to highlight distinctive features of the social representations evident in the two communities.

This chapter, then, like Halla Beloff's, shows us that adopting qualitative analysis as a research technique lends itself as readily to the analysis of the visual image as to that of the spoken or written word—a type of analysis which has been largely omitted from psychological research. Both researchers explain the procedures involved in such an analysis, and in so doing, open up these approaches to others wishing to adopt a similar approach.

6

Theory-led thematic analysis: Social identification in small companies

Nicky Hayes
Department of Behavioural Sciences, University of Huddersfield

The research which is to be described in this chapter was part of an exploration of some of the social psychological mechanisms which underlie organisational cultures. Organisational cultures have been studied extensively, and, during the 1980s in particular, researchers investigated their various manifestations in great detail. While inevitably management training practices led to the development of some theories of culture which were merely typologies (e.g. Harrison, 1972), other models adopted a more complex and thoughtful approach. The study of organisational symbols, rituals and heroes gave rise to semiotic analyses of organisational cultures (e.g. Barley, 1983); the study of organisational practices and strategic decisions gave rise to systems theories (e.g. Allaire and Firsirotu, 1984); while studies of metaphor, anecdote and organisational myths led to a belief that the core of an organisation's culture was a set of implicit assumptions about the nature of causality and even reality (e.g. Schein, 1990).

By the 1990s, culture was increasingly being viewed as a layered phenomenon (e.g. Lundberg, 1990). According to this approach, the surface layer consists of the overt manifestations of culture: its symbolism, rituals, metaphors and socialisation practices. Beneath this is the strategic layer, which is expressed in patterns of typical management practices and decision-making. But underlying both of the others is a deeper layer, which is a shared set of values and assumptions which is used to explain the world and why it is like it is. It is this deeper layer, shared throughout the organisation, which both expresses the culture and guides the organisation's members to operate on a personal level in ways which are characteristic of their organisation.

Looking at these ideas using theories available from social psychology, I argued that it is both possible, and helpful, to see organisational cultures as social representations which are shared by the organisation's members (Hayes 1991). As Moscovici and others have shown, social representations form an important basis to the way that we evaluate and understand the world. They arise (perhaps it is more proper to say they are negotiated) as an interaction between the cultural/ideological values of a society, the values and beliefs operating in a social grouping within that society, and the individual's own social and personal experience. Moreover, social representations express, often indirectly, deeply-held ideas about the nature of reality, and of causality (Moscovici, 1984).

A second strand of research into organisational culture addresses diversity within the organisation. Some large organisations, such as IBM or Mars, seem to have coherent, unified cultures which are shared by all members. Other equally large organisations have more fragmented cultures, in which members of one department may share entirely different values and beliefs to members of another. With some, indeed, it is questionable how far a single organisational culture actually exists. Counter-cultures and canteen cultures can operate with values and goals entirely opposite to those held by the senior management of the organisation. Since newcomers to the organisation are socialised at the departmental level, the existence of counter-cultures can be self-perpetuating, and challenge the notion of a single organisational culture.

Van Maanen and Barley (1985) argue that it is useful to think of an organisation's culture as a series of separate "subcultures", centred around different groups within the organisation. Each of these groups develops its own set of shared beliefs and assumptions about the way that people are, and how to go about getting things done. The beliefs and values which develop in different groups may or may not overlap with one another, and if they do, they may overlap to different degrees. A "strong" culture company, Van Maanen and Barley argue, is one in which there is a great deal of overlap in the values and beliefs held by different "subcultures", whereas a company with a less coherent culture is one in which there is little such overlap (Fig. 6.1).

This way of looking at organisational culture has a number of methodological as well as theoretical implications. One thing it does is to emphasise the importance of the working group—the significant people with whom an employee interacts from day to day—if we are to look at how shared beliefs, or social representations, develop in the first place. Again applying theories available from social psychology, I have argued that social identity theory provides us with a framework which we can use to under-

A "weak" culture company

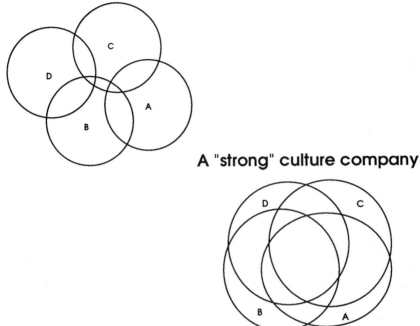

A "strong" culture company

FIG. 6.1.   Working groups and organisational cultures.

stand how membership of their own group becomes important to people, and why this encourages shared beliefs to develop (Hayes, 1991). Social identity theory can also show us how and why in-groups and out-groups can become so important in working life, and so may help us to understand how one organisation may maintain a more unified culture than another.

It can be seen, then, that this approach to understanding organisational culture places a great deal of emphasis on the working group, and on which day-to-day interactions produce shared understandings. These understandings are concerned with fundamental issues, such as human nature and the nature of causality. They are used to explain why people are like they are, why the organisation works as it does, and why it is or is not worthwhile to take a particular course of action. But they are often expressed indirectly, and not explicitly.

This part of my research, therefore, was all about looking for a way to explore the shared understandings within a working group. The investigation reported here took place in two small companies, on the grounds that the number and range of possible social identifications in that working context would probably be fewer, and perhaps less complex, than those to be found in a larger organisation. Since at this point I was particularly interested in seeing how any shared understandings which might emerge were related to social identification, my research questions were about happenings within the organisation which might relate to that.

Consultancy and Social Identification

The research utilised a consultancy model, which operated on the idea that social identity theory can provide a conceptual vehicle for understanding many of the issues and events which go on in everyday working life. In terms of the consultancy itself, three facets of social identity theory were operationalised into practical areas of application for working life, and these were used as a framework for interpreting staff experience. The three principles were emphasised as providing a conceptual basis which the company directors could use, in order to generate positive human resource management strategies in the company.

The three principles draw on three different aspects of social identity theory. The first of these is categorisation, or the tendency of human beings to classify people and events into different categories. The second is the question of intragroup cohesion, and the way in which people come to perceive themselves and others as belonging to the same group. The third is the need for group membership to provide a source of positive self-esteem for the individual. These three features were operationalised for the organisational context in terms of (a) the setting of "them-and-us" boundaries which would help the company to progress rather than hinder development; (b) the establishment of effective formal and informal communication so that all could feel they "belonged"; and (c) providing opportunities for employees to take pride in their company and their working group (Fig. 6.2).

Most of the recommendations which emerged from the consultancy visits took the form of familiar human resource recommendations, which have become well established as sound organisational practice over time. The difference here was that they were presented to the company directors as ways of expressing underlying psychological mechanisms, rather than as practices which had little or no connection with theory. Presenting them this way helps to make sure that the practices which are adopted will suit that particular context.

For example: there are many ways of establishing good communication in an organisation, and many forms that such communication can take. Any consultant rapidly discovers that practices which work well in one place often fall flat in another. But what is ultimately important in social identity terms is not the particular technique, but that all employees should have a general awareness of what is going on, and of how different people con-

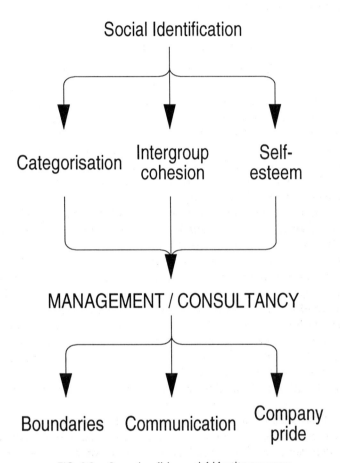

FIG. 6.2.   Operationalising social identity processes.

tribute to the whole, so that they can feel themselves to be part of a dynamic whole. Knowing that this is the purpose allows a manager to experiment, to find the practices which will best suit their particular organisation.

The investigation, therefore, was concerned with whether shared beliefs would emerge from accounts given by members of a small working group.

In order to look at this, social identity theory was used as a framework, both to inform the practical consultancy service which was provided and also, as we shall see in the next section, to shape the analysis of the data.

Methodological Background to the Research

Any form of qualitative analysis is likely to raise issues about comparability. On the one hand, we want to compare people's experiences, in order to find out what they have in common. Yet, on the other hand, we want to find a method which will allow us to appreciate and acknowledge each person's own experience, and to recognise different viewpoints. In the approach described in this chapter, the gathering of the initial data, the framework for the analysis, and the questions which were asked as part of the analysis were all established by prior theory.

The Use of Action Research

There is an argument which states that it is both naive and impractical for psychologists working in the real world to convince themselves that they have no impact on that which they are studying. In the case of organisational research, this is particularly so. People working in organisations are naturally curious about researchers, and develop their own theories about what is going on. As Lewin (1947) showed, it is more sensible for researchers in such contexts to acknowledge this as a factor, and to design their work acknowledging that they are having an effect, than to pretend that their work is somehow immune to such effects. Acknowledging this, the research project as a whole took the form of action research within two small companies.

As we have seen, the research followed a consultancy model, in which the directors of each company were given advice on human relations issues within their company, based on interviews conducted with their staff. The theoretical framework informing the consultancy report was about how social identity processes occur in day to day interactions within the company. The consultancy was provided free, on the understanding that the staff interviews (which would remain entirely confidential) could then be used for further analysis on the part of the researcher.

Social Representations

Since the research focus was on the shared understandings of members of working groups, that meant that I was primarily interested in people's own experience of working life within the company. Consequently, it was decided that the best way to go about this was to collect accounts from the employees themselves, about the company, and what it was like to work in it. This selection of research method was informed by Rom Harré's ethnogenic approach, which emphasises account analysis as one useful way of collecting information about social being (Harré, 1993).

The analytical method which was used to make sense of the interview data was a thematic qualitative analysis, in which the explanations which had been given by employees during the interview were related to different themes. Each part of this analysis was driven by pre-existing theory, reflecting the theoretical context of the research.

As we saw in the previous section, one theoretical dimension of the research was concerned with social representations, and the way that these are used to explain everyday experience. Social representations, at their most fundamental level, effectively constitute shared theories about why the world is as it is, and why people are like they are (Moscovici, 1984). It is the power of social representations to explain and make sense out of day-to-day experience which forms their social attractiveness, and which allows the central core of the representation to remain reasonably consistent even though peripheral elements are negotiated and adjusted to fit particular situations. So when looking at the interview data in this research project, I was particularly interested in the explanations which people gave for why things happened, or why they were like they were.

The explanatory nature of social representations has methodological implications. It implies that there is value in seeking methods of analysis which can focus on the shared explanations which people give. This leads, in turn, to the use of attributional analysis. For example: Moscovici and Hewstone (1983) used attributional analysis to explore the emergence of social representations concerning split-brain research. The method allowed them to look at the type of explanations people were giving, and also to see what these explanations had in common. The link between group-based attributions and social representations led me to focus particularly on the causal attributions which were made during the course of the interviews. These formed the basic data for the analysis.

Social Identity

A second theoretical dimension of the research concerned the question of social identity within the company. Three processes of social identity theory had been identified as being of particular interest, and were reflected in the questions asked in the interviews. These three themes formed the basis of the qualitative analysis, and only those causal attributions which related to one of the three themes were selected for analysis. The selection of data for the analysis therefore involved theory-driven themes, rather than the analysis being based on themes which arose spontaneously from the data.

This, then, was not the type of grounded theory approach to the data which is discussed in the later part of this book. Instead, the theory, or theories, which were under investigation directed the research in three ways: through the selection of the material which was analysed, by restricting the data for analysis to causal attributions, and by providing the themes which formed the framework of the qualitative analysis. In many ways, this can almost be considered as a hypothetico-deductive approach to the research question, but one which uses qualitative data to provide its evidence rather than quantitative information.

The Design of the Study

The study took the form of a longitudinal, action-research-based investigation of two small companies. The companies concerned were small computer software houses, with between twenty and twenty-four employees each at the beginning of the study. They had similar histories, having each been started by a small group of software experts working in a much larger organisation, who had decided to operate independently. The companies had been able to lease their services to the parent organisation for the first few years, but were also able to gain other contracts for their work. As they had matured, these other contracts had become more significant for their work, and the original support from the parent organisation had become less and less important.

In both cases, the original small group who had founded the company had found that they needed to take on additional staff. At the time the research began, each company had roughly two dozen employees: a number too large to be managed by informal communication and personnel systems. This growth had meant that the directors found themselves faced with an increasing number of non-technical problems of human management. As technical people, they found these difficult to handle. They were also slightly reluctant to spend much time dealing with them, on the grounds that this would detract from their "real" work. However, neither company was large enough to support the employment of staff in a purely management capacity, and nor could they support an expensive human resource consultancy programme.

The consultancy, therefore, adopted a "catalytic" approach, based on the idea that a relatively limited contribution at a fairly early point in the company's development could generate a sensitivity to human resource issues in a receptive management, and that this would help them to find their own way of dealing with such problems until they were large enough to employ specialists with the appropriate skills. However, in a small company time is money, and money is not in large supply. This meant that the consultancy needed to be limited and focused, taking up as little working time as possible.

It also meant that it was necessary to emphasise explaining some of the underlying reasons why problems occurred, rather than providing solutions for individual incidents, since the consultancy was as much of a training process for the directors as a trouble-shooting exercise. There was also a need for follow-up visits, to help the company directors come to terms with the fluidity of human resource questions, and to provide some feedback as to how their efforts were being received by staff. Each company, therefore, was visited three times.

The Two Companies

The two companies involved in the research were very similar in many objective characteristics. They were, as has been mentioned, both small software houses with similar histories, and at the beginning of the study were both of a similar size. Both groups of directors contained individuals of an extremely high level of technical competence. But they differed greatly in the way that they went about the business of directing their companies, in respect to business development, staff management, and technical organisation (see Table 6.1).

In general, the orientation of CompuSys (*the names of the companies described in this chapter have been changed, for obvious reasons*) was towards high expectations of staff, accompanied by high technical standards and a generally positive attitude. The directors described the company's policy as people-oriented, and expressed aims for the company which included not only technical excellence, but also a commitment to their staff's well-being and job security. They intended to expand, and engaged in some planned diversification, but were aware of the pitfalls in over-expansion too soon. Their business plans were based on the premise that the company should remain on a firm economic base at all times. When the consultancy began, no-one had left the company, which had been in existence for just over three years; and by the end of the fourteen-month period only one person had left.

The orientation of TechnoComp, by contrast, was much less planned. Unlike CompuSys, the directors of the company did a great deal of "hands-on" work themselves. Consequently they were constantly busy and gave little thought to the long-term management of the company. High levels of staff turnover, however, had alerted them to the fact that there was a problem, so the consultancy was welcomed. Their lack of systematic business planning meant that they were entirely market-led, responding to opportunities without systematic planning and allocation of resources. It also meant that the work load was highly diverse, which increased the work loads on the directors, and increased their reluctance to spend "unproductive" time on the demands of management.

Employees in this company appeared to be rather over-controlled. For example, the directors operated a strict timekeeping policy, according to

TABLE 6.1
Comparisons Between CompuSys and TechnoComp.

CompuSys	TechnoComp
Clear differentiation of directors' responsibilities	Nominal differentiation of roles but some overlap
Not all (6) founders as directors, directorships task-dependent	All (4) founders as directors: Some role differentiation but also overlap
MD has overall responsibility for leadership	No single leader: decisions taken by director consensus
Each member of staff has a single line manager	Nominal line manager but staff answerable to all directors
Loose company policy regarding timekeeping but high expectations about commitment	Strict company policy about timekeeping: staff reprimanded if late
Staff explicitly rewarded if extra effort/time put in	Appreciation of extra staff efforts only acknowledged intermittently
Lunchtime taken according to member of staff's own decision	Lunchtimes pre-set by directors; no allowances for lost time
Staff at work from 7.30am and frequently stay late	Staff arrive after 8.45; 1 person in about 8.30; all staff leave at 5 prompt
Office arranged with task-appropriate working areas	Desks arranged school-like, facing supervisor
Explicit technical standards	Implicit technical standards
Staff seen as company's main asset	Directors' own expertise seen as company's main asset
Detailed plans for expansion	No business plans
Leased premises to allow for moves as company grows	Owned premises
Plans include regional office; also for mergers/takeovers	No plans for expansion
Planned decisions about taking contracts (e.g. refused large but questionable contract).	Market-led, responding to openings as they arrive.

which staff were reprimanded if they arrived late. This policy seemed to have resulted in an unwillingness at TechnoComp to do any more than was compulsory: everyone stopped work on the dot of five, and arrived no more than ten minutes before nine. This contrasted with the approach at CompuSys, where it was simply assumed that staff would make up any lost time during the course of the working week, so nobody checked working hours. There, staff frequently arrived early, worked late, and sometimes even came in at weekends.

The Analysis

These differences between the two companies meant that it was worthwhile to draw comparisons in terms of the responses which were obtained from the interviews. Table 6.1 documents some of the overt behavioural differences between the companies, and it was hypothesised that congruent differences would also become apparent in the shared beliefs held by employees. It was, therefore, hoped that the contrast between the two ostensibly similar companies might produce an appropriate context for analysing differences in group beliefs between the two companies.

The ultimate design of the entire study, therefore, included five different sets of analyses. Two of these were longitudinal: one from each company. Three involved cross-company comparisons, looking at the accounts obtained from staff in the two companies on the first, second and third visits. For reasons of space, however, we will only be able to look at the cross-company comparisons in this chapter. More detailed information can be obtained from Hayes (1991).

The Conduct of the Study

The two companies were each visited three times, at seven-month intervals. This meant that developments and changes in each company were followed up over a fourteen month period. The visits consisted almost entirely of private interviews with members of staff, each lasting 20–30 minutes, conducted over a period of three days. This was then followed up by a report for the directors which summarised the views expressed by the staff, and highlighted human resource issues which they should consider. The report in turn was followed by a meeting between the researcher and the directors, to discuss its implications and the company's general policy and progress.

The interviews with staff consisted of semi-structured rapport interviews (Massarik, 1981). In other words, they were interviews which took the form of conversations, but in which I made sure that the conversation covered half a dozen specific points (see Table 6.2). Each employee was given this schedule when they began their interview, to establish the context of the interview, and had it in front of them throughout the time. Since all of the employees were aware of my visit and curious about it, there was no attempt to hide the object of the exercise, as far as the company's management were concerned, and many employees appeared to welcome the opportunity to talk about the company. In such cases, it was often only necessary to bring the conversation back to the schedule in the last five minutes of the interview, so that we could both ensure that all of the relevant topics had been covered.

TABLE 6.2
The Interview Schedule

When did you first join the company, and how did this happen?

How would you describe your role within the company? Who do you answer to mostly?

How do you get to hear about new developments or arrangements within the company?

Do you enjoy working here? Can you give me any examples of events that are typical of working here?

Does CompuSys/TechnoComp have any social events outside of working hours?

How would you compare CompuSys/TechnoComp with other, similar companies?

How do you think CompuSys/TechnoComp is likely to develop in the future?

Almost all interviews were tape-recorded, on the understanding that I could then use the material for further research. It was made clear that being tape-recorded was entirely optional on the employees' part, although it would be helpful to me as a researcher to have the interviews. In two cases, the staff members requested not to be tape-recorded, which meant that their opinions contributed to the consultancy report but could not be included in the theoretical analysis. Five more interviews were lost from the analysis as a result of equipment malfunction or unclear recordings which prevented transcription. In total, 67 interviews contributed to the analysis (see Table 6.3).

The questions on the interview schedule were intended not simply to initiate conversation about the company, but also to cover aspects of company life pertaining to the three themes of the consultancy which were described earlier in this chapter: categorisation, intragroup cohesion, and opportunities for positive self-esteem. Since it was the causal attributions which were of interest in this research, for the reasons given above, the first stage in applying the analysis was to go through the transcripts identifying

TABLE 6.3
Number of Interview Transcripts Obtained From
Each Company.

	CompuSys	TechnoComp
First visit	14	9
Second visit	12	10
Third visit	16	7
Total	42	26

causal attributions where these appeared. The heuristic which was used to help to identify attributions was the principle that if the statement could be meaningfully rearranged into a statement involving the word "because", without changing its basic structure—in other words, if it had been offered by the interviewee as a reason why something happened—then it could be treated as a causal attribution.

The application of this heuristic generated a large number of causal attributions. However, these covered many diverse facets of organisational life. Any causal attributions which related to the three theoretical themes were therefore extracted from the rest, and used in the analysis. Using a theoretical framework of this kind to structure the analysis also meant that comparisons could meaningfully be drawn between the two companies, since attributions which were concerned with issues specific to the individual company were omitted, and the themes of the analysis were the same for both sets of data. As a result, it was possible to explore specific issues, such as the opportunities for positive self-esteem presented by each company on the first visit. It is not possible to offer the full analysis here, for reasons of space, but examples of comparisons relating to the question of positive self-esteem are given in the next part of this chapter.

Outcomes of the Study

Social identity theory, as we saw earlier, argues that it is important that membership of a particular group should represent a source of positive self-esteem. If it doesn't, people will seek to leave or distance themselves from the group. In the context of a small company, there is little interpersonal space for people to distance themselves. However, high rates of staff turn-over are generally taken as indicators that all is not well in a given orga-nisation; and in this respect, the two companies were very different.

Although they were both doing very similar work, in the same region of the country, so it can be assumed that employment opportunities were similar for both sets of personnel; one company (the one referred to here as CompuSys) had not lost a single member of staff in its three years of exis-tence, whereas the second company (referred to here as TechnoComp) had lost more than ten staff during the past two years. Although it had been in existence longer than CompuSys, enquiries revealed that a high rate of staff turnover had been characteristic of the company throughout its seven year history—and indeed, this was mainly why the directors had been responsive to the proposed research.

Attributions to do with sources of self-esteem, as revealed in the staff interviews on the first visit, showed some very clear differences between the two companies. As can be seen from the analysis, these differences had become even more extreme by the time of the third, and final, visit.

CompuSys—First Visit

The attributions which were made about the company as a whole showed that employees took a general pride in it:

> "I know CompuSys was good because everyone you mention it to knows it as a good company, and they know it puts out good quality work"
>
> "I think we give good service because we are all conscientious about what we do"
>
> "Any growth that we achieve will reflect a sound approach to expansion because we've got a managing director who's got his head screwed on right"
>
> "You won't get stale at CompuSys because it will always be changing and in touch with new developments"
>
> "You could see forward thinking at CompuSys because they were diversifying the size of the company and looking for bigger premises"

Attributions made about employees' individual concerns were equally positive:

> "CompuSys is great because they look after you, and whatever you do for them is appreciated financially"
>
> "CompuSys is great because they expect you to sell in line with your own ethics"
>
> "I came to CompuSys because I felt this was the company to learn from"
>
> "I think the company must do well, partly because of its reputation as a company, and also because they show an interest and they really do care what you think"

TechnoComp—First Visit

The picture obtained from employees at TechnoComp on the first visit, however, was rather different. When they were talking about their company as a whole, TechnoComp employees also indicated general pride in the company:

> "TechnoComp is good because the people are a bit special"
>
> "TechnoCorp service to the customer is excellent because the problem always gets sorted out"
>
> "TechnoComp professional practice is good because of the software they've got"
>
> "TechnoComp is good because its grown a lot recently which shows it's doing well"

It was noticeable, though, that these attributions tended to be more specific than those offered as sources of pride in CompuSys, and notably lacked mention of future-oriented issues such as forward planning and professional development which had been such a characteristic of the other company. Also, when they were talking about individual issues, a very different picture emerged:

> "People think they're working for nothing because they're not getting any rewards"
> "You wonder if it has been worth it because you don't get any thanks"
> "I know one person left because the wages were a pittance and there was no job satisfaction"
> "We don't maintain programming standards because of staff turnover"
> "There's a tense feeling in the place because promotion doesn't happen here"

CompuSys—Second Visit

It was evident from the attributions made in the interviews during the second visit that the staff retained their sense of pride in CompuSys:

> "You get respect from outside because you actually work for CompuSys"
> "I thought what a super company when I joined CompuSys because I could see that we were going places"
> "The CompuSys way is special because in the working atmosphere you are treated as an individual"
> "We are well thought of because we are honest"

There were, however, some signs that staff were becoming increasingly concerned about their professional development, although not in such a way as to lead them to be critical of the company:

> "My only worry is about my personal development because I want to work for CompuSys as long as I can"
> "People are definitely anxious not to be left behind because they would like the technical development"
> "I don't want to be doing this for a long time because I want to be with CompuSys in the future but I want to get involved in something new"

TechnoComp— Second Visit

The consultancy report to TechnoComp after the first visit, on the other hand, had emphasised the importance of providing sources of positive self-esteem for employees, particularly emphasising professional development and progress within the company. The technical director, responsible for most of the staff, had made a consistent effort to implement these ideas. At the time of the second visit, seven months later, morale within the company was much higher, and this was reflected in the general attributions:

"I like being in this organisation because it's dynamic and says go out and do it tomorrow because we've got to have it"

"I like working here because it's different, because when I get up in the morning I know that I'm going to a place that I like"

"It's a good place to work here now because there's been a lot of improvement and things have got a lot better"

Specific comments, too, were very much more positive, at least with respect to technical work:

"It's good here because they've started to do some in-house training"

"I've been getting good experience here because I've been working on different systems and things"

"Having the chart up spurs people on because it's nice for them to see their achievement"

"Going on site is good because it means that you can get much more involved, because you can see where you're going and you can see the people you're working for"

"It's better that you look after one site because you're talking to the same person and you get a better rapport"

Non-technical staff, however, had not experienced the same changes and were less sanguine:

"It is frustrating because I have got a lot more potential than I am using here"

"I am going to look for another job because it's not doing my career any good staying here"

"The technical people can do well because they can get on with things that they are proud of"

CompuSys—Third Visit

By the time of the third visit, the company had continued to grow, but it was very apparent from the attributions made during the course of the interviews that staff retained a very high degree of pride in the company:

"I think CompuSys has still got distinctive values because it's always been there, it's the way we've been brought up"

"I like it here because it's a very good company"

"I was glad when I landed at CompuSys because CompuSys is a dream place to train"

"The people who work here are really first-rate because they know what they're doing and they're good at what they do"

"I was impressed because I could see straight off that CompuSys had people who were really of top calibre"

"I think CompuSys will expand in a big way in the future because the market seems to be there"

"CompuSys is going to grow and grow because the company as a whole is managed in a very professional way"

"CompuSys is going to grow and grow because it's got very marketable skills and highly professional people"

"The managing director won't allow us to grow too fast because he's nobody's fool and a good businessman, and he's making sure that CompuSys has managed growth"

It was evident, then, that the directors of this particular small company had managed to retain, and if anything enhance, their employees' pride in their company. To CompuSys employees, working for the company represented a positive source of self-esteem, as a direct consequence of the directors' policy on technical excellence, explicit reward of staff efforts, and highly ethical business practice. Working for CompuSys, employees felt, earned then respect from those working in other companies, as well as providing them with a sense of personal achievement because their own efforts were appreciated.

Techno-Comp—Third Visit

By the time of the third visit to TechnoComp, by contrast, many of the innovations introduced by the technical director had lost their momentum. In addition, some very real interpersonal problems apparent on the non-technical side of the company had also had an effect, and morale was low. Positive attributions were very few, and highly specific in nature:

"I think the new way is good because it's allocated by sites"

"My client support isn't the same as before because now it's much bigger"

"I can leave the development side because Robert makes sure everything gets done"

For the most part, however, comments were much more negative, and even pessimistic in tone:

"I would describe this as just a small computer company because I wouldn't say there's that much special about it"

"Not a lot has been done about halting staff turnover because the company's so small, it's hard to see what can be done"

"I can't answer customer support questions because I haven't had any training and it makes me feel stupid"

"They have to do some more internal training because some people in here still don't know what they should do"

"Doing some internal training would be a weight off my shoulders because it's needed and it's been dragging on for ages"

In this company, then, it appeared that the lack of systematic planning from the directors, and the inconsistencies between those responsible for different sectors of the work had meant that even positive innovations had little momentum, and were not sustained. Well meant efforts by one director were unconsciously sabotaged by inconsistent demands from others, and by awkward working practices. Overall, there seemed little opportunity for employees to take a positive pride in working for the company, despite their willingness to do so. Perhaps the most telling attribution was made by one employee, who, when asked what he thought of the company, responded:

> "I don't think about this place much because I leave it behind when I go out of the door"

Discussion of the Analysis

It is apparent from this analysis that the type of attributions about self-esteem made during the interviews at CompuSys were very different from those at TechnoComp. The implications of this for the companies concerned were considerable, and were reflected in the appropriate consultancy reports. In the one case—CompuSys—the aim of the consultancy was to confirm the existing successful managerial practices which the directors had undertaken, and to ensure that they could continue these, and develop them, in the future. Various mechanisms for doing so were discussed, such as the use of training to encourage a sense of professionalism, feedback to the employees about company successes, and the recognition of company standards.

In TechnoComp, on the other hand, the attributional analysis revealed a very different situation. There were relatively few opportunities for employees to take pride in belonging to their company, and these decreased further as the inconsistencies between directors had become even more apparent. The technical director of the company was receptive to the messages in the consultancy reports, and worked to build up pride and professionalism among her staff. Some success in this respect was reflected in the attributions made during the second consultancy visit. But by the third visit, the tensions produced by managerial inconsistency, and the personal resistance to "coddling" staff on the part of another director had significantly undermined these improvements.

In theoretical terms, the findings are in broad agreement with what might have been expected from social identity theory. The general attributions made about both companies indicate a degree of pride, at least at first, which would be expected given the motivational nature of the self-esteem dimension. People actively seek ways of feeling positive about the groups to which they belong. But Table 6.1 reveals very different approaches to management made by the directors of the two companies, with the result that when it came to specific aspects of company practice, CompuSys was demonstrably richer than TechnoComp. This meant that although improved managerial practices produced an increase in positive attributions of this type in the second visit, their negation through other factors had resulted in a demonstrable decline by the third visit. Systematic differences between the companies with respect to company pride and self-esteem were reflected by systematic differences in the attributions relating to this theoretical theme.

The connection with social representations is a more complex one. It requires an analysis which can explore degrees of "sharedness" between the various company members. Although this analysis would normally be undertaken on a more extensive data-set, it is apparent even from the limited amount of data provided here that the attributions made by CompuSys employees showed a higher level of consensus, and also of consistency, than those from TechnoComp. The implication is that employees of the former company had generated, or at least had begun to generate, consensual social representations about the company. The consensus had, in fact, been quite striking during the conduct of the interviews; but it also emerged through the thematic analysis. It contrasted sharply with the diversity of views expressed at TechnoComp, which reflected the different ways that the company was perceived by its employees.

Given the theoretical connection between social representations, social identity theory and organisational culture (Hayes, 1991) there would be some grounds for concluding that CompuSys was in the process of creating the consensual basis for the later development of a full-blown organisational culture. Whether that culture eventually emerged, of course, would depend on the nature of the company's later development; but the implications of the analysis were that such a possibility existed.

Conducting this type of Research

Conducting this type of research raises a number of issues about what we are doing when we are doing research "in the field", and about the ways that we go about doing it. One of these issues concerns the use of action research, rather than a more static research paradigm, in which events are supposedly "monitored" by a dispassionate and uninvolved observer.

The latter approach to research is quite simply impractical in the small company, where staff are well aware of the normal state of affairs, and where a stranger attracts interest, gossip, and theorising about the purpose of the research. Indeed, it could be argued that it is impractical in many more contexts too: as Silverman (1977) showed, research participants are rarely the passive respondents to stimuli that they are traditionally assumed to be.

Using a consultancy model, with genuine outcomes for the company, makes it possible to ensure that people's curiosity as to the purpose of the interview is satisfied, and, by and large, people are quite happy about the idea of the same information being used for subsequent research purposes. Having the interview schedule openly available throughout the interview helps people to see the exercise as a consultative, rather than a manipulative venture.

It is, of course, necessary to secure permission from the individual to tape-record the interviews and use them for subsequent research purposes, but most people will co-operate with this if their permission is asked. In this case, as discussed above, this resulted in only two refusals out of 74. It does mean, though, that you need to have reasonably good interview skills, to ensure that people feel able to talk freely during the course of the interviews.

It is also important, naturally, to ensure that the content of the interviews remains completely confidential. Although information from the interviews was given to the directors in the report, this was done in such a way as to ensure that no single individual could be identified. This was probably essential in making sure that staff felt able to give free and candid information. Although directors often assert that anyone can say what they want to them, the reality is often very different, and in a small company those who come out with unwelcome ideas or information can become very vulnerable.

The process of extracting causal attributions from interview transcripts is one with which it is best to have a second point of view. Independent judgements from the same transcripts done by two different people can help to identify attributions which might otherwise have been missed, and also to clarify those instances in which it is unclear whether a causal attribution is actually being made. A second opinion in the process of categorising the attributions is also useful, for similar reasons.

The use of pre-determined themes to structure the analysis gives a researcher a technique for dealing with the very large amounts of data which can emerge from conducting rapport interviews, and reducing these to manageable proportions. While a full research project of this kind will still involve an extensive qualitative analysis, as different theoretical questions are explored, it also becomes possible to investigate a single issue—such as the self-esteem question illustrated here— and to undertake meaningful comparisons between different accounts. In this way, an investigation can combine the use of qualitative analysis, with the richness of data and interpretation that this involves, with specifically targeted research questions.

Using theoretically-informed themes for analysis also allows the researcher to deal with the question of reflexivity which arises from the use of action research. Inevitably, the actions of the researcher will influence that which is being researched. This means that there is a very real question about how far the researcher has actually created the data, rather than collected it. This issue has been dealt with extensively elsewhere (e.g. Lewin,

1947; Reason and Rowan, 1981), and is one with which psychologists undertaking real-world research need to come to terms. However, it may also be seen as a consequence of all psychological research, not just action research: as Silverman (1977) and several others have shown, there is a strong argument that psychologists undertaking controlled laboratory-based experimentation also unwittingly create their data. The use of established theoretical themes can provide a manageable route through this maze: by providing clear theoretical links, and also some theoretical predictions, the social process of data collection/generation may become more systematised, and less an outcome of random or unidentified social factors.

In summary, then, the method of research discussed in this chapter combines qualitative analysis with many of the features of "traditional" hypothetico-deductive psychological research. The use of qualitative analysis means that much of the richness and meaning of the data can be explored. It also ensures that the material which is being analysed originates from the interviewees, rather than being a function of a specific measuring instrument (as might be the case with a questionnaire or structured interview, for instance). It can be applied to spontaneous conversation, as well as to interview material.

The strongest link with traditional psychological research, on the other hand, occurs through the use of psychological theory. Theory is used throughout: to derive research questions and predictions; to inform the data collection process; and to structure the qualitative analysis itself. As such, the approach can be used as an empirical, systematic "test" of a theory, in hypothetico-deductive terms.

There is a price to pay, of course. Novel material, in appropriate to the theoretical themes, will not be included in the analysis—unlike the grounded theory approaches described later in this book. It is for the would-be researcher to decide whether this cost is outweighed by the advantages of the technique. The method also requires a dynamic, fairly broad-ranging theory with real-world applicability, in order to generate appropriate themes for the research. Not all psychological theories would be suitable for this purpose. But the advantages are that it offers a combination of the traditional theory-driven approach to research with the flexibility and richness of qualitative analysis. It is an integrative approach, which may allow us to build bridges between quantitative and qualitative research paradigms, rather than seeing them as in opposition to one another.

HOW TO DO THEMATIC QUALITATIVE ANALYSIS

1. Establish the themes of the analysis, on the basis of the theoretical background to the research;
2. Transcribe the interviews;

3. Identify all the causal attributions made during the course of the interview (you may like to bring in a second opinion at this stage);
4. Extract the attributions into a separate list;
5. Sort the attributions according to the themes of the analysis;
6. Examine the attributions within one thematic category, and identify their general orientation;
7. Compare the attributions within one category made by one set of research participants, with those in a similar category made by another set;
8. Identify the general themes and conclusions which may be drawn from this comparison.

7

Attributional coding of interview data: Meeting the needs of long-haul passengers

Peter Stratton
Department of Psychology, University of Leeds

This chapter describes a particular approach to the analysis of qualitative interview data. The method is grounded in attribution theory, and provides a rigorous analysis of expressions of causal beliefs offered during interviews, therapy sessions, or any other verbal material. The method is illustrated by describing its application to a set of group interviews commissioned by an airline. People who had regularly flown on long-haul routes were interviewed, and attribution analysis used to unravel the values, beliefs, fears and wishes which were waiting to be discovered in the transcripts.

Qualitative data contain human responses in something like their full richness. This feature is both their strength and difficulty. A full human response is likely to be a complex and elaborate thing, and an attempt to describe it in detail can be very unwieldy. For example, Barker and Wright (1951) attempted to describe an ordinary day in the life of a boy and the report filled a complete book. Even so, it is clear from the book that they still had to be selective in what they reported.

Present day technology allows us to record the raw material rather easily, but a researcher discovers very quickly that a stack of video-tapes or transcripts of interviews covering tens or hundreds of hours of recording is not easily digested. The task of qualitative research is then to find ways of extracting the essential information from qualitative material. Qualitative researchers place great emphasis on validity, but this term will have different meanings depending on the paradigm being assumed. As will be clear from preceding chapters, especially those by Rom Harré, Mick Billig and Carol

Sherrard, validity in this book is unlikely to be thought of as "corresponding closely to reality". Validity needs to be redefined in terms of shared meanings within certain kinds of discourse.

In this sense, reliability, which is perhaps overvalued in quantitative research, has an important role in qualitative research. It can be a useful indicator that researchers are able to operate definitions in similar ways and are creating the same meaning within the data. Often, a person reading a report of the results is likely to want to know that it would be possible for a different researcher to have reached similar conclusions from the data. In his excellent account of qualitative research, Silverman (1993, p. ix) argues for the primacy of "authenticity" but also says:

> I insist on the relevance of issues of validity and reliability in field research: we cannot be satisfied mere with ... "telling convincing stories". Contrary to the assumption of many social scientists, as well as funding bodies, generalisability need not be a problem in qualitative research.

Most ways of attempting to deal with the richness of qualitative data use the extraordinary capacity of the human cognitive system to identify patterns in complex stimuli. Researchers need to immerse themselves in the data and use their full range of understanding to identify the significant aspects and underlying structures. There is no question that we have a great capacity to carry out such tasks successfully, but on its own this approach leaves the results difficult to evaluate. All of the influences on selective perception that have been studied within psychology are likely to operate: motivational factors, expectations, familiarity, avoidance of discomfort may all have free play because in the complexity of the task we cannot easily monitor our own processes. The result is that the product of the analysis may be strongly influenced by personal factors. This would not matter if the analysis was repeated independently by a number of researchers who all came to the same conclusions, but such replication is not usually possible.

GROUNDED THEORY AND CONSTRUCTIVISM

One of the most coherent and fully articulated qualitative methodologies at present is provided by Grounded Theory (Henwood and Pidgeon, 1992 and Chapter 12, Strauss and Corbin, 1990). Briefly, the idea is to deal with the potential arbitrariness of selecting examples from qualitative data by having the data processing guided by a clearly defined procedure. If the basis for selecting and portraying material is strong and clear and grounded firmly in the data, there is much less scope for unrecognised distortions to creep in.

Grounded theory is based in a constructive paradigm. In a basic form, also called an interpretivist framework, this position recognises that meaning is not something inherent in a reality "out there" but is constructed by the individual (Segal 1986). Research is not seen as finding things that are there, but of creating meanings. This way of thinking does not deny that there is a reality, but it claims that, at least for some purposes, it is more useful to think of research as negotiating ways of understanding. The job of qualitative research must then be thought of in terms of creating meaningful descriptions of what people do during interviews and other data gathering exercises.

When research is based on interviews, the interpretivist position means giving up the idea that an interview is a way of finding out about some reality— objectively recording the beliefs, attitudes or cognitive processes of a person. It is not just a matter of recognising that the observer inevitably affects what is being observed, so that what is discovered is contaminated by the presence of the interviewer. It is that the material is created through the interviewer's involvement. Without the research, the phenomenon of the interview would not have happened. But we are not usually just interested in describing the interview: we want to use the interview to gain an understanding of some aspects of the lives of the people involved. The interview is a context in which people will give accounts, and it is the job of the methodology to enable us to use these accounts to say something useful about the chosen aspects of their lives.

A full qualitative methodology will therefore include a detailed specification of the interview process so that the context in which meanings are created is fully understood (Stratton, 1992). The analysis can only report on what is co-created between the people involved in the given circumstances. Interpretation then involves deciding what conclusions can be drawn from the presence or frequency of various aspects of what is produced. So the emphasis shifts from a minimal interviewer to a fully specified interview situation: the context, the explanations, the interactions, as well as the interview schedule. As a very simple example, the statement of a suspect to a policeman is not necessarily best regarded as a (questionable) account of reality, but as something interpretable as a product of a well defined situation. More generally, we cannot assume that content is determined by the choice of subjects and the topic of the interview.

For example a discussion of family mealtimes will produce very different material depending on whether it is understood by the family to be market research or a study of children with eating difficulties.

Our Context

In 1981 a research group at Leeds Family Therapy and Research Centre (LFTRC) set out to construct a method of qualitative research which would take account of the kinds of considerations just described (though we had not at the time heard of grounded theory). We wanted to do justice to the constructivist ideas that were around in both social and developmental psychology, but we wanted to tackle very practical issues of relating the ways that families described themselves during therapy to the difficulties they were experiencing. And of course we wanted the method of analysis to tell us what to do in the therapy.

There were often strong influences on what families would report—many were blaming one family member for all their problems; some were abusing their children; in others traditions of secrecy around some areas had built up over many years; in nearly all there was an investment in denying that certain issues had anything to do with the problem. So simply recording the stories that the families were telling would not necessarily tell us enough about what influenced their behaviour towards each other. Whereas grounded theory tends to treat theory as something that may interfere with an accurate perception of the data, the position we have taken is that it is impossible to perceive or understand without using a cognitive framework of some kind. Refusal to specify the framework simply keeps it hidden and unavailable for examination. We therefore chose to use theory very explicitly to guide the analysis of what the families said during therapy so that we would know what assumptions were being made and could question them if necessary. So we set out to create a method of analysing sessions which would use a powerful theoretical basis to get below the surface of what was being said.

The approach described in this chapter makes full use of the human capacity to identify patterns within a clearly defined framework. The advantages are that the process of the analysis is fairly visible, and that once the conclusions are reached, it is possible to work back to see how they were obtained. The approach is unusual as qualitative research because it includes a phase of counting frequencies and then using the frequencies of different kinds of statements to examine the relationships between them. Because it is unusual (this is the only chapter in the book to report frequencies in tables, pie charts and histograms) it needs some comment.

"Qualitative research" is not a well defined and agreed term. Sometimes it is used to refer to any research which uses qualitative data, but rather obviously qualitative data can be used for any kind of research. More fundamentally, most researchers would accept that qualitative research is about generating meaning through relating descriptions and explanations of phenomena to their context. It is quite different to a traditional experimental approach which would be labelled positivist and/or hypothetico-deductive. This approach uses data to test theories about reality and could clearly use either qualitative or quantitative data. What makes qualitative research exciting is that it takes a whole set of radically different positions.

First, the idea that "reality" can be discovered is abandoned. This is the constructionist position that, both in research and in the rest of life, we are about creating meanings, not discovering facts. From here, we have the idea of the researcher "interacting with the research participants and then with interview data in producing the research account" (Costain-Schou and Hewison, 1994, p. 49). Meaning is created within an interview and it is then the task of the researcher to provide an account that is meaningful and helpful to other people. Constructionism, at least within the systemic framework, makes a strong claim that alternative accounts can be added together to enrich our understanding rather than be assumed to be incompatible alternatives. What is called a "both-and" rather than "either/or" position. Incidentally, this would make it very odd for a systemic constructionist to be told that they are prohibited from counting how often things happen.

It may be useful to divide qualitative research, if not into two categories, then at least along a continuum. At one end the product is the revelation that a certain phenomenon exists, while at the other is a claim that a certain population has a certain probability of a certain characteristic. An example of the former in our work would be studies of families which are each a unique phenomenon, and qualitative research can demonstrate aspects of a specific family which stand as interesting without any claim that any other family is similar. At the other extreme, qualitative methods (for us, identical methods) can be applied to a large sample of people with the possibility that aspects will be discovered sufficiently consistently to allow a claim that the findings can be applied to people other than those studied. There are critics who would claim that this extreme is not longer pure qualitative research, but so long as we are talking about qualitative methods (rather than just qualitative data, cf Costain-Schou & Hewison, 1994) it is difficult to see how a method can cease to be qualitative simply because its output is used in a different way.

We see our research method as fundamentally qualitative because it is not pitching theory against reality but is interpreting selected aspects of human functioning in relation to their context, in order to create meanings that can be shared and used. "Selected" is important because we do not have an idea that something can be completely known. This leads us back to the other strategy that differs from most other qualitative research. We use a clearly identified theoretical base, attribution theory, to guide our selection. Our claim is that you cannot avoid being selective, and unless you clearly specify the basis for selection, you will not know what assumptions you have made. Worse, the person trying to use your findings will not know either. We have therefore used the analysis of attributions as a framework within which we can use any technique we find useful in achieving the objectives of qualitative research.

A Synthesis: Attributional Analysis

The multidisciplinary team of LFTRC brought perspectives from developmental psychology, systems theory, psychoanalysis and clinical psychology. From combining these perspectives, a concept emerged that was in fact being studied outside of any of these areas in social psychology. We identified the perceptions that people have of each other and of events in their lives, and particularly the beliefs held about why things happen as they do, as a core phenomenon in determining how people react to events.

The methodology most suited to analysing these perceptions was at the time (and is still) being provided by attribution theory. Appropriately, attribution theory owes its origins to Heider (1958) whose work originated in the attempt to take seriously the "everyday psychology" by which ordinary people (i.e. non-psychologists) operate. Today attributional analysis has been shown to be an extremely powerful technique for predicting behaviour, having the potential to avoid the limitations of traditional attitude studies and of attempts to predict behaviour from hypothesised structural characteristics (traits or personalities) of individuals.

The LFTRC research group took the basic structure of attribution theory but then found it necessary to spend several years developing and refining a set of techniques which would enable attributional beliefs, as expressed in any verbatim material, to be identified and comprehensively analysed. The system (Stratton, Heard, Hanks, Munton, Brewin & Davidson, 1986) is still the most comprehensively validated and tested procedure to do this within either the clinical or the social psychological fields. The technique uses content analysis and has taken account of the advances made in various areas of discourse analysis. It is however unique in providing a comprehensive account of all the important and more-or-less coherently expressed beliefs made during interviews, and converting essential aspects of these to a numerical coding which can then be processed statistically. We call it *attributional analysis*, or *attributional coding* when just referring to the central component of coding the verbal material.

A technique that will help the researchers to get beyond the content of events described by extremely disturbed families and identify their core attitudes and emotional reactions, should have a wide range of application. In order to explore the range of possible applications we created a business (The Psychology Business, what else?) as a context in which to work. We have discovered that attributional analysis is an extremely versatile tool which can be applied to a great variety of conversational material for a variety of purposes. However, we started with market research because we knew this area was very limited in the techniques used for analysing interviews.

The technique is easier to understand if seen working in practice. I therefore describe how to conduct a research study using attributional analysis and then describe a specific application in some detail, and give some examples of the kinds of results obtained as a way of getting a feel for the method. The description covers the main issues that are likely to arise using attributional analysis, so it can be used as a framework (a kind of "worked example") on which specific pieces of research can be based. At the end there is a checklist of the steps to take when using the method in practice.

The study

One application of attributional analysis which needed to have a highly practical outcome was research into the needs of long-haul air passengers. British Airways had been conducting regular research to try to find out what passengers most wanted. This kind of research is run continuously by all major companies in order to discover what their customers want. In some cases the results of the research are used to decide how best to advertise, while another use is in "New Product Development"—finding out whether there would be a market for something that does not yet exist. Bradley (1987) gives detailed examples of a variety of marketing research projects. In the present case the interest was in improving an existing service. The international airlines compete fiercely for customers, and are all trying to find an optimal balance between giving passengers what they want, while keeping prices as competitive as possible.

The piece of research that we used was part of a series of studies in which people who had experience of flying, and the crews of the planes, were interviewed to discover their wishes, complaints and general attitudes. British Airways would also have been conducting survey research in order to quantify the more measurable needs. The focus in our study was on long-haul flights in which the passenger would be on the plane between six and maybe fourteen hours, and would be paying an economy fare. Keeping in mind the constructionist approach of this research, we were not concerned with what kind of thing a long-distance passenger is, but with making a particular kind of sense of the accounts about the context of flying that they constructed during an interview. If the airline can make sense of the sense that passengers make about flying with the airline, there is a good chance that they will both achieve their objectives.

A series of interviews with groups of passengers, and with cabin staff, had shown that passengers could list any number of facilities that they would like on the flight. These ranged from bacon and eggs for breakfast to individual television screens with a wide range of programmes and games for each passenger. This was not much help to the airline which was already finding the best balance it could between what was given to passengers and the cost of the flight. While the airline undertook a large-scale conventional qualitative market research study, we took a small sample of their interview material and conducted a parallel attributional analysis. At the end we could therefore compare conclusions and test whether, as we claimed, attributional analysis would give a deeper analysis of the material, and do this more efficiently in the sense of needing less data to reach its conclusions.

THE METHODOLOGY OF ATTRIBUTIONAL RESEARCH

The Sample

The first stage in any research procedure is to specify the sample. When qualitative research is used merely to give a rough indication of behaviours that might be expected, sampling has been regarded as relatively unimportant. So long as the subjects belong to the population of interest—native adult English speakers, for example—the data are valid for the purpose. Unfortunately, especially in commercial uses, the low expectations of what qualitative research can offer have sometimes resulted in sloppy methodology, which has in turn reinforced the idea that the results from qualitative research are unreliable (Stratton, 1991).

As we are claiming that much more rigorous qualitative research is possible, and that the results are transferable to significant contexts, the issue of sampling becomes more important. You will have to go to texts on experimental or quantitative research for detailed accounts of sampling methodology, but all of these methods are applicable in qualitative research. In fact the difference is that, because qualitative research is more intensive it will inevitably use fewer participants, and so sampling becomes even more important. Sometimes just a few extreme and unrepresentative participants can skew the results. In the present study the sampling had already been done by selecting participants who made regular long-haul flights on business. One of the advantages of doing research with commercial organisations is that they often have extensive data-bases of information about the people—customers, employees etc.—who can be recruited for the research.

The Interview

There is much to be said about techniques of interviewing for qualitative research which cannot be covered in this chapter. Basic interviewing technique can be found in many psychology textbooks, there are general accounts of interviewing; and even books on interviewing for quantitative research have much to offer (Fowler & Mangione, 1990). There are some texts specialising in qualitative interviewing, for example Mishler (1986). Others deal with interviewing specifically for market research (Robson and Foster, 1989; Weiers, 1988).

Conducting interviews to provide data for an attributional analysis imposes its own additional requirements. As you will see later, we use the amount of time spent talking about each issue as an indication of the person's concern with that issue. Attribution research provides good evidence that people offer more attributions about the issues that concern or confuse them. For this aspect of account-giving to have full scope, the interview must be set up in such a way that the expectations and perceptions of the respondent become clearly defined. A schedule must be constructed which specifies areas of interest to just the right level of detail. Participants in the interviews use the questions asked, as well as the way in which they are asked, as information about the purposes of the interview, and to guide their responses.

It might be helpful to think about the extremes here: if the interview was completely open-ended the interviewee would have no idea what the interviewer wanted, would not know what to talk about, or in what detail, and would feel unable to give what was wanted. At the other extreme, if an interview schedule asks every possible question about a topic, the amount of material gathered would be almost precisely defined by the number of questions about the topic. In other words, an analysis of which aspects were discussed most would amount to an analysis of the amount of detail on each topic in the schedule. This "extreme" can go further. Some interviewing procedures, especially those based on projective techniques, can delve so deeply that the respondent starts creatively inventing all kinds of ideas and attitudes that they had never contemplated before. Here we have the interview being truly co-creative, but there may be no sense in which the meanings created could ever have influenced the respondent in the past. In some contexts the researcher would also have to be concerned that as a result of the ideas produced in the interview, the future functioning of the interviewee might be affected. Interviews with employees about their jobs would be one example.

A general account of interviewing from a constructionist perspective has been published (Stratton, 1992) and perhaps two ideas from systemic therapy give the flavour of what is needed most clearly. Cecchin (1987) proposes a stance of curiosity in which it is the understanding of the participants that is endlessly fascinating. If the therapist (interviewer) can think in this way, the respondent will not feel interrogated or evaluated, but will respond openly. Another idea about the stance to take comes from Anderson and Goolishian (1988, p. 382) who state that a therapist should *"be a respectful listener who does not understand too quickly (if ever)...."*

With this general orientation you are likely to avoid traps such as feeding the answers you want, negotiating an agreement about what is the truth, and arguing with the respondent to try to persuade them to adopt a more sensible position.

ANALYSIS OF THE INTERVIEW

This is the core issue in this chapter. The Manual of the Leeds Attributional Coding System (LACS; Stratton, Munton, Hanks, Heard, & Davidson, 1988) provides detailed instructions for identifying causal beliefs within verbatim material and then coding them. What follows is a summary procedure which will be entirely adequate for a basic analysis. For more advanced applications, please write to the author for more details.

Stage 1: Extracting Attributions

For our purposes, we want to list, in the speakers own words as far as possible, every statement of a causal belief. We take as our definition:

> Any statement in which an outcome is indicated as having happened, or being present, because of some identified event or condition.

Fig. 7.1 shows a segment of a transcript with the attributional statements identified. Note that sometimes the cause is offered first, but at least as often people mention an outcome and then explain why it occurred. Also, connective words such as "because" may or may not be present.

Identifying attributions is a matter of practice. Our experience is that there is rarely dispute about whether a pair of statements meets the criterion. Differences between "extractors" come about mostly because some search much harder for cases. For example, sometimes a cause is offered for an outcome that was mentioned several sentences earlier, and some extractors will attempt to include all such cases while others feel that there is an element of judgement involved, and so they should be left out. For most purposes reliability is increased, and little is lost, by keeping to clear and direct expressions of a causal belief.

To start with, extractors need to work from a transcript of the interview. With practice we find that it is perfectly possible to extract reliably directly from an audio or video recording. This cuts down the work considerably and removes one of the major disincentives to the detailed analysis of interview material.

As a rough guide, attributional statements are offered at a rate of at least two per minute, and may run at five or six per minute in some circumstances. This high rate is clearly a function of the perception that explanations are appropriate in an interview, and would not be found in other kinds of conversation. Incidentally, it is almost never necessary to ask "why" in order to elicit an attribution. Just ask people to describe a situation with which they are familiar, and they spontaneously go on to offer explanations.

Once the attributions have been extracted they can be listed in order of occurrence. We adopt a convention of putting the cause on the first line and

SAMPLE TEXT

If you go to the toilet you get stuck behind the meals trolley.

It also blocks the aisle up for a good forty-five minutes. They are very awkward for the air hostesses to use.

Also, two hostesses serve, one from each end, so if one goes away to answer a query then the other hostess cannot move the trolley down.

Perhaps there should be someone else who could answer the queries.

It always seems like a down-market restaurant—banging and rushing about it isn't conducive to sit down and have a nice meal. And quite often they come to take the trays away before you have finished and you are made to feel as if you should have finished.

You shouldn't be rushed because you've got nothing else to do up there.

I've become worse at flying over the years—the more flying I've done the more nervous I get. I don't actually think about the flying, I just want the flight to be as enjoyable as possible and I just tend to think I've got to get from A to B and once I get there I'm fine.

Attributions extracted from the material

(The cause is stated first, in *italics*)

If you go to the toilet you get stuck behind the meals trolley.

It (the meals trolley) blocks the aisle up for a good forty-five minutes.

[two hostesses serve, one from each end, so] *if one goes away to answer a query* then the other hostess cannot move the trolley down.

Because the hostess cannot move the trolley [while the other is answering a query] there should be someone else who could answer the queries.

banging and rushing about like a down-market restaurant isn't conducive to sit down and have a nice meal.

quite often they come to take the trays away before you have finished and you are made to feel as if you should have finished.

because you've got nothing else to do up there You shouldn't be rushed

over the years I've become worse at flying

the more flying I've done the more nervous I get.

once I get there I'm fine.

FIG. 7.1.   Sample text from group discussions with passengers.

the outcome on the second, regardless of the order in which the statements were made. You may construct a coding sheet, or configure a computer to take the text and the codings to be associated with each one.

Stage 2: The Coding

Each attributional statement is coded for certain basic information, and for the standard dimensions of attribution.

Personnel Coding

Construct a list of the significant people and other events. In some circumstances you will want to code the identity of the speaker (for example in a family interview). You may also wish to identify the person responsible in the cause (who we will call the agent) and the person whom the outcome most affected (the target). In our example we coded (among others):

- The speaker;
- Passengers in general;
- The crew;
- The airline.

It is essential to code the personnel first because the attribution coding that follows must be done in relation to a clearly specified person.

Attribution Coding

Each statement can be coded on up to five "dimensions" of attributing. These dimensions are the major characteristics of attributions that have been found in previous research to say something important about the causal belief. In each case we make a judgement about which pole of the dimension applies most strongly and allocate that aspect to the statement. For ease of coding we score a 1 if the dimension applies and a 0 if it does not. Each statement can then be summarised by a series of numbers which a computer can use to identify patterns.

In any particular piece of research it will not usually be necessary to code all five dimensions. You should decide on theoretical grounds which are most likely to be important, and just code these. The five dimensions are described here, but more detailed descriptions are given in the LACS Manual (Stratton et al. 1988). Five dimensions are more than other researchers specify. An account of the five dimensions was first provided by Stratton et al. (1986). Briefly, that analysis started from existing definitions such as that by Abramson, Garber, & Seligman (1980) but found it necessary to make further distinctions to deal with inherent contradictions in those definitions. In their attributional reformulation of learned helplessness Abramson et al. used three dimensions (aspects) of causes which had already been identified in previous attributional research. These dimensions are used in the Attributional Styles Questionnaire (Peterson, 1982) and remain the basic set in most subsequent research. They refer to:

- *Stability:* whether the cause will apply in future;
- *Globality:* whether the cause tends to have significant consequences;
- *Internality:* whether the cause originates within the individual or comes from outside them.

A standard example: if you fail an exam and attribute this to your stupidity, this is a *stable, global, internal* cause. If you attribute the failure to the fact that a concrete mixer was operating outside the window during the exam, this is an *unstable, specific, external* cause.

Major considerations which led us to expand these dimensions were:

1. That control was not being recorded as a dimension of attributing because it had been assumed that internal events are controllable and external events uncontrollable—an assumption that is clearly unjustified;

2. The definition of "internal" was sometimes based on a distinction between events originating within the person, versus external circumstances, and sometimes on whether the event occurred just because that specific person was involved. The two are certainly not identical: for example, being able to remember your own name originates internally but is not unique to you. We retained the label "internal" for the former distinction, but chose to add a separate dimension called "personal" for the latter;

3. The existing literature was inconsistent over whether it was the cause or the outcome that was being coded for certain dimensions. In some cases it was neither, for example reference might be made to the stability of the link between the cause and the outcome—revising *always* improves exam results. Our coding system is therefore explicit about which part of the cause–link–outcome sequence is being considered for each dimension.

Basic Definitions of Attributional Dimensions

STABLE [1] / UNSTABLE [0]
Will the cause apply in future? Attribution to stable causes implies an expectation that whatever caused this event will continue to be a causal factor in future events.

GLOBAL [1] / SPECIFIC [0]
Does the cause have a significant range of consequences? The choice of global causes means that events of this kind tend to cause significant consequences.

INTERNAL [1] / EXTERNAL [0]
Did the cause originate within the person, or was it an external circumstance? When people attribute internally they see the cause arising from themselves or their actions rather than being caused by people or events outside.

PERSONAL [1] / UNIVERSAL [0]
Did the event happen because this particular person was involved, or would it have been true for anybody? People who attribute personally have a belief that they are especially likely to experience these events.

CONTROLLABLE [1] / UNCONTROLLABLE [0]
Could the person have exerted a significant amount of influence over the outcome? Complete control is not necessary, and control may be exerted other than through the specified cause.

These definitions are sufficient to undertake a basic coding of attributional statements. The fundamental rule is to keep in mind how the coding will be interpreted. For example, when deciding whether an outcome is controllable, remember that a coding of control will contribute to an interpretation that this person sees themselves as able to influence that outcome.

In order to start thinking in attributional dimensions you might try working out the implications of different patterns of dimensions for some of your own events. What follows will only be helpful if you are going to take some time to work on it. If you prefer to read on I suggest you skip the rest of this paragraph...

- What would it feel like if you believed that your exam results were mostly explained in terms that were stable, personal and uncontrollable?
- Or suppose you habitually thought in terms of explanations that were unstable, specific, internal, universal, and controllable?
- Suppose someone applied the first pattern to failures and the second pattern to successes. Would you be able to predict their revision strategy for an exam they expected to be easy? Would they behave differently if they expected the exam to be difficult?

There are no definite answers here: the idea is for you to practise thinking in terms of the dimensions.

Some Further Issues in Coding

The major source of confusion in attributional coding arises when it is not clear whose perspective is being coded. The simplest case is when our interest is in the speaker, and so each of the dimensions will be applied from the speaker's perspective. In this case be very clear that when Jane says "the house is a mess because John is untidy" the cause (although being untidy is an "internal" kind of thing) is coded as external because it is external to Jane.

Both to avoid confusion and as a refinement in the coding, we sometimes code from the perspective of the speaker and separately from the perspectives of the agent and/or of the target. Each possibility gives different information but you can see that we may rapidly be generating a lot of coding, and a complicated set of data to analyse.

There is also confusion in the attribution literature because it is not always clear whether it is the cause or the outcome that is being coded, or maybe the connection between them. Think of the example "I failed the exam because you cannot spot questions in that subject". The cause, which relied on spotting questions, was not under this person's control. But they might already have indicated that they knew they could easily have passed the exam if they had done some revision. In this case the outcome was controllable.

Look again at the five definitions of the dimensions above. There is a progression from coding the cause in the first three, to coding the whole attribution for whether it indicates something *personal* about the individual, and then to the outcome for whether it was *controllable*. Other researchers code only the cause for all dimensions. You should feel free to choose which approach will be most likely to be useful in your particular study. The only essential is that you should be clear and consistent, both while coding and in your report, about which way you are doing it.

Content Coding

Each attributional statement can also be coded for its content. The most basic form is to code whether the outcome was positive, neutral, or negative. Attribution theory claims that there is an essential distinction here—an attributional style which is unproductive when applied to negative outcomes may have quite different significance when applied to positive events.

In most research it will also be useful to code some aspects of the attribution. In abusive families we may want to know whether the outcome was an abuse incident so that the causes associated with such incidents can be grouped and examined. Interesting questions would be:

- Did the incidents follow from stable causes (which will therefore be a problem in future)?
- Who had control over the outcome?
- Who was most often the agent (person in the cause) when abuse was the outcome?

In studies of drug use we code the social activities and influences of friends as well as the different types of drugs to see how these different factors are associated. The broad decisions about what to code must be taken in terms of the objectives of the study. When specifying the items it is helpful to list a sample of extracted attributions and scan these to discover the kinds of content that people have talked about. As with the attributional dimensions, each item of the content is allocated a number for its coding. The account of the airline study will give an idea of what a content coding can look like.

It may be helpful to give an idea of how much work should be involved in constructing an index. For a study in which the index is simply used to identify major contexts to which the attributions apply, the process may only take a few minutes. At the other extreme, an index for coding aspects of attachment processes in the verbal content of therapy sessions has taken a group of three researchers (Dorothy Heard, Helga Hanks, and the author) several hundred hours of repeated cycling between a provisional index which is applied to sample data, modified or maybe completely recast, applied again, then tested in terms of the data it generates, and then reformulated in order to increase the potential to describe aspects which are judged to be clinically significant. Finally it is applied to a substantial sample of data to establish the reliability of the coding; to ensure that the ways people have expressed themselves lead to unambiguous choices in the content index; and to identify any significant aspects which are not being identified by the coding. Any problems emerging at this stage mean that the "finally" was premature, and further work is necessary.

In such a case the index itself is a major research product because it incorporates considerable detail about ways of conceptualising and recognising various phenomena. In most cases an index will fall between these two extremes and it is the simpler kind of index which is most common and most practicable. Even so, for truly exploratory research, many of the processes listed for the attachment index will be essential, and we find that an experienced researcher will take about 20 hours to complete the task.

The Analysis

Once the attributions have been extracted and coded they can be processed to identify significant patterns. Because all of the information (apart from the original statements) has been recorded numerically, it is easy to enter the data into a computer statistics package in order to explore it. As indicated, we are looking for consistent tendencies which appear in the data, so we need a method which allows us to explore freely. The most general-purpose package for this work is SPSS—Statistical Package for the Social Sciences. In fact any system that works out cross-tabulation will do the job but SPSS makes it easy to include the verbatim text along with the numerical codings and this has real advantages. Spreadsheets usually offer the same facility.

The Interpretation

Once the strongest patterns have been identified they need to be interpreted. In fact, as a grounded theory approach the two parts of the process are interdependent. There is a continuous cycling round the data finding patterns, making tentative interpretations of them, and following up hypotheses and other patterns that might help in understanding them. Some tendencies will be found that are not especially interesting. For example, finding that 90% of causes are internal to the agents is (if you think about it) rather obvious. Agents tend to be taking action (internal) or causing events by their nature. However, others may lead to some interesting conjectures which can then be explored further in the data. For example we discovered that psychological needs tended to result from causes which were stable and global. Does this mean that the most important influences on passengers tend to have psychological outcomes? And if so, what kinds of consequences are expected when psychological needs are operating as causes? A great strength of the method is that you can go back and run further analyses to answer such questions.

The Airline Study

Three groups, each composed of between six and eight regular flyers, were given an extended interview. The interviews in fact lasted well over four hours but not all of the discussion could be used for our analysis. In this section the basic structure of the analysis is presented through the most direct findings. In the next section the more detailed analysis and the progression through to the practical applications are presented.

Extraction

The three interviews yielded 1039 attributional statements. An idea of the kinds of material captured by this process is given by the examples in Fig. 7.1.

Coding

Personnel: When coding the agent and target, we concentrate on people if any are mentioned. So the index has various kinds of people, and a few other essential categories. The respondents themselves, passengers in general, and cabin crew were the most significant. The airline was sometimes mentioned, and aspects of the quality of service also figured. Apart from these, food and drink seemed very much on the minds of passengers. Altogether there were 234 (out of 1039) attributions in which food or drink was either the reason for an aspect of travel, or a consequence of some aspect.

One question that can be asked early in the analysis is how often different persons feature as agents or targets. In this study, respondents and passengers in general were agents 153 times, but targets 648 times. So they were much more often seen as experiencing the consequences of a causal sequence than initiating it. Although the crew were more often agents (240 times) than targets (181 times) these figures indicate a lot of interest in the influences on their behaviour as well as in the effects they have. Most of the interest in the airline was in the effects it had—it figured in 83 causes but only 19 outcomes.

Attribution Coding: Each of the 1039 statements was coded for all of the attributional dimensions described above. As this research was exploratory there was no basis for selecting some dimensions and not others.

As an example of the use of an attributional dimension in relation to the personnel coding, Fig. 7.2 shows the percentage of statements for each kind of agent in which that agent had control. You may find that attributional analysis rapidly gets to a level of complexity that is rather confusing, so let us unpack that statement. We are not giving the proportion of statements through the interviews that showed control by each type of person or influence. We are, for each category (passengers, crew etc.), taking all of the attributions in which that person was an agent, and then seeing how many of those statements were of a kind that allotted control to that person. For example:

people want drinks with their meal
you shouldn't have to ask for them

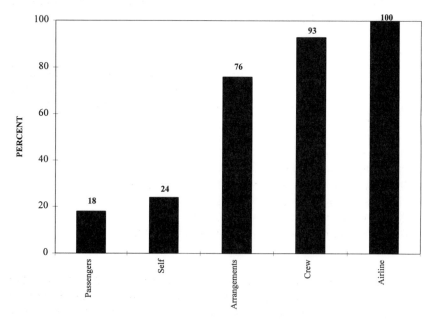

FIG. 7.2.   Who has control?

or more generally:

When the customer has particular needs
The hostess should be sensitive to them

In these two attributions the "passenger" is the agent, but they do not have control over the outcome (which depends on the "hostess" (steward). In contrast:

British Airways have good training programmes
so you get competent service

Here the agent is the airline, and the outcome is very much under their control.

It is clear from Fig. 7.2 that passengers are rarely seen as being in control of events. Typically, the respondents saw themselves as having a little more control than passengers in general. It is a very common tendency for the worst complaints to be made, and the worst situations to be described, on behalf of some general class of people rather than the speakers themselves. At the other end of the continuum, cabin crew are seen as highly likely to be able to influence (remember, total control is not required for this coding) the events with which they are involved. Strikingly, every single statement which identified British Airways as involved in the cause presented them as having some control over the outcome.

Content Coding

It is very easy to set up an index to code aspects of each statement. For example, in this study we coded the cause and the outcome of each statement separately in terms of the kind of provision or resource being described. Items were:

1. Physical need;
2. Psychological need;
3. Physical or psychological state other than a need;
4. Standard in-flight facility or factor;
5. Standard out-flight facility or factor;
6. Special service (beyond what is basic and paid for);
7. Practicalities.

To achieve reliable coding each item is accompanied by a brief definition and examples. For example, physical need was defined as "mention of any requirement to do with bodily functions, sustenance, physical comfort (e.g. seating, air quality), and physical safety."

Other codes may apply to the attributional statement as a whole. Some indicator of overall positive or negative evaluation is invariably used. An overall coding in this study was whether the attribution indicated a met or unmet need. The specific categories are shown in the report of overall frequency of use of the categories during the interviews (Fig. 7.3). It is clear that using ratios of attributions falling into different categories can provide clear insights into the relative emphasis given to different concerns. "Essential requirements" are not frequently discussed, but rather taken for granted, and are rarely said to be missing. But there is a high level of reference to unwanted features and events.

If you were an airline manager looking at these results you would want to know more. How does my airline compare with the general figures for satisfaction in Fig. 7.3? What kinds of needs are met by standard care and what kind by special care? What are the implications of the low level of control experienced by passengers? Such questions are answered by the detailed exploration of data prescribed by the grounded theory approach, and it is this process that takes attributional analysis beyond a simple quantification of content coding.

Extending the Analysis

The basic analysis reported above provided some important pointers to the issues that concern passengers. First, there is a disturbing lack of perceived control. It is probably significant that the tendency to uncontrol is even stronger for passengers in general than it is for the respondents. People will often attribute their more disturbing or unacceptable thoughts to the population in general and not complain about, take the blame for, or be seen to be not coping with these aspects themselves.

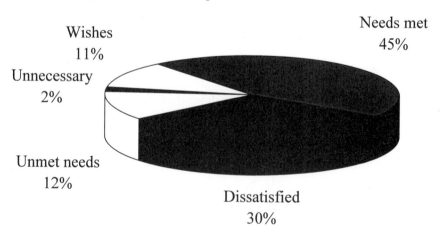

FIG. 7.3.   Levels of Satisfaction.

The lack of control even when they are agents must be interpreted in relation to the fact that passengers are more than four times as often described as targets than as agents. Meanwhile the crew and the airline show the opposite pattern and are very much in control. Together these findings indicate a considerable dependency felt by the passengers.

There is also a high level of dissatisfaction (Fig. 7.3). But the dissatisfaction, and the suggestions for dealing with it, are not about essential requirements (such as not wanting the plane to fall out of the sky) but about mundane provisions: constant supply of mineral water; games to stave off boredom; possibility of walking around and talking to the crew; and above all, better food, more food, less food, different food, special food. And the same for drink.

Taken together these findings led to a hypothesis that long-haul flights induce a powerful sense of handing over control, even over life and death, to the airline and its staff. Passengers then try to deal with this anxiety by demanding to be looked after. If they are cosseted, fed, and generally cared for, they feel they would have greater confidence that the airline and staff had their interests at heart. This confidence could then be extended to essential requirements such as safety which are too frightening to question directly. (Several talked about anxiety and fear but none ever questioned the safety of the plane.) We formulated this hypothesis in relation to attachment theory and the idea that passengers were seeking evidence that they were provided with a "secure base" (Bowlby, 1988). More simply and crudely you could think of the message when passengers become dependent on the airline for their physiological needs, safety and even dignity, as being "I want my mummy".

The hypothesis was well supported by the basic analysis but it indicates that the airline had a dilemma. Apart from the cost of providing what the passengers were asking for, they were caught in a paradox. The more they responded to these expressed needs the more they moved towards making the passenger dependent on the crew for every aspect of their functioning. So just providing what was asked for could actually have the effect of making the underlying problem of helplessness worse. This dilemma provided a focus for one aspect of the more intensive analysis of the data. For our purposes here we will follow just one aspect of that exploration.

Attributional Patterns

Once attribution dimensions have been coded, they can either be analysed individually (as above) or taken in combination. From the perspective of the passenger the most common pattern was:

STABLE (1);
GLOBAL (1);

EXTERNAL (0);
UNIVERSAL (0);
UNCONTROLLABLE (0).

This pattern occurred 363 times out of 1039 attributions. If you code as described above this pattern will appear in the computer as 11000. You can see that any pattern of the five dimensions can be expressed as a five digit binary number of this kind.

The 11000 pattern refers to important causes (they will recur and they have significant consequences) but they originate outside the respondent, do not identify the respondent as a unique individual in any way, and are not easily influenced by them. So these statements do not involve the respondent—they are someone else's business.

The frequencies with which the pattern applied to different kinds of outcomes are given in Fig. 7.4. In this kind of analysis it is possible to compute what the expected value, statistically speaking, of the frequency would be. So, for example, although psychological needs were the outcome 36 times, we would have expected a figure of 61 occurrences based on the frequency with which this factor was discussed. For each outcome the actual number of statements is indicated by a number: the expected value is preceded by an E.

The 11000 pattern most commonly applies to "special service", and the level is substantially above what has been statistically predicted, even given the great importance attached to this type of outcome.

Remembering that "special service" refers to a special degree of being looked after, its prevalence with the 11000 pattern is highly significant. Factors leading to special service are regarded as important and likely to continue to operate. However the respondents feel that they have no

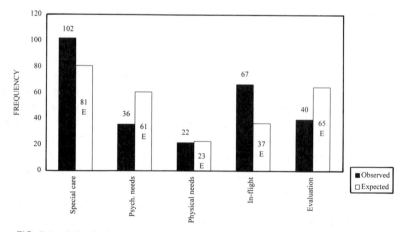

FIG. 7.4. What is characterised as stable-global external-universal-uncontrollable.

involvement in how this kind of service comes about, and that it is not geared to them personally.

Another pattern strongly associated with special service is 11010 (stable, global, external, personal, uncontrollable). This differs from the previous pattern because there is an element of individuality of the respondent involved. In this case psychological needs and evaluation also occurred above the predicted level.

It would seem that where psychological needs such as relaxation are concerned, the respondents are much more aware of their own specific requirements. However they will see the causal factors as external to them and outside their control.

The prevalence of special service with the 11010 pattern also indicates that respondents find a number of instances in which service can be related to them as individuals. However the frequency with which this pattern was associated with special service was only 44, compared to 102 for the 11000 pattern.

A crucial pattern is 11110 (stable, global, internal, personal, uncontrollable). These events are important and seen as arising from the individual and unique to them. However they are not under the person's control. Try to imagine how you would feel if every time something went wrong you believed that it was a cause of this kind that was responsible. Wouldn't you become rather pessimistic? Clinically, when causes of things going wrong are consistently attributed in this way, the pattern is associated with depression. In the present data the pattern is rare, as might be expected (22 instances), but the most common association is with the psychological needs.

Altogether nine patterns were identified as occurring significantly frequently. What is striking is that every one of these patterns ends with the respondent not being in control of the outcome.

Special Care

The dominance of special care in the highly significant and common attributional pattern of 11000 led us to explore this issue in more detail. One comparison in Fig. 7.5 examines the role of the crew vs. food and drink, in whether the passengers felt they were getting special service or just standard in-flight provision. It can be seen that while food and drink predominate in perceptions of standard provision, special service is seen as coming almost exclusively from the crew. This reliance on the crew for special care was consistent throughout the analyses.

The next finding is that psychological needs dominate in relation to special service. When special service is a cause, 25% of the consequences related to psychological need, but none related to physical need. It is notable

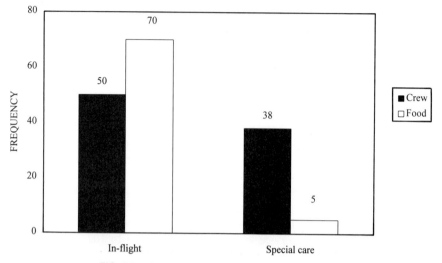

FIG. 7.5.   Routine in-flight provision vs special care.

also that the strongest expressions of dissatisfaction were associated with psychological needs (10%) but never with physical needs. Finally, 34% of the cases in which crew were agents resulted in an aspect of special service, 29% of these cases related to psychological need, but only 3% related to physical need, and 5% to standard in-flight provision.

Back to the Attributions

Emerging from the numbers, we then used the significant tendencies in the data to identify groupings of statements. It is at this point that a statistics package that will include the numerical coding and the text of each attribution becomes most useful. Fig. 7.6. lists some attributional statements selected for the pattern of attributional dimensions and identified from the content coding as dealing with particular issues.

By reading through the statements in different groupings, it becomes possible to formulate a description of the range of content covered by, for example, 11010 attributions in which the cause is a psychological need and the outcome is a requirement for special service. In practice, after the first pass of this stage of the analysis, further hypotheses will be suggested, and other combinations of variables will be checked for their prevalence, and significance, as indicated by the dominant attributional patterns associated with them. Then we return to the statements with a new grouping. This cycle may be repeated several times before drawing our overall conclusions.

Special service

If you get into a conversation with staff in the bay area
It's genuine friendliness

They don't have to talk to you
you feel as if you belong

You get into a conversation with staff
you feel it's a family type of environment

They apologise then bring your drink
you think "she recognises my needs"

If you are treated as an individual
it makes you feel like you are a valued customer

The stewardess makes an effort with kids
you feel they are caring

Psychological need

You can pick up vibes from the way people look
crew should be aware of non-verbal communication

when you have a problem
the crew should comfort you straight away

if you feel claustrophobic on the plane
the crew could offer you a drink

passengers with a problem
the stewardesses should not embarrass them

FIG. 7.6.   Sample attributional statements

Outcome and Evaluation

It has only been possible to offer a small proportion of the available findings from this study in order to illustrate the process. However, this restriction applies also to what can realistically be presented in a journal article or a report to a client. Hopefully, here as in our reports, the selection of data is sufficient to indicate the sort of basis on which we can then make recommendations for action.

Although other themes were identified in the analysis, many of our recommendations derived from the aspects of the analysis presented above. We have indicated a detailed exploration of the relationships between the passenger's feelings of handing over control, the requirement for special service, and its association with psychological needs, combined with the particular involvement of cabin crew in providing or failing to provide what was needed.

In reporting to the client we pointed to the risk that a simple response to the request for special service might be counterproductive. If it took forms that increased the passengers' lack of control, and their dependence on the airline, it would increase the sense of vulnerability. But it was vulnerability that we felt was driving the need for special service in the first place. We offered a series of action points designed to avoid the potential vicious circle, and to meet the needs indicated in this research without incurring substantial extra costs. The summary action points were as follows:

1. Recognise passengers as individuals. Personal greetings;
2. Extend passengers' sense of control where possible. Choice offered during the flight, for example choice of seating, food and drink and so on;
3. Explore the kinds of attention to detail and special service that will make passengers feel more individual and better looked after;
4. Train crews to recognise psychological needs and relate them to special levels of care. Emphasise that they, the crew, are the main channel through which these fundamental needs such as reassurance, a sense of individuality, and the ability to make a relationship, can be met;
5. By implementing action points 4 and 5, allow passengers to feel that they have an appropriate, non-dependent relationship with the crew;
6. Train crews in procedures to ensure that requests are not forgotten;
7. Continue to emphasise the airline's total commitment to safety and reliability.

Often an attributional analysis will uncover aspects of attitude and feelings that would be very hard to detect using conventional qualitative methods. In other cases the value of the analysis is to confirm, in a more precise way, what was already known or suspected. We feel that this analysis was of the latter form. Our metaphor for this kind of consequence of attributional analysis is that of the GP who gains an intuitive idea of the problem from observing the patient describe their symptoms. Such intuitive ideas will often be correct, but if much depends on the decision, a careful practitioner will call for more extensive tests. Doctors are rarely disappointed if the tests confirm their original intuition, but they are enabled to proceed with greater confidence, and sometimes with a clear judgement about the probability of error in the preferred hypothesis.

The three interviews that we used were part of a larger sample which had been analysed by a leading qualitative market research practitioner. The conventional analysis of the full sample was the culmination of two years of research and provided the basis to set up a relaunch of the airline's economy service. The new initiative was reported in the Financial Times (5/11/90) and included the following descriptions. We would invited comparison of the terms used with the main action points summarised above:

"... the flight is more than just food and drink for the passengers; it's an experience. We're trying to build in much more customer contact; to make the crew a lot more conscious that they should be talking to the passengers"

"trials of ... the choice of a pasta main meal instead of just the chicken or beef option..." "... a new seat ..."

"... list of names of passengers by seat displayed in they galleys ..."

meet the *"emotional expectations of passengers, viz. to enjoy themselves; to trust the crew; to feel at home; have their individuality recognised; to feel valued and respected; and to be served by people who possess a flexible approach."*

The attributional analysis not only included all of the major conclusions from the conventional study: it provided a clear understanding of the underlying processes and also offered a number of extra findings.

CONCLUSION

This project was unusual in that we had the results of a very substantial research effort, including field trials, with which to compare the conclusions that we were able to reach based on three group interviews. We would claim to have demonstrated that attributional analysis can take a limited amount of data and achieve the same kinds of implications for action as much more extensive research. Furthermore, we feel that as we understand more about the ways that people operate and express their causal beliefs, this approach gives a much greater prospect of understanding the sources of, and constraints on, people's actions, for example, the contradictory wishes for more care and more control in the BA study. It would have been difficult for other methods to discover this conflict, let alone to specify how it might be overcome.

Attributional analysis has been successfully applied in a wide variety of contexts. Our own work has included dysfunctional families, child abuse, families coping with chronic illness, General Practitioner perceptions of illness and treatment, conceptions by men and women of sexual harassment and intimidation, criteria for graduate recruitment, the family processes involved in decisions about and attitudes to eating, attitudes to the stories and characters in a television "soap", and audience perception of quality in international broadcasting, as well as a whole range of consumer issues for market research.

Attributional analysis is emerging as a powerful tool to relate beliefs about cause to the values that people hold, and the expectations that lead to certain forms of action rather than others. It is a more complex form of analysis than many others used in qualitative research and so would only be recommended for use where other, less arduous, techniques will not do the job. But from our perspective, the detailed insight that it offers into the ways that people conceptualise their world and decide on their actions makes it well worth the effort.

CONDUCTING ATTRIBUTIONAL CODING

1. Decide who you want to make claims about and choose a sample to represent them
2. Construct an interview guide
3. Record interviews
4. Extract the attributions from each interview
5. Set up a coding index identifying those aspects of the extracted attributions that relate to your interests
6. Code the personnel and the dimensions of attribution for each statement
7. Code the content of each statement using your index
8. Do the analysis
    8.1 Examine the tendencies in the attributional coding
    8.2 See how these are related to different people and different content
    8.3 Do the same for overall attributional patterns
    8.4 Develop hypotheses about how the interviewees understand the context
    8.5 Check these hypotheses out through further exploration of the data
    8.6 Use the significant combinations of attribution dimensions and content to select groupings of statements. Check that the statements selected in this way have the expected meaning.
    8.7 Continue this cyclic process until you are confident that you can give a meaningful account of the interview material.
9. Draw out the implications by relating the account of meanings within the interviews to the context the participants were discussing and the concerns that gave rise to the research.
10. If appropriate, use the conclusions and the verbatim material as a basis for survey or hypothesis testing research.

NOTE

Data from this study were originally published with the permission of British Airways in Stratton, P. (1991). Attributions, baseball, and consumer behaviour. *Journal of the Market Research Society, 33,* 163–178.

8

Qualitative analysis of murals in Northern Ireland: Paramilitary justifications for political violence

Gerry P.T. Finn
Department of Educational Studies, University of Strathclyde

INTRODUCTION

The research reported here is part of a wider psychological examination of the ideological dimensions of the conflict in Northern Ireland (Finn, 1990a, b, 1994, 1996, 1997). A special interest lay in exploring the wider societal beliefs that could be drawn upon to justify the use of political violence, and the interrelationships between these beliefs and the construction of social identities within the two opposed communities.

A brief critique is presented of the dominant theoretical and methodological approaches used in studying the Northern Irish conflict. The research reported here shows how different qualitative methods can be enlisted together to explore intergroup conflict. The approach blends elements of social representations (see chapter by Hayes) with rhetorical analyses (see chapter by Billig) in the study of the visual imagery (see chapter by Beloff) of the Northern Irish conflict. Northern Ireland's wall paintings display representations of the communities and their conflict.

MURALS AND POLITICAL VIOLENCE IN NORTHERN IRELAND

The power of the murals is attested to by Brian Keenen (1992). One of Keenan's last acts, before going to Beirut where he was to be held captive for four and a half years, was to travel around Belfast. The murals had a real impact on him:

"I particularly remember those stark murals, colourful and grotesque, which have become a part of Belfast, and part of the historic expression of the people and their city."

For Keenan it was the grotesque and negative characteristics that were most evident and became best remembered. Murals were

"images imprinting something vague, political and half-believed in the minds of people".

He continues:

"(T)he images have become more than just paintings on the wall, more than just a statement of belief. They seemed to have taken on the form of icons, but not icons generating different gods, more like a loud discordant orchestra of crude images clashing and jarring in the dark; our history, our past and our violent present twisting and kinking out of proportion and out of harmony. There was no interlacing relationship between these images: what people thought they meant and what relationship they bore to each other was lost in garbled clichés of tribalism. These were the icons thrown up in the collective mind of a kind of epileptic turmoil. And they reflected my own turmoil about the place.

"Those nightmare images that so possess us in our sleep had moved out of mind and into time. They had become our reality. On every corner the impress on the mind was reinforced. Underneath the skin of the city there was contagion. A kind of malevolence festered and spread uncontrollably and unseen. Out of a sense of frustration, of fear, of a raging thirst for identity and purpose, it seemed that people were drinking in the poison: some unconsciously and some by choice until they became intoxicated by rage and despair and helplessness" (Keenan, 1992: 15–16).

That is one interpretation of Belfast's wall paintings. Keenan's words express the power of the murals and display their ability to interact with an individual's own emotions and beliefs. There are many negative aspects to them. If many murals, with their clashing beliefs and justifications for violence, are viewed within one period of time, then despair and depression are inevitable, as Keenan experienced. But the message of the murals, as we will see, is much more than that.

However, Keenan's comments do serve to identify the extent to which the murals convey messages to the community. To do this they must draw upon and reflect aspects of the widespread beliefs commonly found within the community. And that is the clear intention of those who produce them. The process of production is usually collaborative and muralists see murals, not as an art form, but as a means of communication, drawn with specific ideological intent and content (Rolston, 1987, 1988, 1992). The identification of the social process of production and the ideological content of the product enabled Finn (1990, 1996) to develop an argument that murals could be seen to be visual representations of social representations. Murals openly display the images and symbols of the social representations from which they are composed. The wall paintings are of special significance because of their relationship to the role of political violence in Northern Ireland.

Political violence has been common throughout much of the history of Ireland. English attempts to colonise and rule Ireland met with numerous attempts at resistance, that then resulted in the confiscation of lands from the Irish and the creation of a new aristocracy. Still resistance from below could not be halted, with the Province of Ulster being the area most resistant to English rule. A new policy of replacing Catholic Irish with Protestant British was undertaken. The planned plantation of Protestants from England and Scotland into Ireland in 1609, especially into the province of Ulster, was believed to be one means of controlling Ireland. British Protestants, especially those in Ireland, were greatly relieved when King William III defeated Catholic forces under James II in 1690 to ensure that the British crown and British state would be Protestant. Protestantism was the cement which held together the newly emerging British state formed by the Union of the Crowns of England and Scotland (Colley, 1992). And Ulster became the province in which the Protestant plantation proved most successful, but rebellion against British rule was not stilled in either Ulster or the rest of Ireland.

The republican United Irishmen, formed by Belfast Protestants, gained the support of the Catholic peasantry. Their attempted uprising in 1798 was savagely quelled by British forces aided by other Irish Protestants. Almost three years before the insurrection of the United Irishmen, a section of Protestantism had already begun to organise against Catholics and any Protestants whom they judged to be disloyal to their crown, country and religion. The victory of King "Billy" at the Boyne and other significant events during his Irish campaign became central elements in the belief, images and symbols of what became the Orange Order. The action of the United Irishmen failed, but it had alarmed the British government. Full integration of Ireland with Britain, which meant the dissolution of the Irish parliament, was proposed as a means of bringing Ireland under more direct London control, and sections of the unrepresentative, pro-British Irish establishment agreed. (Intriguingly Orangemen were divided and remained officially neutral towards the proposal.) The Union of Ireland with Britain did not have majority support throughout Ireland. But support for it did come from the Irish churches, Catholic and Protestant alike, in return for political favours and promises, and the support of sufficient Irish parliamentarians was bought or obtained by patronage and titles. The closure of the Dublin parliament in 1801 proved to be no solution. Agitation for the return of an Irish parliament and for Irish self-government increased throughout the nineteenth century.

Irish opinion was to be divided between those who advocated the use of force to overthrow British rule and those who advocated the use of constitutional means and the force of argument to achieve the same end: these differences have continued to divide Irish politics. The former approach is the physical force tradition, associated with the United Irishmen, the Fenians, the Irish Revolutionary Brotherhood, and now the Provisional IRA and Sinn Fein: the latter approach, the moral force tradition, is linked with the Home Rule League and the Irish Parliamentary Party, and Irish constitutional parties such as Fianna Fail and Fine Gael (though both of these parties also have a physical force past) and Northern Ireland's Social Democratic and Labour Party. But in Ireland both nationalist and unionist politics have had their moral force and physical force wings. The argument about the future of Ireland dominated British politics for much of the last quarter of the nineteenth century, but the crunch came in the first quarter of the twentieth, with 1912 being a crucial year.

By then unionists had built on their own earlier physical force traditions. For example, in its early days, the Orange Society, the forerunner of the Orange Order, had demonstrated a willingness to use force when required. From the time of the first Irish Home Rull Bill in 1886 unionist gun clubs had sprouted up. That bill had been met with outright threats of violence from unionist and British-based Conservative politicians. The political uproar divided the Liberal Party and a previously weakened and discredited Conservative party re-emerged as a strong political force. Irish unionism had its own divisions. In the South the unionists were very small in number. And even though their political influence was greater than their minuscule electoral base, Southern unionists remained very dependent on support from elsewhere. The position in the North was different. In the nine counties of the Northern Province of Ulster, the unionists were believed to constitute a small majority. Soon not only did unionist opposition to Irish Home Rule in Ireland centre on Ulster, but the opposition of Ulster's unionists began to focus on the future of Ulster. As the political circumstances for unionism worsened, unionists in the rest of Ireland rapidly came to be seen as expendable by unionists in the North, but unionism would not surrender Ulster to Irish Home Rule.

By 1912 the various unionist gun clubs had become the armed wing of loyalism, the Ulster Volunteer Force (UVF), and in 1913 the UVF became the Army of Ulster, when unionists formed a Provisional Government to show that they would resist Britain rather than become part of a self-governing Ireland. The UVF was involved in gun-running and open military exercises as unionists threatened insurrection and the secession of the nine counties of Ulster from Britain. Despite increased unionist noise and threatening actions, the Irish Home Bill was signed by King George V in January 1914, leading some unionists to solicit the support of the German Kaiser. Then, in the political turmoil produced by the "Great War" of 1914–1918, nationalists and unionists agreed with the British Government that the implementation of the bill would be delayed. The UVF was incorporated as a whole into the British Army. Most members of the Irish Volunteers, the nationalist militia force established in imitation of the UVF, also enlisted, but the British Army did not accept them as a discrete military entity; and not all wished to enlist.

Some of the small proportion of Irish Volunteers that refused to join the British Army became part of the body of Irish revolutionaries that staged the Easter Rising in 1916: they took the name of the Irish Republican Army (IRA). Impatient at remaining under British Rule, frustrated by the still unresolved question of Ulster, angered by reports of the possible extension of military conscription to Ireland, and believing Britain to be using political violence to determine the future of other small nations, these Irish republicans tried to seize power. An independent Irish Republic was proclaimed and a Provisional Government announced. After little more than a week of fighting, Britain regained control: but its role had been seriously challenged and its moral authority haemorrhaged as the Irish rebels were transformed into martyrs by the heavy-handed British reaction. No longer would the offer of Irish Home Rule be enough. Republican victory had been gained from bloody defeat.

Sinn Fein, a radical republican movement demanding Irish independence, won a landslide victory in Ireland in 1918. But Ulster had retained a unionist majority: Ulster Unionists had won their own landslide in six of the nine counties that formed the Province of Ulster. Elected Sinn Fein members did not go to Westminster. Instead they established an Irish parliament in Dublin. Britain refused to recognise the Irish parliament and the War of Independence began. In 1921 a treaty that could not satisfy Irish republican demands was proposed by Britain. Agreeing to the treaty meant agreeing to the partitioning of both Ireland and the Province of Ulster. A new entity, to be named Northern Ireland, would be based on the six counties with a solid Unionist majority. It would be controlled by a Belfast parliament under the overall control of Britain. For many republicans this was totally unacceptable. Under threat of war by Britain the Irish representatives agreed and signed the Treaty.

The Treaty was approved by a small majority in the Irish parliament, but civil war erupted as republican organisations split. After the civil war had ended in victory for the pro-Treaty side, many republicans still refused to accept the legitimacy of either the treaty or the Dublin parliament. But over time more became reconciled to the political reality of the situation they found themselves in. Eventually only a small, purist membership remained in Sinn Fein or the IRA. By comparison the UVF had been dissolved in Northern Ireland, but its members had been incorporated into the all-Protestant Ulster Special Constabulary committed to the defence of Northern Ireland. One source of attack was the IRA, which, though outlawed on both sides of the border, continued to mount sporadic attacks against the "Protestant parliament and Protestant state" that unionist politicians had declared Northern Ireland to be.

The traditional Protestant supremacy in Northern Ireland was seriously challenged in the 1960s. Ecumenism challenged conventional religious attitudes: broader socio-economic change challenged the traditional ethnic structuring of the economy and civil society. Some leading unionists advocated some modernisation of Northern Ireland. Local Civil Rights movements, inspired by the struggle for black civil rights in the USA, campaigned for social justice and equal rights for Catholics. Their activities were often violently halted by loyalist groups or by the Special Constabulary. Unionism itself was split. The liberal wing of unionism (some had even participated in the growing Civil Rights movement) recognised the justice of the demands and wished to offer some reforms and attempt an accommodation with the minority community. Others did not. Signs of majority discontent appeared at a very early stage. A new loyalist paramilitary group was formed in 1966, but took the old UVF name. It planted bombs which were for some time attributed to the IRA. After the UVF killed two Catholics it was made an illegal organisation. Unionist discontent was also expressed by other means. By the end of the decade it was clear that hardline Unionist politicians were gaining the upper hand.

Throughout this period the ever-shrinking IRA was in the midst of an internal debate about its transformation. Just as the conflict was intensifying in the North, the IRA proposed to discontinue the use of political violence and concentrate on political and community initiatives: that did not meet with universal agreement. The split formally occurred in January 1970. The dissenting minority became the Provisional IRA and the same division also led to a new Provisional Sinn Fein. As the conflict continued and became more violent, both Provisional organisations grew in strength, becoming so dominant in Northern Irish republicanism that references to the IRA or Sinn Fein now usually refer to these organisations alone; a convention followed in this chapter. Smaller republican groups have also formed: usually after a dispute about the ideological value of armed struggle in relation to conventional political activities. Ultra-unionist groups, usually self-described as loyalists, also emerged. Apart from the UVF, the other main body is the Ulster Defence Association (UDA), which was formed in 1972 to co-ordinate the activities of local armed groups that had been established across Northern Ireland. Some of its sections, such as the Ulster Freedom Fighters (UFF), were quickly outlawed, but the UDA remained legal until 1989.

This brief and overly simple historical outline demonstrates the considerable part played by political violence in the history of the relationships between Ireland and Britain, between Ireland, Britain and Northern Ireland, and between the different communities within Northern Ireland itself. And it is this history that forms the backdrop to the justification of political violence by loyalist and republican paramilitaries alike.

Theoretical Background to the Research

The aim was to investigate the nature of intergroup conflict in Northern Ireland. In this chapter particular attention will focus on understanding political violence. Tajfel, the originator of the most useful psychological model of intergroup conflict, social identity theory, had emphasised the importance of understanding ideological factors in conflicts. Indeed Tajfel had gone even further. He stated that psychological analyses of inter-group conflicts are necessarily flawed if the wider socio-cultural circumstances are neglected. Specifically discussing the Northern Irish conflict, Tajfel (1982, p. 8) had stated that:

> The social, historical, political and economic causality of the present situation must undoubtedly remain prior to the analysis of any of its psychological concomitants (emphasis added)

In this statement Tajfel drew attention to the direct effect of these societal factors on the psychology of group conflict. Moscovici (1984) has related how such factors are reflected in the content of social representations (also see Scarbrough, 1990). It is indeed through social representations that social, historical, political and economic factors are given some psychological reality and it is through social representations that they are re-presented in the ideologies which present idealised patterns of the social world for inhabitants who struggle to make practicable sense of it (Billig, 1987; Billig et al., 1988; Doise, 1986). So, ideologies are dependent on the interlinking of social representations, and ideologies are similar phenomena to widespread beliefs (Farr, 1990; Gaskell & Fraser, 1990; Scarbrough, 1990).

To begin to understand conflicts then, it is essential to recognise that the psychological concomitants of Tajfel's identified societal factors must be socially represented in the content of ideologies of the conflict. And it is the ideologies of the conflict, that define, maintain and sustain that very conflict. As a result, the nature of widespread communal beliefs about the conflict must be explored before other psychological dimensions to the conflict in Northern Ireland can be adequately examined or interpreted. To follow this sequence is to pay heed to Moscovici's advice that the usual progression of psychological investigation and explanation should be reversed: a broad societal approach should precede those less social, much narrower, more individualistic and much more common foci of psychological attention. It is only by understanding these wider ideological processes and their impact on human actions that specific group or individual actions can make any real sense.

Billig (Billig, 1987, 1992; Billig et al., 1988) has shown that the ideological nature of everyday social thinking is highly complex. The on-going processes of the social construction of reality depend on doing some ideological work. But ideologies are not simple rules that determine a specific outcome. They are complex and dilemmatic. Making sense of the world means grappling with complicated issues and resolving apparent contradictions. So the exploration of ideological thinking about conflicts will inevitably come across conflictual thinking about the conflict itself.

The need to explore these beliefs firmly points to the need to adopt a qualitative approach, informed by the theoretical perspectives of Moscovici and Billig. Research into social representations and argumentation in everyday social thinking in Northern Ireland should be the first step in aiding understanding of the psychological dimensions to the violent conflict there. That means that approaches based on social representations and rhetorical analysis can usefully be employed to examine the relationship between communities' general beliefs, the legitimisation of psychological violence and different senses of communal identities.

There are important points of convergence between the research orientation of Moscovici and the rhetorical approach (Billig, 1987, 1991) used by Billig et al. (1988) in their exploration of the social reality of everyday thinking. Moscovici may have tended to emphasise the consensual nature of social representations (or at least he has been judged to do so, e.g. Potter & Wetherell, 1987) but he did also discuss their plasticity and dynamic structure. The identification of the potential for ideological change, even transformation, was one of the important findings of Billig et al. and their findings direct research towards the discovery of argumentation and contrary themes in common social thinking.

Methodological Background to the Research

Until relatively recently (Beloff, 1980) there was little psychological investigation of the Northern Irish conflict. The increase in research has relied largely on questionnaire studies or experiments employing Tajfel's social identity model (see Cairns, 1987; Harbinson, 1989). Much of this research has been both interesting and valuable, but it is also limited. Questionnaires do give a crude overview, but one which can all too often obscure the diversity of social thinking within what is erroneously believed to be a discrete group and which hides the complexity in individual social thinking (Billig, 1991). The social identity research has usefully explored the outcomes of intergroup conflict and indicated some of the processes by which group preferences and discrimination occur but, as Tajfel stated, by itself this research can say little about the wider backdrop to group formations, their interrelationships, or communal beliefs about the legitimacy of the use of political violence. Communal beliefs about the conflict remain to be explored (Beloff, 1989). To understand these processes the nature of Northern Ireland's communities' widespread beliefs must be investigated.

Gallagher's (1986, 1987) pioneering studies explored some of these issues by interviewing prominent individuals within local political organisations. He interviewed leading activists from the Ulster Unionist Party (UUP), Paisley's Democratic Unionist Party (DUP), the paramilitary Ulster Defence Association (UDA), the Social Democratic and Labour Party (SDLP) and Sinn Fein (SF), the political wing of the republican movement associated with the IRA. Gallagher also supplemented these findings by analysing the literature produced by these political organisations. From these sources Gallagher was able to demonstrate how different ideological positions were crucial to judgements about the legitimacy of both the Northern Irish political entity and the different courses of action, including political violence, to be taken to maintain or transform it.

Gallagher showed that ideologies and social identities were interrelated in complicated ways. Interviewees in the SDLP and SF both agreed that the social identity of the minority community was Irish and nationalist, but differences in the precise social identity of activists reflected their different ideological perspectives. The interpretation of the history and symbolism associated with Irish nationalism was strongly disputed. The SDLP identified constitutional nationalism, working through elections and parliament, as the only route to achieve a united Ireland: SF advocated the revolutionary overthrow of what was presented as being the illegitimate and unreformable political entity of Northern Ireland. Activists' ideological beliefs were presented as a characteristic of that group identity (also see Scarbrough, 1990; Turner, Hogg, Oakes, Reicher, & Wetherell, 1987).

Two quite different social identities were present in the social thinking of the activists in both unionist parties. There were expressions of a British identity rooted in a sense of belonging to the United Kingdom and a Protestant and Ulster identity that was located in Northern Ireland. There were different emphases placed on these social identities within the accounts of representatives from the two parties. The British identity was slightly more prominent in the social thinking of the UUP interviewees, with the Ulster identity being more stressed by the activists from the DUP. Nonetheless, elements of both social identities were found in all accounts. And that mixing of social identities, albeit with a stronger emphasis on an Ulster identity, was also true of activists in the UDA, whose political programme has often advocated the non-unionist position of independence for Northern

Ireland. Gallagher comments on the dilemmatic ideological nature of these discourses and shows how they co-exist in unionist thinking. Paradoxically, the different emphases explain the ideological fragmentation among unionists, but their common dilemma over identity also helps explain why a common ideological front can sometimes be achieved.

Gallagher's research indicated the complexity of social identities and showed how they interlock with ideological beliefs. That complexity has been largely missing from social identity research into the Northern Irish conflict (Cairns, 1987). As a result only a limited understanding of the diversity of potential social identities and their sustaining ideological beliefs has been gained (Beloff, 1989). Even less has been learned about the inter-relationships between social identities, ideological beliefs and the justification of armed struggle; nor is much known about how these justifications resonate with the widespread beliefs of the wider community.

One possible approach suggested itself. Wall paintings proliferate in Northern Ireland. They do at least deal openly with the conflict. Moreover, many openly celebrate the conflict from the perspective of the opposed paramilitary movements. Many murals highlight republican and loyalist armed struggle: support for political violence is explicit. The murals are based upon social representations and are constructed from the images and symbols that constitute social representations (Finn, 1990a, 1996; see Moscovici, 1984). Drawing upon Billig's work, it is to be expected that some of the ideological complexity of everyday social thinking about the conflict will be captured by the wall paintings.

The inevitable dilemmas in ideological thinking need to be explored. But the dilemmas in ideological thinking need not be explicit: there is a continuum. Some dilemmas will be clearly expressed, whereas others will remain subtly implicit (Billig et al., 1988). And the analysis of the wall murals is aided by Beloff's important research into visual imagery (Beloff, 1985, 1988, 1994 a,b; Billig, 1994; Canter, 1994; Robinson, 1994; Sayers, 1994; Wetherell, 1994). Lessons learned from her explorations of visual rhetoric can be used to illuminate the social meaning of murals and bring into a sharper focus the interrelationships between widespread beliefs, ideologies, different communal identities and the justification of political violence in Northern Ireland, which is the main focus of this chapter.

The Design of the Study

The design of the study was relatively open-ended. Some preliminary examination of murals suggested the different dimensions of the still ongoing study reported here.

Two independent elements proceeded together at the beginning. Wall paintings were located and studied. Simultaneously, efforts were made to discover more about the history, processes of production and supposed purpose of murals. Both of these aspects were necessary in order to confirm that the murals could be judged to be social representations.

In addition it was hypothesised that it might be possible to interrelate murals to specific political issues or general political developments in Northern Ireland. Much of that would depend on being able to date the production of the paintings, if any remained in a sufficiently viable form that allowed for interpretation. Research on murals carried out by others proved to be valuable here.

Murals can be found in many locations in Northern Ireland. Some limitations on the scope of the study had to be set. The collection of murals was restricted to specific if substantial areas of Belfast, parts of County Antrim to the North of Belfast, and to Derry and some areas of County Londonderry. This sample had the merits of including the two main Northern Irish cities and a range of different population centres in the two counties that contain these cities. It also included populations which varied considerably in their proximity to the Border.

An all-inclusive collection of murals is not possible because of their ephemeral nature: they remain in existence for very variable time periods, with some being very short-lived indeed. In an attempt to gain a broad overview of the social significance of murals, it was decided to make a special study of the production of murals in one area. West Belfast was chosen as it is an area of considerable paramilitary activity and provided a variety of murals representing both loyalist and republican images. It was not feasible to undertake a longitudinal study of the diverse geographical areas that comprise West Belfast, so this part of the study was restricted to similar areas immediately proximate to the Shankill and Falls Roads, the central roads in the loyalist and republican areas respectively. Murals produced in these areas were examined and recorded (Finn, 1990a).

Another aim of the study was to develop a historical dimension to the analysis. This proved to be possible because some murals had remained in existence for some years. Some recording and analyses of the murals (e.g. in 1983 in the Irish art journal, *Circa*) had taken place and had been supplemented by some recent publications (Loftus, 1990, 1994; Rolston, 1987, 1988, 1992), which have presented further details and examples of wall paintings. In addition, some specified areas in Belfast, especially West Belfast, were visited at different time intervals.

The Conduct of the Study

To study the wall paintings in sufficient detail it was necessary to record them and the most obvious means of doing this was by photography (Beloff, 1985; Canter, 1988). So once a mural was located, it was recorded by a photograph. There is no scientific method to the location of murals. Some sites were identified by helpful suggestions made by people in Northern Ireland. Often local inhabitants would advise on other nearby locations. Some murals were found by the simple method of driving around and looking for them.

The first exploration of murals commenced in late February 1989, continued until June and was recommenced in September and October of that year. Further visits to locate murals in Belfast alone took place in June 1992. One new Belfast site was visited in February 1994. A new site for murals in 1992 was revisited in both February and June 1994, but no new murals had appeared there.

Some background to some of the local murals was obtained by talking to local people. Although locals were nearly always very helpful in a general way, little detailed information was obtained. Sometimes information on the muralists was given. Pride in the murals as products of the local community was displayed. It was a common experience to be informed of other murals in the general area and, if they were not already known, to be given precise directions on how to find them.

Understandably, despite generous help in locating murals, actual comments on the content of the wall murals were much less forthcoming. However, numbers of older children and younger adolescents would openly voice support for paramilitary groups and some would claim, sometimes honestly, some involvement in the production of murals.

Some further information on murals was obtained from *Combat*, the unofficial monthly of the illegal UVF; from *Ulster*, the official UDA monthly; and from *An Phoblacht/Republican News*, the weekly newspaper of Provisional Sinn Fein. Some other publications also included an occasional brief reference to wall murals.

A range of articles and commentaries on the murals have now been produced: they present considerable information about the development of murals. More recent publications have proved helpful: the collection of photographs in Rolston (1992) has proved to be invaluable.

One of the aims was to use the murals to understand more about those widespread societal beliefs that could be drawn on to justify political violence in Northern Ireland. That meant, as argued earlier, that Tajfels' prior societal factors and their own psychological concomitants needed to be understood. Effectively that meant gaining an understanding of the history of the conflict and the role of political violence.

Consequently, considerable background reading into the history of the conflict and into the history of the various political and paramilitary organisations was undertaken. Commentaries on the organisations and analyses of the varied literature produced by these organisations were studied. West Belfast was a significant site of the intergroup conflict and an important location for murals, and particular attention was paid to its socio-political history.

It was also important to gain an understanding of the social and political background of specific murals. Often the message on the wall was, at least at one level, very overt. Yet some murals were more obscure and additional scholarship was necessary to identify the significance of elements of the mural. This scholarship had some very limited overlap with the art historian's more dedicated investigations of the painterly history of artistic work (see Beloff, 1994a). A knowledge of contemporary political events and the broad ideological context at the time that the mural was produced was essential. But, as the importance of murals lies in their capacity to communicate a clear message to the local community, the main aim was to ensure that those immediately accessible images were recognised, and their history understood.

OUTCOMES

One interpretation of the murals has already been presented and others will follow (Finn, 1990a, 1996, 1997). In this chapter murals from a variety of locations, produced at different times, will be analysed with the intention of examining the dominant content of the social representations that constitute the ideological justifications for loyalist and republican political violence. The full range of contrary themes will not be explored in detail, but only in so far as they contribute to an understanding of the reasoning that has sustained paramilitary political violence; nor will this analysis explore the important ideological dilemmas over group identities experienced by Northern Ireland's communities.

The Propaganda Value of Murals

Some have suggested that murals act as territorial markers, but murals are not painted on the perimeter of community areas. Instead they are located well within them. This location may serve as a daily reminder to all who live in that community that there is strong support for the paramilitaries and their campaigns of political violence (Gallagher & Hanratty, 1989): it also provides some limited protection for the murals. Damage to murals would be much easier if their location was on the periphery. Nonetheless, damage still occurs, even when murals are centrally placed. Republican murals are often the targets for paint bombs thrown by the security forces. Loyalist murals, with a few exceptions, escape this treatment.

Damage to republican murals often leads to a determination to repair it and reinstate the message. That can lead to a continuing sequence of repair by muralists and damage by security forces. Sometimes damaged murals are turned to the muralists' own advantage. One paint-bombed mural in Derry was left damaged. Rolston (1988, p. 16) explains that a wooden wall plaque was attached. It stated:

> *This mural was designed and painted by the creative talents of republicans. It was vandalised by the destructive talents of the RUC and British Army. July 1982.*

The propaganda potential of wall paintings is clear. However, the propaganda value normally lies in the intended content of the mural itself.

Loyalist Murals

The need to be careful in interpreting murals is exemplified by the images on the wall of the Orange Cross social club just off the Shankill Road (Fig. 8.1). This mural had been painted in 1986 to commemorate the role of the UVF in the Battle of the Somme seventy years before. The mural shows the original UVF, which had become the 36th Ulster Division, serving Britain in the "Great War". However, on 18th February 1989 the Orange Cross social club was attacked by the Irish People's Liberation Organisation (IPLO). Steven McCrea, who had just been released after a long prison sentence for his role in killing a Catholic in 1972, was shot dead and the building was

FIG. 8.1.   Soldiers at the Somme (and Britain's prisoners of war).

© *Gerry Finn.*

severely damaged. Over half of this mural was destroyed and is missing from this photograph (see Rolston, 1992). Under the heading of the Ulster Volunteer Force, the missing section had shown UVF members as prisoners of war, held behind barbed wire in prison camps. But these were contemporary UVF prisoners held in British prisons. The juxtaposition of the two images was a clear identification of the ideological dilemma faced by the contemporary UVF. The earlier paramilitary organisation named the Ulster Volunteer Force had received considerable support and had eventually been incorporated into the British Army. Although the UVF and its supporters see themselves as the inheritors of the past, that is not recognised by others, and especially not by the British state.

The contemporary UVF's claim of an identity with the past is highlighted by a nearby mural in Dover Place (Fig. 8.2). In 1987 the muralists had taken the opportunity of what was recognised to be the 75th anniversary of the founding of the Ulster Volunteer Force in 1912 to represent the contemporary UVF as its direct descendants. The organisation is identified at the top and the motto "For God and Ulster" is presented along with other insignia. A map of Northern Ireland is rendered as an Ulster flag; and on each side is an image of an armed UVF member, one in 1916 apparel, the other in today's garb, and labelled "1912 then" and "1987 now" respectively. Underneath written in the style of a scroll is "They Fought Then, For the Cause of Ulster, We Will Fight Now."

FIG. 8.2.   UVF portraits in history: 1912 and 1987.

© *Gerry Finn.*

The mural shows visual embodiments of social representations which are used as anchoring devices: they attempt to make the unfamiliar familiar. Present day loyalist paramilitaries are to be seen in the same light as the original UVF. They are to be seen simply as part of the campaign by Unionists to ensure that their religious and political heritage is not surrendered: they fight for God and Ulster. Both murals are an attempt at communal self-presentation of the loyalist paramilitary action as valid: both seek to legitimise paramilitary action. In different ways both point to the dilemma that these actions are treated as illegal by the British state and loyalist paramilitaries are imprisoned as criminals by the state to which they profess their loyalty. This ideological dilemma is acute.

Loyalists identify with the British State, and see themselves not only as loyal, but as the only loyal and law-abiding citizens in Northern Ireland. Paramilitary action needs to be justified within this framework. That is why the historical precedent is essential. The first UVF had an initially uncertain relationship with the British state. It also confronted the legal government, but circumstances changed and soon the UVF and the British government were no longer opposed. The problem is that the attempt to legitimise the UVF by this historical parallel inevitably also draws attention to the differences. Then, the British Army made clear its refusal to act against the first UVF; some leading UVF figures had formerly been prominent British Army officers. When the "Great War" began, the UVF officially became part of the British Army. Now British security forces act against the contemporary paramilitary organisation which has styled itself the UVF, and British courts imprison its members.

Other local murals express similar themes. Murals affirm community support for loyalist paramilitaries (e.g. Fig. 8.3). The proclamation is that the "Shankill supports all the loyalist prisoners." The traditional loyalist image of Union flags hanging from Orange pikestaffs enclose the emblems of various loyalist paramilitaries. In the middle is another outline of Northern Ireland in the guise of a flag. In clockwise order are the paramilitary emblems: the becrowned shield which contains the red hand of Ulster, with the inscription UDA above, and the UDA motto *Quis separabit* (who will separate?) below; the becrowned shamrock of the Young Citizens' Volunteers (YCV), a section of the first UVF but now used as a name for the youth section of the latterday UVF; the red hand against a background of blue in a triangle of yellow on which is written Protestant Action Force (a nomme de guerre sometimes used by the UVF); and finally there is the emblem of the UVF. That is the red hand of Ulster surrounded by the motto "For God and Ulster", which is presented in clearer form in the adjacent mural (also Fig. 8.3). In it, an armed UVF fighter in the now-customary stylised image of the paramilitary uniform of today, poses before the Ulster flag and the UVF colours. To help interpret the message, "This is Loyalist

FIG. 8.3.   Proclamation of community support for loyalist paramilitaries.

© *Gerry Finn.*

West Belfast", "Shankill" and "No Surrender" (the traditional unionist slogan) accompany the images.

The murals give unconditional approval to all loyalist paramilitary prisoners and attempt to represent their actions as if they were little different from the usual strategies employed by traditional unionism to defend loyalism from its perceived threat. However, the murals also display very well the dilemmatic nature of loyalist thinking. The number of murals which represent loyalist paramilitaries as part of the community and its heritage reveal the extent of the need to propagandize around this interpretation. Instead, as the Orange Cross club mural complained, there is an important contrast between the treatment of loyalist paramilitaries today and that received by those they claim to be their forerunners. And that contrast is emphasised by the need to declare (which is in reality an exhortation for more) Shankill support for loyalist prisoners (Fig. 8.3).

Sometimes the justification of political violence draws even more on the past. The tercentenary of the Battle of the Boyne was in 1990. In Blythe Street in the Sandy Row area of Belfast, a mural to celebrate the anniversary equated the Battle of the Boyne with loyalist paramilitary actions in 1990 (Fig. 8.4). In the mural King William not only crosses the Boyne, but seems to travel from 1690 to 1990 as well. Beside one pillar is one of William's soldiers in 1690 dress: at the other, presented as his descendant, is a modern loyalist paramilitary. To the right in the style of a heraldic scroll is written: "We the loyalist people of the Sandy Row remember with pride the 300th anniversary of the BATTLE OF THE BOYLE. No surrender." And the

FIG. 8.4.   Historical unity of loyalist armed struggle: 1690 and 1990.

© *Gerry Finn.*

message is claimed by the Ulster Freedom Fighters (UFF), the then dominant militaristic faction that controlled the UDA (Bruce, 1992). The
dilemma within loyalism about the role of armed struggle in Northern
Ireland is highlighted by the claim that it can be equated to the struggle for
the crown between William and James.

One mural almost appears to have given up on the battle for hearts and
minds. In 1989, in Ballycraigy, just outside of Antrim, a mural had presented
the usual heraldic style display of support for the UVF, along with a 1912
date to suggest historical continuity between the two organisations with that
name. That remained there in 1992, but by then some additions to the wall
painting had also been made (Fig. 8.5). Two silhouetted figures of loyalist
gunmen, painted on boarding, had been attached to the mural. Above the
original mural, on another board, was the Bart Simpson cartoon character
dressed in loyalist garb against a backdrop of Northern Ireland. The board
was headed Ballycraigy. On one side of Bart Simpson was "You don't like
us." On the other side was "We don't care." Intriguingly, on the same block,
but around the corner, was a message from the paramilitaries. It said:
"anyone causing antisocial behaviour will be severly (sic) dealt with...!"
Whether Bart Simpson's ambiguous comments are directed to those deemed

FIG. 8.5. Images of continuity and loyalism as community security service?

© *Gerry Finn.*

to be "antisocial", to the wider community or even to both remains uncertain, and a matter for careful interpretation by all local residents.

Possible symptoms of some local difficulties in Ballycraigy are not necessarily indicative of communal feelings towards loyalist paramilitaries elsewhere. In parts of Belfast claims for the legitimacy and the powerful effect of loyalist political violence certainly meet with local support. A compound mural in Meekon Street in East Belfast conveyed a multiplicity of messages (Fig. 8.6). Union and Ulster flags form a traditional quasi-heraldic backdrop to a mid-1980s "Ulster Says No" to the Anglo-Irish agreement. Constitutional unionists and loyalist paramilitaries were then involved in some joint opposition to the agreement (Bruce, 1992) and campaigned vigorously against the British government. In an illustration of the loyalist dilemma over the politics of the relationship with Britain, both the UDA and the UVF issued death threats against the British and Irish politicians and civil servants involved in pursuing this policy. Tom King, the Conservative Secretary of State for Northern Ireland, was attacked by loyalists during his next visit to Belfast.

The top mural here (Fig. 8.6) displays the island of Ireland. The republic is a green white and gold tricolour: the North is represented by an unruffled Ulster flag. But the South is cracking from the impact of a clenched red hand of Ulster, in the form of a fist, which has punched a hole through its middle. On one side of the island is the more usual representation of the red hand, Ulster's traditional emblem, and on the other an armed loyalist paramilitary is outlined. The projected relationship between a secure Northern Ireland, loyalist paramilitaries, and their capacity for defence and offence is clearly drawn, and then underlined by the proclamation of support for "all loyalist prisoners".

Some very complicated and complex strands are woven into the justification of violence conveyed in this mural. In 1974 Britain set up a power-sharing legislative assembly in Northern Ireland, proposed a joint Council for Ireland which would involve the Irish government, and had agreed with the Irish government that no change in the status of Northern Ireland would occur without majority agreement. Despite that last assurance, loyalist outrage led loyalist workers to strike against British government policy, while loyalist paramilitaries erected barricades, and blocked roads. During the strike the biggest loss of life in one single day of the Northern Ireland conflict occurred in the Irish Republic. No-warning car bombs in Dublin and Monaghan led to 32 deaths and, although both the UVF and the UDA denied any involvement, Bruce (1992) has firmly attributed responsibility to the UVF. Nonetheless, apart from these bombings, and despite voiced threats, loyalist paramilitary activity directed against the Irish Republic has been limited: it has, of course, been the British government that has carried out the political developments in Northern Ireland that have been opposed by loyalist paramilitaries. So, in the context of the Anglo-Irish agreement, as with other proposed political initiatives, it was the British government that remained the main focus of loyalist political attacks and that poses ideological problems for loyalist paramilitary activity.

That is why the red hand of Ulster that smashes up the Irish Republic visually represents a multi-layered metaphorical message. The metaphorical

FIG. 8.6. Loyalist physical force and flags of loyalty and treachery.

attack expresses general opposition to any political moves that increase Irish influence on Northern Ireland. Republican paramilitary force will be met with even mightier loyalist paramilitary force. One powerful proposed justification for loyalist political violence is that it is directed against republican paramilitaries, who publicly identify with the Irish tricolour and are often represented by loyalists as indistinguishable from the Irish Republic itself. Real dilemmas are raised here: many loyalist attacks have actually been simply against Catholics (Bruce, 1992). And even when the use of avowedly pro-state violence is directed against republican paramilitaries, that brings loyalists back to the dilemma that it is opposed by British state. But this mural also conveys a powerful message of supposed loyalist intent: if it becomes necessary, loyalist paramilitaries will attack, and even overcome, the Irish Republic. Thus do loyalist paramilitaries represent themselves as the true defenders of Northern Ireland and, amidst fears of future abandonment by Britain (Bruce, 1992; Finn, 1990b), as the only force that can be depended on to be loyal to that cause; this justification of present loyalist armed struggle by promising true-blue commitment to the cause in the event of a future Irish Armageddon is often a sub-text in other murals that directly focus on the past.

In a loyalist world-view, often coloured by conspiracy theories (Finn, 1990b), in which individuals continuously plot on behalf of pan-nationalist fronts, the mural's Irish tricolour becomes a flag of convenience for loyalists to cover all those they believe threaten Northern Ireland. Inevitably those suspected of involvement in republican politics join those suspected of being republican paramilitaries. In its most extreme version, the belief in the pan-nationalist front means that political violence is justified against many diverse targets. Innocent, often randomly-chosen, Catholics and constitutional nationalist politicians, openly opposed to republican violence, become the "legitimate targets" of loyalist paramilitary operations: republican plots become plots by the Irish republic and loyalists flag its legitimacy as the target. And when conspiracy theories converge with a religious belief in the inevitability of the biblical Armageddon, past battles and the present conflict become mere harbingers of that unavoidable conflagration to come (Finn, 1990b). From this religio-political viewpoint, dates are irrelevant, time is one, and King William's victory at the Boyne is merely an example of that same earthly battle between good and evil that does stretch from before 1690 to the 1990s and after (cf. Fig. 8.4). For some, usually those who do not seek religious solace in predestined heavenly delights, but who do still accept a secularised version of these events, the defence of a politicised Protestantism from what they perceive as a historically continuous catholic (and Catholic) assault does justify continuous loyalist armed struggle (Beattie, 1992; Guelke & Wright, 1992; Nelson, 1984; Parker, 1993).

This small selection of murals identifies some of the devices by which loyalist political violence is justified. Mainly this is by making some identification with its use in the past and, in the case of the UVF, by claiming some nominal descent from the original organisation. The problem is that the dominant ideological argument used to justify loyalist armed struggle also pinpoints the dilemmas in loyalist thinking. The dominant argument is that if the proposed historical parallels are accepted, then loyalist paramilitary organisations are necessary, and loyalist political violence is justified. Yet, the historical parallels are not strong. Moreover, in the past, loyalist paramilitary organisations received support either from the British state or from significant sections of that state and its civil society. So it was the unionist elite in Northern Ireland, backed by the British Conservative party, that proposed overt military action in opposition to Irish Home Rule Bills in the early 20th century and formed the first UVF. Early UVF actions, admittedly preparatory rather than actively offensive, met with tacit support from influential sections of the British state, especially the British Army.

That is not the contemporary position. Loyalists justify their armed struggle by claiming that it is pro-State violence (Bruce, 1992), but loyalist paramilitary political violence is opposed by the British state. And that dilemma is poignantly symbolised by mural proclamations of support for all loyalist prisoners, each of whom is imprisoned by the State on whose behalf they claim to fight. So these loyalist justifications of paramilitary violence simultaneously declare the dilemma loyalist ideology faces today. The best justification for loyalist armed struggles lies in hints of a deteriorating situation, which plays on communal fears of a future British withdrawal, and a bitter civil war in which loyalist paramilitaries are the only remaining defenders of loyalism. Yet this is the core ideological dilemma at the heart of loyalism: a belief in potential British betrayal of the self-perceived most loyal of Britain's subjects. That places loyalism in the horns of a crucial strategic dilemma in evaluating whether the present use of loyalist political violence to attempt to influence Northern Irish politics now does not make British withdrawal, and a potential civil war, more likely in the future.

Republican Murals

A republican mural on Belfast's Falls Road again shows the need for careful analysis and some understanding of its background (Fig. 8.7). The mural honoured Mairead Farrell, Sean Savage and Daniel McCann, three local Belfast IRA members who, in Gibraltar in 1988, were shot dead in a controversial undercover SAS operation that raised the question of whether a "shoot to kill" policy had been in operation (see Urban, 1992).

FIG. 8.7.   Republican armed struggle: sacrifice for a new dawn

Interpreting this mural was difficult. Bad paint bomb damage had occurred and the boarding supporting the wording had been broken off. (Some local residents claimed the damage had been done very noisily by security forces very early one morning.) Nonetheless, some aspects were clear. The Fianna sunbursts around the scene symbolised the dawning of the new day (and new order) that republicans believe will be won. The central figure was a representation of Mother Ireland in distress. The completed wording was discovered to have been:

> *"I have always believed that we had a legitimate right to take up arms. From an interview given by IRA volunteer Mairead Farrell. Executed with her gallant comrades Sean Savage and Dan McCann."*

But the rest of the mural was so indistinct that numerous interpretations were possible.

Research disclosed that the central theme of the mural was based on the Ballyseedy republican memorial (*An Phoblacht/Republican News*, 19.5.1988). That knowledge helped, but there are either small errors in its reproduction or small deliberate variations. The actual Ballyseedy memorial (see National Graves Association, 1985, p. 56) depicts in the centre a desolate, ashamed, Mother Ireland. Her loose cloak is pulled down beneath her naked breasts; she just manages to hold onto an infant by her fingertips. She stands with her head hanging, looking in the same direction as the infant, who has turned and is gazing much more directly at another figure. There, at Mother Ireland's feet lies a man in a pain-racked position. His clothing has been roughly pulled away from his torso, bare ribs protrude. His hand still touches her cloak, but his position suggests that he may now be dead. On her other side, but facing the other direction, stands a man in heroic pose, and clenched fist at his side. Various interpretations can be made of the original, but the dominant message of the mural, underlined by the additional symbolism, is that the struggle for Ireland is renewed in apparent defeat and destined for eventual victory. This is a common republican message, as the frequent use of the phoenix arising from the flames demonstrates.

The mural's general theme represents the "executed" IRA members as heroic victims of deliberate state violence, martyrs for the new Ireland that is soon to dawn. Farrell's quote justifies political violence and, in the context of the mural and her death, implies that other options are not possible. But the very need to proclaim this justification identifies the dilemma in thinking about political violence. The mural asserts the legitimacy of armed struggle and challenges its opponents by reminding them of the way that these IRA members had been killed. Yet the choice of the Ballyseedy Memorial to remember Farrell, Savage and McCann is as intriguing as its historical significance is double-edged: it commemorates eight anti-treaty republicans killed by Irish soldiers in March 1923. As a reprisal against IRA landmine attacks during the Irish civil war, nine republican prisoners were tied to a landmine which was then detonated. Astonishingly, one prisoner was blown clear and survived.

By making the Ballyseedy Memorial the centrepiece of the mural, the intensity of earlier deep divisions among nationalists, indeed among republicans, is recalled. To the shame of Mother Ireland, those divisions in the fledgling Irish Free State led to Irish atrocities against Irish republican rebels. It reminds republicans of the continuing divisions among nationalists and of the condemnation of the present IRA's paramilitary activities by the Irish Republic. Nonetheless, recognition of the Ballyseedy memorial and its significance is limited in the local community. Passers-by in the Falls Road were unable—some perhaps unwilling—to identify the origins of this wall mural. For republicans it is, however, a reminder of what is judged to be the treachery and deceit of sections of the republican movement and the perceived illegitimacy of the establishment of the southern Irish state.

So a range of ideological dilemmas are conveyed in the imagery of this wall mural. Some were made even more explicit in a 1991 mural in Whiterock Road, painted to celebrate the 75th anniversary of the Easter Rising (Fig. 8.8). The year 1916 appears as flames, with the armed leaders of the

FIG. 8.8.   Picturing the Easter Rising: 1916 and 1991.

© *Gerry Finn.*

Easter Rising waving a tricolour in the foreground. To the side, the Dublin GPO, where the Irish revolution began and the Irish Republic was first proclaimed, is ablaze. At the top are classic republican emblems: the phoenix, the symbol of revolutionary commitment being continuously reborn in adversity and struggle; the starry plough, the symbol of Connolly's Irish revolutionary socialists; and the sunburst, signifying the new day to come. In the middle, written in a contemporary graphic arts style, lower-case, was "who fears to speak of Easter week," without a question-mark: for only a rhetorical question was asked.

State celebrations of the Easter Rising in the Irish Republic have been increasingly scaled down during the northern conflict for fear that public events would be hijacked by IRA supporters. In 1991 there was controversy at the determination in the south to play down the 75th anniversary. Radicals and republicans instead joined together in Dublin to mount their own celebration of the Easter Rising. In drawing attention to this attempt to play down the past, the mural drew attention to the contemporary debate about the legitimacy of the IRA use of political violence, and the refusal of many to countenance any equation between 1916 and the political situation in Northern Ireland; a refusal so strong that it had indeed led many in the Republic to "fear to speak of Easter week."

So this mural overtly comments on the dilemmas in nationalist thinking about the legitimacy of armed struggle and reminds people that the Irish constitutional parties were themselves sprung from the 1916 Easter Rising and the bitter strife of the Irish civil war. An independent Irish state had eventually emerged from the Easter Rising, but no thirty-two county Irish Republic had yet been created: the six counties of Northern Ireland remained British. Yet the raising of these points in the mural also high-lighted the opposition to republican political violence from the Irish Republic and Irish constitutional nationalists. They dismiss arguments for any historical legitimacy for the contemporary IRA, by denying any comparison between the circumstances of 1916 and Northern Ireland in the 1990s and by castigating the IRA for using indiscriminate tactics against a widespread range of "legitimate targets" in its campaign of armed struggle.

Unlike loyalist murals, relatively few republican murals have sought to represent the past to justify the present (Finn, 1990a; Rolston, 1992). Paradoxically, despite the constitutional nationalist dismissal of IRA actions as historically legitimate, republicans do not need to insist that the orga-nisation can legitimately claim some historical continuity from the past to the present. Despite considerable splintering and fragmentation within the IRA and the republican movement, a direct lineage can be demonstrated; anti-state political violence on behalf of Irish revolution against British rule can be accepted as having been a historically justifiable strategy and is represented now as a continuing necessity. So the ideological justification for the perceived continuation of armed struggle against Britain is, therefore, largely sought in the present. References to the past are more oblique, less central.

In that sense the Whiterock mural does not depart too much from the republican focus on present-day events: it directs attention to today's ideological dilemmas within constitutional nationalist thinking about the heritage they share with today's physical force, revolutionary republicans: a past in which political violence against the British state met with common approval. Yet that ideological focus is also dilemmatic for republicans: Irish nationalist critics do indeed share a common heritage, but still they condemn the republican armed struggle today as unnecessary and illegitimate; a betrayal of that past. So this mural (and others) hinted strongly at the growing internal republican dilemma over the ideological value of armed struggle as a political strategy (Finn, 1990a, 1996).

Republican justifications for political violence usually centre upon contemporary events. The state is portrayed as being guilty of political violence, making republican political violence necessary in return. An old mural in Rossville Street, in Derry's Bogside district, recalls the death of eleven year old Stephen McConomy, killed by a plastic bullet fired by security forces on 16th April 1982 and questions the state's definition of civil order (Fig. 8.9). Three murals painted side-by-side in Toomebridge in Antrim show republicans as victims and officers of the British state as brutal, bestial oppressors (Fig. 8.10). To highlight the issue of strip-searching of prisoners (and the treatment of Ireland in general), a partially naked young woman, metaphorically another representation of Ireland, cowers in a dark cell, desperately hiding from the bright light as she pulls some strips of clothing around herself. Next a snarling pig, with very large teeth, represents the RUC. To emphasise the image of police brutality, the club carried by the caricatured policeman has nails sticking out of it. The final mural has a British Army officer, carrying a baton shaped like a club, caught in an adapted road traffic sign that signifies "No Brits". The image of the officer conveys an impression of a snorting bull. Around the image is the legend "Brit Busters". In Northern Ireland that allusion is clear. It is not always the case that republican muralists present the security forces as less than human. But here this visual imagery is used to explain their behaviour, represented as brutally repressive, and to justify the need for a response from the "Brit Busters", the IRA, to ensure that British soldiers are removed.

Contemporary international comparisons were drawn in some murals. Just off the Falls Road was a mural of Nelson Mandela (Fig. 8.11). It had been painted to celebrate his 70th birthday in 1988 and was repaired throughout 1989 following paint bomb attacks. A pre-prison-release image of Mandela is the central feature, as African National Congress (ANC) colours of green, yellow and black intermingle with republican green, white and orange. He is acclaimed as a "comrade" and future victory is foretold.

FIG. 8.9. Victim of rubber bullet: a question of civil order?

© *Gerry Finn.*

FIG. 8.10. Portraying victims and oppression to justify armed struggle.

© *Gerry Finn.*

FIG. 8.11.   Mandela: icon of struggle and international solidarity.

© *Gerry Finn.*

The implicit message is of a common struggle by Irish republicans and the ANC. Other murals elsewhere represented this image of Irish republican political violence as being at one with other contemporary armed struggles. Effectively these murals feature a rich complex of ideological dilemmas around the justification of political violence in general, identify specific circumstances in which there is some agreement about its legitimacy, but raise the issue of whether, in the context of Northern Ireland, republican violence does satisfy these requirements.

The general legitimation of republican political violence is represented in imagery that presents a picture of a community that is abused and on whose behalf the IRA fights back. That interpretation does not convince all at whom it is aimed. Some locals reverse the causality: they do see themselves being badly treated by security forces, but believe that treatment is made worse by the actions of the IRA. Yet there does also remain a general sense of injustice based on past discrimination and abuse at the hands of the Northern Irish state (Osborne, 1991) and the present behaviour of the army and the RUC (Brewer, 1992; Gallagher, 1992). That general communal self-image of being victimised (O Connor, 1993) is something around which the republican movement can mobilise. The community accepts that it is, and has been, oppressed and victimised. Republicans argue that, if they are not to remain forever victims, there is no option but to fight back against what they represent to be an inhuman system perpetuated by British force. They portray defence and resistance in different forms and identify them with the actions of the IRA.

There is much scope for internal communal disagreement with this analysis, and much occurs. Yet this does provide the general framework within which republican political violence is justified. Eventual victory will not be achieved through armed struggle itself, but by willing self-sacrifice for the good of the community. The dangers taken by IRA members are not disguised in the wall paintings. The IRA dead are proudly proclaimed and honoured. They are represented as a special case of communal victims: those who risked much, and then sacrificed all, for their community. That is perhaps best represented in what is strictly speaking not a mural, but a memorial on the gable-end wall of an Ardoyne house used as a Sinn Fein advice centre. This North Belfast garden also contains a Celtic cross and is enclosed by metalwork railings incorporating various Celtic designs (Fig. 8.12). Local dead IRA volunteers and local members of the community who have died are listed there together. The plaque in the middle has a phoenix rising out of the flames of a community on fire. Around it is written a poem which explains the means by which "Freedom has arisen".

Oft from prison bars, oft from battles flashes
Oft from heroes lips, oftenest from their ashes.

A rough approximation of a quote from Terence MacSwiney, Lord Mayor of Cork, who died on hunger strike against Britain in 1920, is inscribed around the eaves:

"It is not those who can inflict the most but those who can endure the most shall win."

The republican justification of political violence is that it is a response to the ongoing British mistreatment of the minority community in Northern Ireland, an entity denied political legitimacy by the minority community. And despite the deaths and injuries caused by republican armed struggle, it is the minority community, including IRA members, who are represented as victims in republican murals. That is who is portrayed as suffering oppression, and represented as those who, enduring most, will eventually win. The republican justification of political violence lies in the present and

FIG. 8.12.   Communal deaths, but eventual victory through adversity.

© *Gerry Finn.*

the murals continually depict present injustices to the minority community. Republican dead (Figs. 8.7 and 8.12) are simply represented as (a)part committed to the whole ill-treated community: a very potent message lies in the representation of republicans using political violence in the expectation that, as a result, they will suffer imprisonment or death. Republican para-militaries are victims left with no option but to take up armed struggle, despite the potential cost. But the very persistent symbol of the phoenix reminds all of the belief that it is in adversity that the republican movement grows in strength and commitment. One early mural slogan represented these sentiments succinctly: "You may kill the revolutionary but never the revolution" (Rolston, 1992, p. 35; cf. Loftus, 1990, 1994).

So the most effective justifications of republican political violence are that it is the only response to the victimisation of the Northern Irish minority community by the British state and that it will inevitably lead to a united Ireland. Most splits in republicanism have involved disputes over this analysis: armed struggle has historically been dilemmatic for republicans. At the core of the debate are questions about the legitimacy and availability of other political strategies, the effects of armed struggle on the whole Northern Irish society, and on British and Irish governments, and questions about the status and treatment of the minority Northern Irish community itself. Internal debate on the role of republican political violence intensified from the late 1980s (Finn, 1990a; 1996). Republicans determined to resolve their ideological dilemma over the use of political violence by ending it: they called a ceasefire. That decision, in turn, made it more difficult for loyalist paramilitaries to justify their own armed struggle. The end of republican anti-state violence intensified the contradictions inherent in the pursuit of loyalist pro-state violence and eventually led loyalist paramilitaries to declare their own ceasefire.

Crucial practical political problems need to be resolved, if the ceasefires are to be permanent and a solution to the Northern Irish conflict constructed. Profound social and economic change is necessary if old ideological dilemmas are to be displaced by new ones (Billig et al., 1988). The actions of both British and Irish governments are the key to the creation of the political changes which can aid the peaceable resolution of the ideological dilemmas that surround the use of political violence in the Northern Irish conflict. But the potential for other, different decisions about the role of political violence in Northern Ireland remains strong.[1] Murals still display the content of the social representations used to justify armed struggle. There remain republicans and loyalists who still advocate and justify armed struggle; others envisage scenarios which leave them with "no choice" but to return to political violence to further their cause. Outsiders can adopt an optimistic or a pessimistic view of the future course of events. But we can all hope that the writing on Northern Ireland's walls may now, even if ever so faintly, read "Peace".

Conducting this type of Qualitative Research

This research uses a blend of qualitative techniques which are well described elsewhere (see chapters by Beloff, Billig, and Hayes, this volume). Only by adopting a rich mix of qualitative methods is it possible to research complicated and sensitive topics, such as the Northern Irish conflict. Qualitative approaches ensure that a sufficiently deep approach can be taken to the understanding of the widespread beliefs that underpin justifications of political violence.

The most important element in doing this research was the decision to treat visual images as a serious topic for psychological investigation. That allowed an entry into the range of potential justifications of violence and into community identities. Research of this nature requires the adoption of an approach that is non-intrusive, but which is evidential and sensitive to the concerns of the local communities.

In carrying out this type of research investigators must be very aware of the possibility of their own prejudices influencing their interpretations. Instead it is essential to attempt to enter into the subjective world of those communities that are being explored. To do this researchers must immerse themselves in the literature and art produced by these communities. Only then can the rich symbolism of visual imagery be understood.

Seldom is it the case that dilemmatic thinking will be presented in explicit terms in murals. Billig et al. (1988) explained that there is a continuum from implicit to explicit in dilemmatic thinking. Most of the examples in the murals were much more implicit than explicit. Dilemmas were more explicitly topicalised in the mural that asks "who fears to speak of Easter week" (plate 7) and in the original full mural, before it was partially destroyed (plate 1), that contrasted images of UVF members in 1916 and 1986. To identify implicit dilemmas it is necessary to uncover those contrary themes that mural messages are meant to oppose, but which remain unspecified by them.

In interpreting murals it is essential that accounts of local widespread beliefs are thoroughly explored. Interpretations of murals by the researcher need to be interrogated by setting them against general analyses of the conflict drawn from historical and contemporary reports about the conflict. It is also important that the background to an individual mural be explored. Often the necessary information is presented in the mural itself: sometimes that is not the case. For example, the mural based on the Ballyseedy Memorial (plate 7) was only inadequately understood until the original on which it was based was identified. One danger for the researcher, however, is that a single mural is over-interpreted. It is essential that murals are tested against one another. Only when there are demonstrably common themes in a number of murals can an interpretation be offered with any sense of authority: singular themes in individual murals may be indicative of dilemmatic themes and new departures but, without some corroboration in other murals or in spoken or written policy statements, they have to be treated with great care. The collaborative production of murals ensures that murals can only emerge after going through a process of consensual validation and scrutiny, but that does not guarantee that a single mural does not contain some features that are at best tangential to the conflict. Even muralists are allowed some artistic license.

Carrying out this Form of Analysis

The precise use of these qualitative techniques is described in the chapters of Beloff, Billig and Hayes.

1. Clarify the nature of the issue that interests you. Refine and define the precise question(s) you wish to ask and then consider how you can answer it (them).

2. Consider the methodology that is best employed. Qualitative approaches can be used for most problems. Quantitative approaches can be appropriate when analysing specific aspects of societal phenomena, if they can be genuinely isolated as independent variables (Doise, 1986). However, they are seldom appropriate in gaining a true understanding of those wider societal phenomena themselves (Moscovici, 1984; Finn, 1992).

3. Are there visual representations associated with the social phenomenon you wish to study? Normally the answer will be yes! Is it a reasonable hypothesis that these visual representations will provide an opportunity to explore social representations related to your question? Again that would often appear to be the case, but one drawback could be the source of these representations. If they are drawn from media sources, they will present some of the most commonly available social representations, but not necessarily those in which you are most interested.

4. If you are going to explore visual representations, you will need to undertake considerable reading about, and considerable viewing of, relevant and related visual artefacts in order to understand the iconic and symbolic aspects of the visual data you obtained. Effectively that means making an effort to use other sources of information to help you identify the social representations on which the visual representations are based.

5. Analyse your visual representations using the psychological insights offered by social representations and visual rhetoric. Identify what are the dilemmatic themes related to the representation. With visual data, like verbal statements, it is almost inevitable that there will be contrary themes. That does mean that there will certainly be other ways of "seeing" the situation.

6. Consider: what evidence would negate your interpretation? Once you have decided what this is, go through your data set to see if your interpretation can be invalidated. If it can, consider again: if it cannot, think again and repeat the exercise. By this process of self-criticism, you ought to be able to arrive at a better view of your visual materials. Then test out your interpretations based on the visual representations against the literature on your topic. Again test out your evidence for your interpretations.

7. Note the paradox of doing research into visual material and then writing about it. Ensure that you can report and represent some of your evidence visually. One of the problems with this research is that the richness of the visual content makes it difficult to substitute words for the power of the image. That is why others have used visual images to make their case. Consequently it is necessary to create meaningful

word-pictures of the visual world you have studied, even though the word-pictures often cannot possibly do justice to the richness of visual representations, as is the case with murals in Northern Ireland.

8. Remember again that visual representations contain alternative visions. So, once you think you are finished, analyse and re-analyse your data set again. Remain optimistic. Every visual representation is a fragment of some social vision: every visual representation tells you something of at least one good story.

NOTE

1. This chapter was completed a few months after republican and loyalist ceasefires were called. Unfortunately the continuing history of Northern Ireland has indeed demonstrated that these ideological dilemmas have not yet been finally resolved, which supports the socio-political analysis offered in this paragraph.

III | GROUNDED THEORY AND PHENOMENOLOGY

INTRODUCTION TO PART III

The final group of chapters deals with a very different orientation to the field of qualitative analysis. In these chapters, the analysis is not driven by prior theory, but instead seeks to adopt a "bottom-up" approach, in which the data themselves suggest theoretical insights, and these are developed through an iterative process which ultimately leads to theory which is firmly grounded in, and derived from, human experience.

Jonathan Smith

The research by Jonathan Smith presented in Chapter 9 is also data-driven, and not structured by prior theory, at least in terms of its content (though he provides a strong theoretical grounding for the methodology adopted in the study). His exploration of self-reconstruction during and after pregnancy illuminates many themes—about the process of identity construction, and also about the value of qualitative techniques for producing in-depth and detailed analyses of significant life-experiences.

The study operates within a phenomenological context—exploring human experience from the inside, as it were. By allowing the individuals participating in the study full opportunity to describe and explore their feelings at various points during the course of the pregnancy and afterwards, Smith is able to gain insight into nuances of personal experiences which would be unreachable using traditional quantitative techniques. The strength of the phenomenological approach becomes apparent in the comparisons of current and retrospective accounts of experiences during the pregnancy: the way that an individual describes her feelings at nine months, for example, is very different from the way that she describes her feelings of that time, five months after the birth.

The differences, moreover, take a specific form, and allow Smith to follow an interactive process in the development of theory, as each case enriches and enlightens earlier hypotheses. By doing so, he produces an account of the way that identity becomes constructed and re-constructed through the course of a significant life-transition. This approach to understanding pregnancy is entirely at variance with most traditional research into the experience, which has tended to focus on the medical approach and thus clinical/abnormal issues. In Smith's research, pregnancy is seen as a major life-experience, but not in any sense an abnormal one; and it is the personal meaning and nature of that experience which is the focus of interest and of theory-building.

One of the strengths of qualitative research is the way that it permits researchers to engage in idiographic analysis in a systematic and meaningful way. This chapter gives a particularly good illustration of this strength. Smith is not attempting to produce a nomothetic account, but rather to explore developments in personal identity for four specific individuals. The use of an iterative process of theory-development strengthens these insights, and so permits a certain measure of generalisation, but this is not the goal of the research. Nomothetic research is notorious for permitting only grossly general outcomes, and it is questionable how usefully these can be applied to the particular experiences of individual human beings. The idiographic approach allows the richness of experience to be explored. In the case of research into real-life experience, such as the experience of pregnancy, it is arguable that only an idiographic approach has the subtlety to give us the insights needed for an understanding of that experience.

Smith uses a combination of methods of data collection in the analysis. One of these is the use of diary material: studying the records which the women kept of how they were feeling and their day-to-day experiences. A second was the data generated by in-depth, open-ended interviews, which were structured so as to allow the women to talk as freely as possible, with minimal prompting from the researcher. This particularly rich form of data is the source of some interesting contrasts between current and retrospective accounts. In addition, the women were asked to complete repertory grid assessments, which enabled the researcher to explore some of the values and personal anxieties associated with the changes through which they were passing, or had passed. The use of these different techniques allows a form of triangulation: issues raised in the interviews can be explored from a different angle by examining the alternative sources of data; and in this way, the researcher can develop a richer and more multi-dimensional picture that might be possible from just one type of data.

The Drugs and Family Research Group

The Drugs and Family Research Group (Chapter 10) adopt yet another approach to qualitative analysis: an approach which draws on the strength of having an active research group, as opposed to a single individual conducting research. The technique described in this chapter involves the use of vignettes to understand the experiences of families of drug users. It is perceived as complementary to the use of quantitative measurement, rather than in opposition to it: the researchers use the vignettes to add enrichment and insight to their understanding of the issues.

Traditionally, research in the area of families of drug users has been concerned with the apportioning of responsibility, or blame, for the problem of drug abuse; but this is not the approach adopted by the DFRG. Instead, they emphasise the need for a fuller understanding of the experience of those who are close to, and share their lives with, drug users. Their research methods seek to identify significant themes and issues which arise from that experience. This goal, of course, facilitates a deeper understanding of the individuals concerned, but it is also hoped that such an approach may highlight commonalities between the experiences of different families, and so enable the researchers to develop a deeper general understanding as well as an understanding of particular individuals.

The use of vignettes as a form of qualitative analysis is distinctive. The vignette is the view of one person with regard to the key issues in a particular case, summarised in a relatively short paragraph. These views are developed from a study of interviews conducted with the people involved, but the constructor of the vignette may or may not have been directly involved in the interviewing. If they are, of course, their vignette will be informed by their interview experience as well as the interview material itself, but those who are not directly involved in the interviewing, and who therefore must deal only with the interview material, can also provide unexpected insights. For this reason, the researchers have generally opted to produce more than one vignette of the same case for their analysis.

The comparison of vignettes constructed by different individuals raises a number of research issues. In particular, it highlights the levels of description used by the researchers concerned, and the way in which these show systematic differences between researchers. The four levels of description which emerged from the research project are named, in order of abstraction, descriptive, deductive, thematic, and speculative. The descriptive style is the most basic, consisting essentially of factual material without any particular inference or abstraction. The deductive style involves drawing conclusions or inferences from the material, such as inferring underlying or recurrent patterns of interaction. The thematic style involves the researcher standing back from the material even more, in order to identify consistent themes such as complexity of relationships, or recurrent concerns with anger of love. The speculative style involves high-level abstractions, such as the development of hypotheses about unconscious motives and needs.

These levels of description allow the researchers to interpret and, where appropriate, to integrate the different viewpoints obtained from different vignettists. Commonalities which emerge from the comparisons often indicate issues of particular significance to the individuals concerned, and these can provide particularly valuable insights. However, a lack of commonality between different vignettes of the same interview material is also not uncommon, particularly in instances where three or more vignettists are involved. The researchers liken such discrepancies to a photograph of an object taken from different angles: there may be little in common between the various images, yet taken together, they help to provide a three-dimensional picture of the whole.

It is apparent from this chapter that the use of vignettes in this way has a considerable potential for the research process, especially in real-world research dealing with complex issues. In particular, vignettes provide a rich source of ideas for deepening a researchers' understanding of the issues, as well as providing an aide-memoir for other forms of analysis, and an indication of appropriate orientations for such research. They can be used to highlight themes and features in particular cases, and across cases in general; and these themes in turn may be used to structure further analysis. But vignettes are not just complementary: they are also, as is apparent from the chapter, a useful qualitative research tool in their own right.

Nigel Lemon & Helen Taylor

In the study of nursing care in an accident and emergency unit described in Chapter 11, Nigel Lemon and Helen Taylor utilise a phenomenological approach. Phenomenology has a long theoretical history, challenging as it does the positivistic and objectivistic orientation of much conventional scientific research. Its emphasis is contained in the idea that meaning occurs through subjective experiences (phenomena), rather than through the accumulation of supposedly objective "facts"; and that therefore in order to understand human experience, we need to explore the nature of that experience as closely as possible.

Phenomenological research involves four basic steps, and what follows is a very simplistic attempt to describe them (a fuller account is given in the chapter itself). It begins with the step known as bracketing, which involves a continuous attempt to suspend prior knowledge about the phenomenon, such that the researcher can approach it with as open a mind as possible. This is not done through denial, but through an attempt to bring that prior knowledge to the surface, in order that it may be recognised and separated out. The second step is about analysing, and is concerned with making the choices about which experiences should be the focus of the study, and the methods by which they should be gathered and recorded. The third stage, intuiting, involves exploring the data without preconception. The researcher needs to feel what it would be like to live in the informant's world, in order to be open to insights or themes which may be contained within the data. The fourth step involves describing the insights obtained from the study, and the experiences from which they are derived.

The phenomenological orientation has rarely been applied in this type of research. Studies of Accident and Emergency units have tended to focus on quantifiable features of the situation, rather than on the experience of nursing care from the point of view of those experiencing it. Lemon and Taylor show that this can be a productive approach, bringing up ways of understanding the situation which can do much to clarify essential yet previously overlooked features of nursing care. Their study involved the systematic analysis of interview transcripts, from interviews which had been conducted in such a way as to provide as rich a phenomenological account as possible. Perhaps inevitably, this meant that only certain patients were available for study. Since it was vital that those participating in the study should be able to articulate their experience, those with clinical problems which might impede either memory or articulation could not be included. This, however, is simply an aspect of the phenomenological approach, which is concerned with the uniqueness of experience, and makes no claim to representativeness.

Lemon and Taylor provide a lucid and informative description of the various stages of qualitative analysis involved in the project, and show how this methodology, systematically applied, provides a rich source of insights into the nature and processes of caring. In particular, it leads them into a distinction between "caring for", and "caring about", which permits a much clearer differentiation between the behaviours and practices associated with caring, and the human meaning underlying the experience. In a context in which simplistic behavioural definitions of the nature of nursing practice are becoming increasingly prominent, while recognised as inadequate, such clarifications help to provide us with both insight and vocabulary which may in time help in the foundation of an enriched understanding of the nature of nursing practice.

Nick Pidgeon & Karen Henwood

In Chapter 12, the final chapter, Nick Pidgeon and Karen Henwood bring together the significant principles of grounded theory, and produce a thorough and invaluable discussion of the assumptions and implications of the method. Their chapter is structured into six parts, beginning with a brief but clear discussion of the three theories of knowledge which form the epistemological background for the emergence of grounded theory. This is followed by a discussion of the role of qualitative research in providing an alternative paradigm from the received, positivistic approach to scientific knowledge The discussion examines the need for a more "human" psychology, the need for research which is able to address the quantity–quality debate in meaningful terms, and the need for research which can generate new ideas and new theoretical orientations.

Grounded theory as a technical research term was introduced in the sociological field by Glaser and Strauss (1967). In this chapter, Pidgeon and Henwood discuss the original proposition and some of the changes in meaning of the term which have developed since 1967. One of these, for example, concerns the relationship between research experience and subsequent theory, which was referred to by Glaser and Strauss as being "discovered" during the course of research and analysis. Pidgeon and

Henwood prefer to discuss this relationship in terms of what they describe as the "flip flop" between ideas and research experience, leading to a view of grounded theory as generated, rather than discovered.

From there, the chapter proceeds to a discussion of the various steps involved in using a grounded theory approach to qualitative analysis, which the authors illustrate with examples drawn from their own research. The first step involves a systematic inspection of the data with a view to the construction of an array of concepts and categories which can meaningfully be used to describe it. However, this is unlike traditional content analysis, since the categories do not represent a pre-defined set of mutually exclusive categories, but are generated from the data themselves.

Pidgeon and Henwood draw on two of their own studies to illustrate the steps involved in conducting grounded theory with qualitative data. The studies themselves are very different: one was concerned with engineering decision-making, and the other with the relationships between mothers and their adult daughters. But these differences in the studies in themselves illustrate how the method can be applied to a range of areas; and the examples give practical illustrations of how the various analytical steps are manifest in practice.

The fifth part of the chapter is a discussion of some of the possible goals of grounded theory work. While the approach is eminently suitable for the development of large-scale theoretical structures, such a goal is extremely labour-intensive, and requires a major research commitment, not to speak of an ability to avoid simply becoming snowed under by masses of detail. Most people undertaking this type of research will have more limited goals. In this section, the authors discuss some of the issues around using this method in the development of a useful taxonomy; in the development of a more localised but nonetheless creative approach to theory-development; and in the development of a "fully-fledged" grounded theory.

Finally, Pidgeon and Henwood conclude their chapter with a discussion of criteria for assessing research. Since this type of analysis does not lend itself readily to the criteria used for evaluating positivist quantitative research, it is necessary to articulate clearly just what the aims of the research are, and in particular what it purports to achieve, and what it does not. The authors provide a number of helpful and appropriate criteria in this section, which highlight the distinctive characteristics of this form of research and allow forms of assessment which do not, as so many of the received criteria do, implicitly devalue the aims and goals of the research.

9

Developing theory from case studies: Self-reconstruction and the transition to motherhood

Jonathan A. Smith
Department of Psychology, University of Sheffield

The main purpose of this chapter is to introduce an approach to developing theory from qualitative data by providing an illustration of applying this methodology to a specific psychological research area—self-reconstruction: how individuals' perception and accounts of themselves change through time. The data illustrating the methodological approach is drawn from a larger project on accounts of identity during the transition to motherhood. In order to contextualise the application of the more specific theoretical approach being illustrated, it will first be necessary to give an overview of the complete project.

IDENTITY CHANGE DURING THE TRANSITION TO MOTHERHOOD

The central question of this research project was: how do women's accounts of their sense of self or identity change during their first pregnancy and the transition to motherhood? In attempting to address this question, the project adopted certain theoretical and methodological positions. It was felt that it would be useful to attempt to produce a detailed record of a small number of women's experiences, rather than for examples conduct a postal survey of a large number of women. The study was to be longitudinal, collecting data at a number of time points and then seeing how each woman's data changed through time. To help provide the detail, the study would be multi-method, using different sorts of data, to help build a richer picture of the woman's experience. Finally it was decided that qualitative methodology would be appropriate, given the specific aims of the project: that is, the project was concerned with how individual women were thinking and feeling about changes happening to them. The project wanted to capture that experience from the individual woman's own viewpoint, not to measure the frequency of a particular event or response, and therefore a qualitative approach was deemed valid. At the same time, given the wish to employ a multi-method design, some quantitative measures were also used.

The project as outlined can be seen within certain theoretical traditions. It adopts a phenomenological, idiographic and woman-centred approach. *Phenomenological* psychology is concerned with attempting to record the individual's subjective account of reality as opposed to an objective 'reality' itself. (See Chapter 11 for more on this.) The *idiographic* approach attempts to build its claims on findings from individual case studies and only cautiously moves to generalisations for a wider group. The arguments for idiography are quite technical but in simple terms are reacting against the nomothetic approach of most psychology. Jean Pierre De Waele (1986) has argued that most psychological research is based on averaging data obtained from a large sample and that the resulting statistics can only apply to an average person, not to any particular individual. Indeed it may be argued that the notion of Mr and Ms average are themselves problematic, in which case nomothetic results do not hold for anybody at all! The term *woman-centred* (Nicolson 1986) refers to research which centres its analysis on the personal accounts of women who are taking part in the study.

Where does this project stand in relation to existing research on pregnancy and the transition to motherhood? One criticism that has been made of much of the work on the transition to motherhood is that it has been too influenced by the medical or psychiatric model. While pregnancy is a normal life event that most women go through without major long-term physical or emotional difficulties, these types of studies tend to concentrate on, for example, problems encountered during pregnancy, complications during labour, "maladaptation" to mothering. Other psychological studies which do see the transition as a normal—rather than abnormal—event often employ the nomethetic design discussed above. What is lost in this process is the opportunity to find out how any particular woman is responding to the experience of becoming a mother. Some researchers have begun to attempt to fill this gap by conducting intensive interviews with women and these studies can be considered closest to the project described here. Thus Anne Oakley (1979) and Paula Nicolson (1990) both include verbatim extracts from women's responses to inform and support their arguments about postnatal depression.

Conducting the Main Study

The main project is based on data from four women going through the transition to motherhood. The women were contacted through a number of sources such as General Practitioner referrals and ante-natal clinics. At a first meeting the women were told that this was a study about the relationship between pregnancy and identity, and informed of what would be required before they agreed to take part. Each woman was visited four times: at about three, six, and nine months pregnant, and five months after the birth of her first child.

Each of the women met the following criteria: this was her first pregnancy; it was planned; she was in a stable relationship. These minimal criteria were chosen to allow some comparability across cases. Beyond the fulfilment of these however, these women were not selected as being particularly representative of a population. An idiographic study treats each individual as standing for, or representing, herself or himself.

Main Types of Data Collected from Each Woman

Interviews and Diaries.   The woman was interviewed at each visit and kept a diary between visits. The interview was intended as an exploration of how going through the transition was affecting the woman's sense of personal and social identity. Although a pre-set schedule was used in order to facilitate comparison across time, the questions were deliberately open, intended mainly as cues for the women to talk, and the interview proceeded with minimum constraint or comment by the investigator. Each interview lasted between 60 and 90 minutes. The interviews were taped with the woman's permission and the tapes transcribed verbatim.

Instructions for the diary were left very open, the woman being asked to record things she thought and felt during the pregnancy, related to the topics discussed in the first interview. A blank notebook was issued as diary 1 at the first visit. At each subsequent visit the current diary was collected and a new blank one issued.

The tapes were listened to, and the texts read, a number of times, by which point the investigator was very familiar with the material. The transcripts and diaries were examined for identity related themes, some resulting directly from the interview schedule, some clearly emerging from the woman's own accounts. The author would describe this as interpretative phenomenological analysis, an attempt to unravel the meanings contained in the woman's accounts through a process of interpretative engagement with the texts and transcripts.

Repertory Grids.   The repertory grid was devised by George Kelly (1963) as a method for exploring the way an individual perceives or constructs her/his personal and social world. This study employed a standard grid technique with elements provided by the researcher and constructs elicited from the participant. The elements were selected from among those considered as representing important characters for the participant—either aspects of herself or important others:

1. Me on my own.
2. Me at a meal with friends.
3. Myself at twelve.
4. My ideal self.
5. Me as I expect to be in 1 year.
6. My mother.
7. My father.
8. My partner.
9. Somebody I dislike.

In order to elicit constructs the participant was shown three cards at a time and asked to say how two of them are similar to each other and different from the third. Eight sets of comparison produced eight constructs. The woman then rated each construct as it applied to each element (scale 0–10), producing a rating matrix for each grid. This exercise was repeated at each subsequent visit. The woman was asked to rate each of the elements against each of the previously elicited constructs for how she felt now.

A standard computer package calculated the correlation between all construct pairs and various graph plots were made of the significant inter-construct correlations. Similar analysis was carried out on element relations. With this sort of analysis the grid produces quantitative data but it is data from an idiographic and phenomenological perspective.

Retrospective Accounts and Grids.   Five months after the birth of the child, the woman was asked to write a retrospective account of the pregnancy. She was asked to think back to herself at the three time-points she had been visited by the investigator and write a short account of how she thought she was at that time: for example how she felt about the pregnancy, and how it was affecting her sense of identity. She was also asked to complete two more repertory grids, for how she thought she had responded at three and nine months pregnant. The point of this exercise was to find out what the woman thought her pregnancy had been like once she had had her child and to compare these retrospective accounts of the pregnancy with what she had felt during the pregnancy itself. This will be discussed much more fully later in the chapter.

Sequence of Analysis.   The first stage involved constructing a draft case study for each woman, drawing on all the differing data sources. The case study was intended to capture in detail the process of perceived identity change during each woman's transition to motherhood, including an assessment of how the woman's retrospective account compared with what she said during pregnancy. The investigator returned to each woman with the preliminary data analysis in the form of the themes raised in the interviews and diaries with examples from the transcripts and results from the repertory grid analysis. The woman was asked for her reaction to this material; this conversation was also taped and transcribed and incorporated into the final case study. Thus this first stage of the project entails drawing on a great deal of material to write up a detailed case study of each woman's changing sense of identity during the transition to motherhood.

TOWARDS A THEORY OF SELF-RECONSTRUCTION

In the remainder of the chapter I hope to illustrate how I used the case studies already obtained, in order to begin some theory construction. Thus the first aim of the overall project was to produce detailed case studies of individual women's experience of becoming mothers. The second stage then uses those case studies to begin cautiously looking for patterns across cases. I was concerned with a number of theoretical questions but here I will discuss how I explored the notion of self-reconstruction. I was interested in looking at how people reflected back on key events or changes in their lives. Do retrospective reports of a past event or phase differ substantially from accounts the person gave at the time the events were happening? More specifically do women's perceptions of their pregnancy change once they have the baby with them? In subsequent sections I will illustrate the way I went about attempting to answer these questions.

Self-reconstruction: Theoretical Background

The basic premise on which this work is based is that people are active agents who monitor, update and amend their biographies in order to present a certain view of themselves, both to themselves and to other people. Thus, for example, it might be argued that a promising student who had always been predicted to do well at university but who does badly in the final exams may rewrite his/her personal history by downplaying all the excellent school reports and exaggerating the slight problems teachers had suggested. In this way the student can claim that he/she never was in line to do well at university anyway.

An important theorist for this view of how people organise their lives is George Herbert Mead (1934), who suggested that a key aspect of what it is to be human is the ability to reflect on what one is like, and in turn change the view of oneself that one carries around. A number of writers following Mead have gone on to discuss the more specific ways this may affect psychological processes. This dynamic view of what a person is is consistent with a re-constructive model of memory. That is, what we remember is affected by a whole series of factors, including things that have happened subsequently and what is prompting our attempts to remember something new. As Wyatt (1964, p. 315) suggests:

> All I wish to propose is that for all practical purposes the past exists only when we re-create it by training our thinking on it, or that the past as individual and collective history cannot be recovered but has to be reconstructed.

How have psychologists attempted to study this? Not surprisingly most psychological research on these re-constructive processes, in the last 25 years or so, has been in the form of quantitative experiments. For example Conway and Ross (1984) carried out an experiment bearing on the example of the student I mentioned above, by looking at how a study skills programme affected students' actual and perceived performances. While the programme did not lead to an improvement in students' grades compared with controls, this wasn't how students perceived it. The students in the study skills programme overestimated their improvement at test time and six months later, and underestimated their original performance. Michael Ross (1989) claims people carry around implicit theories of the self, for example that individuals are supposed to change for the better and that data is then selected to confirm the chosen theory. Therefore "recall is inaccurate if a theory dictates greater or lesser change than has actually occurred" (Conway and Ross, p. 745). In this instance the students invoked a model of self-development and progress and therefore, because they hadn't actually improved, made themselves look as though they had by exaggerating their previous inability. For an exception to this general quantitative trend, see Neisser's (1981) qualitative case study, looking at changes which occurred over time in John Dean's account of the Watergate affair.

Some work also looks at longer term changes. Lowenthal, Thurner, Chiriboga, and associates (1976) asked people facing important life transitions to reflect on the course of their lives. The transitions were: leaving high school, marriage, onset of middle age, retirement. People in all age groups tended to see the best time of their lives as being within five years of the present, the worst time as distant—in their adolescence for the older groups, in future old age for the youngsters. All groups tended to emphasise the positive attributes of the current period, so that the young describe life now as exciting, the older group life now as easier. Lowenthal et al. interpret their findings motivationally, suggesting people gain self-esteem by assuming that their current lives are at their best and adjusting their autobiographical record to support that. However, Lowenthal et al.'s study is cross-sectional and is not therefore able to distinguish between individual development and group cohort effects. Also there is no account of what the old people thought when they were younger, with which to compare their retrospective stories.

In this study I wanted to address similar questions by drawing on the detailed case studies of pregnancy I had obtained. In this way it may be possible to gain a clearer understanding of the complex processes operating. Are there instances of women retrospectively changing their view of the pregnancy? What would the individual instances of those transformations look like?

Methodological Concerns

While an important function of conducting detailed psychological case studies is to capture the richness of the individual person or group being investigated, researchers will often wish to move beyond the individual to make claims for a group of cases. As Rom Harré (1979, p. 137) points out, working with case studies does not preclude the search for more general truths:

> *I would want to argue for a social science ... which bases itself upon an essentially intensive design, and which works from an idiographic basis. Nevertheless such a science is aimed always at a cautious climb up the ladder of generality, seeking for universal structures but reaching them only by a painful, step by step approach.*

How does one proceed? Firstly it is argued that theoretical claims from case studies should be grounded in the cases themselves. Thus it should be possible to see how a particular theoretical argument has been derived from and/or modified in the light of a close examination of the cases themselves. Rather than using the cases to test a pre-existing fully formed theory, with this approach one is attempting to develop a theory on the basis of the material in the case studies. I employed this type of *grounded theory* approach throughout my project on the transition to motherhood, in that while I had some sense of what I might find, I deliberately chose methods which would be open to discovering something new that I had not predicted or were flexible enough to allow me to modify my preexisting hunches. (See Chapter 12 for a more complete discussion of grounded theory.)

In developing theory from the case studies, I was influenced by *analytic induction* and the related approach of *negative case analysis* (outlined by Kidder, 1981). In the version of negative case analysis used, one starts with a hunch or preliminary hypothesis and then examines the first case study in terms of the hypothesis. The question one asks is: how can the hypothesis be modified in order to take into account what is in the first case? The hypothesis is then changed so that it can fit this case, usually thereby becoming much more specific in the process. Then one moves to the second case study and goes through the same procedure, changing the hypothesis again so it can be said to apply to case two as well as case one. This procedure can be carried on indefinitely. With each case the theory becomes much stronger. The resulting hypothesis or theory can then be said to be true for all the cases that have been included in this iterative process, so that one can make very strong claims for that group, stronger indeed than the actuarial or probabilistic predictions of most experimental work. As Colin Robson (1993) points out: when presented this way, negative case analysis is extremely stringent. In reality one is more likely to make claims that hold for a group with a few marked exceptions. For the purposes of clarity however, I am going to give an example of where negative case analysis did result in a theoretical claim for all cases, although the number of cases in the data set is small.

Using the Case Studies to Develop a Theory of Self-reconstruction

First, a preliminary general hypothesis was proposed, based on the existing literature:

> *People reconstruct their accounts of the past. This manipulation facilitates stories of development or stability.*

The first of my case studies from the pregnancy project was then interrogated in the light of this hypothesis which was modified and made more specific in the process, in order to make a claim which was true for that woman. The investigator then turned to the second case study and tested the modified hypothesis which was again changed in order to accommodate the new data, as outlined in the previous section. This process was repeated for each of the four case studies. The aim of this process, then, is to produce a statement which can be said to be true of all the cases and which can therefore form the beginnings of a theory of the reconstructive self, with particular reference to the transition to motherhood.

The process of negative case analysis or analytic induction modified, clarified and expanded the initial hypothesis. It was indeed found that each of the women actively reconstructed her self-concept as she went through the transition to motherhood. The revised hypothesis:

> *New mothers give reconstructive accounts of their pregnancy. This reconstruction takes various forms and these can be said to produce a set of narratives of pregnancy:*
>
> *1. A positive gloss on their pregnancy, exaggerating the positive and downgrading the negative. Often this takes the form of idealising the late, usually most difficult, stage of pregnancy.*
>
> *2. A progressive narrative suggesting self-development/improvement through the transition—reversing suggestions of decline or divergence.*

3. In a general counterbalance to narratives of development, the reconstruction of order and continuity, downplaying change.

A woman employs a number of narrative constructions. In each case she tells at least one story of progress and change, and one of continuity and stability. Different stories allow the coexistence of different narratives. Sometimes "conflicting" narratives occur in the same story.

Note that this statement is presented as a hypothesis about "new mothers". Until all new mothers had been included it would remain a hypothesis. At the same time, it is also now a true statement for the four women in the study, so we see the beginnings of a theory.

For the purposes of this chapter the details of one of these forms of reconstruction will be provided. In the extracts below, used to illustrate the reconstructing, square brackets [] indicate where I have edited out some of what the woman said, in order to save space.

1. A positive gloss on their pregnancy, exaggerating the positive and downgrading the negative. Often this takes the form of idealising the late, usually most difficult, stage of pregnancy.

While Clare, the first woman in the study, expressed some apprehension and impatience when she was nine months pregnant, her retrospective account of the time presents a much more positive picture. Compare the following accounts:

Real-time 9 Months.   Impending labour exercises my mind somewhat, fairly cataclysmic.[] This emergence of a new life I mean it is very near and impending now whereas whenever it was, back in June, was a sort of floating. []You wonder physically what it's going to be like, actually giving birth.[] Will you be able to cope?[] And I suppose a little bit of fear about whether you will come through it intact.[]The ground is much more uncertain than it was three months ago. You reach out for it but you wonder and you can't wait for it.[] You also feel impatient with your sort of lumbering body.

Retrospective 9 Months.   There is a sense of anticipation—not animated excitement, just gentle waiting. There is very definitely a person, although the veils are still between us. I am a mother, or at least preparing very soon for this stage—there is a dreamlike quality about this last stage of the proceedings with the waiting, and the heavy, lumbering movement which has a grace of its own, despite the discomfort. I am a lady in waiting.

So a contemporaneous account of uncertainty and some anxiety seems retrospectively to be reconstructed as one of idyllic calm. And when Clare uses the same term to describe her body—"lumbering"—it is reinterpreted more positively.

Clare is also able to gloss the late pregnancy as positive by temporal transposition. Thus a phrase she had used in the real-time interview at nine months is placed retrospectively in the account of six months. At nine months pregnant, Clare seems to be concerned at how the new roles associated with being a mother may undermine her sense of identity:

Real-time 9 Months.   Sometimes you feel as though Me is being lost or submerged.

This is echoed in the retrospective account of the middle pregnancy:

Retrospective 6 Months.   I am also one, but that is a little submerged for the moment.

Thus one way of highlighting the positive aspect of the late pregnancy may be reattributing anxieties felt late in the pregnancy to an earlier time point.

Sue, the second woman in the study, described considerable anxiety at nine months pregnant. She expressed some uncertainty about being able to cope, and giving up work seemed to have the effect of jeopardising her sense of self. In Sue's repertory grid data this unease is reflected in a significant correlation between elements "self in one year" and "disliked person" ($r = 0.79$, $p < 0.05$), suggesting a pessimistic view that once she is a mother Sue will become more like someone she doesn't like. Retrospectively, looking back five months after the birth, Sue dramatically changes this relationship—there is a significant *negative* correlation between "self in one year" and "disliked person" ($r = -0.79$ $p < 0.05$), presenting a reconstructed optimistic view that as she becomes a mother she will be *less* like the person she dislikes.

The two examples illustrate therefore how what, in real-time, is often described as a difficult or equivocal point in the pregnancy can be retrospectively reconstructed more positively.

For Diane, six months pregnant seems a time of some difficulty. During the interview at this stage, Diane expresses considerable irritation with other people:

Real-time 6 Months.   People tend to annoy you.[ ]As soon as you've been to the doctor they'll say "Oh how did you get on?" "Oh well he's told me I've, um, I'm anaemic." "Oh well you can't be eating the right food then." And you[ ]feel really angry because you know you're doing your best but it almost makes you feel guilty.[] Some people are just so tactless it's unbelievable. [] For example there was one girl that when I went into work[] when one doctor had said "Oh you seem to have put on a lot of weight over the last four weeks[] what are you eating?"[] this girl said "there's a healthy pregnant woman for you" pointing at this other one, and I could have just kicked her, you know, I thought how tactless can you be?[] They always seem to forget I think what—what it must have been like 'cause they—you can't tell me that they didn't feel like that, you know, that they sailed through, you know, without feeling tired, without feeling sort of irritable.

Diane also seems displeased with how she is treated by the medical profession:

Real-time 6 Months.   When I went up the hospital, I found it you know a bit like being in a cattle market[]"Stand on the scales, do this do that"[]you think to yourself "Well, this is my first baby and they should take a bit more notice of me".

This is just a small sample of Diane's references to being irritated by people at six months pregnant which becomes one of the dominant themes of the interview. At the end of this sequence, the interviewer attempts to see how comprehensive this feeling is:

Q: You've given quite a negative picture of this reaction of other people. I mean is there another side to that?[] Are there other people who will tend to behave or react to you in a more positive way, as far as you are concerned?

A: Yeah I would say three quarters would be negative and a quarter would be what I would put in "Oh aren't they lovely people, they're so understanding".

This is followed by a short section illustrating this positive side which had therefore to be prompted by the interviewer.

Compare this overall picture with the presentation of six months pregnant in Diane's retrospective account:

Retrospective 6 Months.   This is where I really came into my element. At work I had everyone running around for me. If ever anyone asked me to do anything I would just point to my tummy and say tiny tot doesn't want to. All my mates called my baby tiny tot as well. It was lovely to feel my baby moving around inside of me. I couldn't really imagine what she was like but just felt that she was a part of me, the most important part. I wouldn't do anything that I thought would harm my baby inside of me. Most dinner times I would have a lie down, and the girls would try and listen to her heart beat and feel my tummy, hoping the baby would move. I must admit I loved every minute of all the attention. This is also the time I started drawing and making things for my baby, and so happy to be doing it too. Thinking back, this was the time I realised how sensitive I had become, people really got on my nerves. Things that normally wouldn't bother me at all drove me mad. In fact I became quite paranoid about some people. [1] I think in fact this was when I most liked being pregnant. I suppose because I couldn't exactly not be noticed, with my big bump.

There is clearly a shift in the overall presentation from the mainly negative story of the real-time interview to a predominantly positive retrospective account. Thus the irritation at other people which plays a large part in the real-time interview is still there when she looks back but warrants only a small mention in the retrospective account. The irritation also becomes depersonalised, fading in contrast to the particular detail of both the rest of the account and the real-time interview. Also, in the real-time interview, Diane says she finds it hurtful when people refer to how big she is. The visibility of her increase in size is transformed in the retrospective account to a positive attribute [1]. Diane's overall retrospective assessment at the end of her account is clearly different from the pervasive message of the real-time interview.

As with Clare and Sue therefore, we see a positive glossing of a time in pregnancy that at the time was described as quite difficult; for Clare that time point was just before the birth, for Diane it is in middle pregnancy. Space precludes detailing the equivalent transformation of the fourth woman.

CONCLUDING COMMENT

This chapter has been structured to illustrate the stages I went through in developing theory from case studies, from the constructing of the cases themselves to the subsequent phase of hypothesizing and theorising. Hopefully the previous section has indicated how the examination of a set of case studies can help develop and add substance to preliminary hypotheses one has formed. The particular value of detailed case studies is the richness of the support they can provide for the theoretical claims being made.

Here only one narrative reconstruction has been illustrated. All four women provide examples of a reconstructive positive gloss on some aspects of the pregnancy. But as pointed out earlier, each woman shows instances of each of the reconstructive strategies. This therefore points to a complex psychological process: a new mother being able to tell herself and others a number of different stories about the pregnancy. While this type of research usually employs a small number of cases, this is justified by the ability to capture this psychological complexity. And of course one can go on and add more case studies to the data set for theorising, as long as depth is not sacrificed for breadth in the process.

The main aim at this stage has been to document the narrative reconstructions rather than explain why they happen. However one can speculate about causation. In a general sense it may be argued that for these women the birth of their child and being a mother is a generally positive experience. This positive glow once the child is here may therefore colour their recollection of the pregnancy, diminishing the less pleasant aspects. And it might be suggested the new mothers have a vested interest in playing down difficulties they may have experienced because they do not want anything to interfere with establishing this new positive relationship with the child. So the changing perception of the past may both have a cognitive component but also be serving motivational ends. Not surprisingly the complete picture is an even more complex one. The range of reconstructive strategies the women employ suggests that these modifications may indeed be serving a number of different functions (Smith, 1994).

Further Reading

This chapter has discussed a number of theoretical and methodological approaches. If you wish to pursue these in more detail, the following readings are suggested. Chapter 11 in this book discusses phenomenology and Chapter 12 is concerned with grounded theory. Smith, Harré and Van Langenhove (1995) provide a recent discussion of idiography. Earlier introductions to this approach can be found in Harré (1979) and De Waele (1986). Bannister and Fransella (1986) is the standard and very accessible introduction to repertory grids. With regard to the topic of the transition to motherhood, see Smith (1992) for an introduction to the range of approaches employed.

If you wish to read more about the project on motherhood and identity discussed in this chapter, Smith (1991) provides more detail on the qualitative analysis employed and a fuller case study of one woman's transition to motherhood. More on the repertory grid analysis employed can be found in Smith (1990). Finally see Smith (1994) for full details of all the narrative reconstructions and more on the theoretical ideas around self-reconstruction. The examples in this chapter illustrating the reconstructive glossing were first published in that paper.

10 The use of vignettes in the analysis of interview data: Relatives of people with drug problems

Tony Miller, Richard Velleman, Kate Rigby, Jim Orford,
Anne Tod, Alex Copello, and Gerald Bennett
School of Social Sciences, University of Bath

Drug use, and problems arising from that use, are escalating within the UK and elsewhere (Home Office, 1990; Gossop and Grant, 1991). Most drug users exist within a social context which includes family members as parents, partners, or children; yet almost no research has been conducted which examines the impact on families of having a problem drug user as a member.

The fact that so little research has been carried out, however, has not prevented theorising about the family's involvement in the genesis and maintenance of the drug problem. Professionals' (and lay) theories have often held the families responsible for the drug-taking problems of their members (Paolino and McGrady, 1977; Cermak, 1986). One example of this is the blame for the development of drug problems in the young often being placed quite firmly upon the qualities of parenting and the characteristics of the families from which the young people come (e.g. Blechman, 1982). Another example is the current emphasis on "co-dependency" and on "women who love too much", implying yet again that the co-dependent woman is also suffering from a "personality disorder" which led her unconsciously to select a partner who would then develop an addictive problem (Cermak, 1986).

However, the research into the experience of relatives of problem drug users, out of which the use of vignettes as described within this chapter arose, was not based within this theoretical paradigm: it was not concerned with the attribution of responsibility. Instead, it constituted an investigation into the effects of, and methods of coping with, having a problem drug user in the family. We were interested in discovering the nature of the relatives' experience of living with a problem drug user, and in particular the nature of the relatives' coping, support received, and other social-psychological issues. The research was conducted by a group of psychologists (some who were both practitioners and researchers, others who were solely researchers), collectively known as The Drugs and the Family Research Group (DFRG). The research interviews were conducted from a number of centres within Wessex and South-West England.

Given the dearth of research in this field, our objective was simply to interview 50 close relatives of identified problem drug users, with the identification occurring through clinics and self-help groups. In doing so, we hoped to throw some light upon both the similarities and differences between the effects on the families of problem drug users and the effects on the families of problem drinkers, which have been rather more extensively examined in other research (summarised in Velleman, 1992). We also wished to examine any differences in effect on the family if the problem drug use was prescribed as opposed to illicit; and whether or not there were differential effects depending on whether the family member was a parent or a spouse. Some of these issues have been examined in other publications (Orford, Rigby, Miller, Tod, Bennett, & Velleman, 1992; Velleman, Bennett, Miller, Orford, Rigby, & Tod, 1993).

Methodological Background to the Research

The DFRG take the perspective that qualitative and quantitative analyses of complex material (such as detailed interview data) are complementary, not competing: we believe that a combination of methods of analysis leaves us in a stronger position to comment on the issues which we set out to research than we would be in if we confined ourselves to one analytic approach alone. It is with this perspective in mind that we set about analysing the interviews that were conducted in the research outlined above. The interviews were semi-structured; that is, they followed a prearranged set of headings and prompts, but otherwise structure was kept to a minimum. They are described in more detail in the next section.

In line with the pluralistic approach to analysis that we have already outlined, these written up interviews were analysed both qualitatively and quantitatively. Part of the qualitative process was the extraction of key themes which permeated many of the interviews. Analysis of these themes enabled us to develop our understanding of coping processes; these analyses have been published (Orford et al., 1992). The written up interviews were also coded using a structured coding frame which examined 33 codes divided into 10 sections, including such broad areas as: Actions, Attributions,

Feelings, Outcome, Treatment, Expectations/History and the Future. This enabled the results to be analysed quantitatively, and these have also been published elsewhere (Velleman et al., 1993).

The Use of Vignettes

At the same time as the interviews were being coded, however, the DFRG decided to experiment with a totally different way of looking at the information contained in the transcripts. We were interested in reducing the case material into small manageable summaries, highlighting the distinctive features of each case: we termed these "vignettes".

The use of vignettes similar to these (and case study material in general) is not new, of course. In fact there is considerable interest in the use of both case study and vignette material. A recent search of the available psychology database revealed over 3,500 papers in the period 1967–1993 with the words "case study" in the title, and clearly there would be even more papers related to this topic which the search did not reveal simply because the words "case study" did not appear in the title. Similarly, there were over 60 papers in the psychology database with the word "vignette" in the title.

The use of vignettes in the past, however, has been limited. The most common way that they have been used is in relation to *the behaviour of professionals*. For example, they have been used in the training of professionals, or in the evaluation of training; e.g. Stone & Klein (1989) described the use of vignettes as an aid in teaching group psychotherapy; and Sriram, Chandrashekar, Isaac, Murthy, Kumar, Moily, & Shanmughem (1990), using vignettes, examined mental health training for primary care medical officers.

They have also been used to discover how well clinicians would deal with or assess important situations. For example, using vignettes, Yager, Linn, Lweake, Gastaldo, & Palkowski (1986) examined how doctors of different specialisms recognised physical and psychological complaints, and why intervention decisions were made; Misener (1986) investigated the judgements which different nurse specialisms made of the potential seriousness of child abuse incidents; Stelmachers & Sherman (1990) examined how well experienced crisis workers assessed the risks of suicide; and both Routh & King (1972) and Schofield & Oakes (1975) examined the relationship between recommendations for treatment and the perceived social class of the client.

Vignettes have also been utilised *as a more general research tool*. For example, Westman & Etzion (1990) investigated gender differences in explanations for career success and personal failure; Hjortso, Butler, Clemmesen, Jepsen, Kastrup, Vilmar, & Bech (1989) examined inter-rater reliability for psychiatric diagnoses; Sundberg, Barbaree, & Marshall (1991) used vignettes to examine attitudes to rape; and Alexander and Becker (1978) described the use of vignettes in survey research.

Reports have also been made of the development and validation of vignettes for use as *an assessment tool* for either research or therapy programmes; e.g. Ribordy, Camras, Stefani, & Spaccarselli (1988) who described the development of vignettes enabling the assessment of emotional recognition to children; Thayer (1977) who examined which variables might be useful for inclusion in counsellor training vignettes; and Heverly, Fitt, & Newman (1984) who attempted to overcome methodological problems in constructing case vignettes by developing an empirically based process for producing vignettes.

More rarely, reports are published where vignettes have been utilised as an assessment tool with *clinical groups*; e.g. Farrow (1987) who used vignettes to differentiate adolescents who drove while intoxicated from other groups of adolescents.

One of the important differences between almost all of these reports cited above and our own use of vignettes lies in the fact that our vignettes were summaries of actual research interviews, whereas the majority of vignettes used for research purposes utilised composed vignettes—ones specially written to aid a particular training or investigatory project.

It is in the clinical literature that examples of the use of vignettes as ways of summarising real data occur and there have been a very small number of publications which use vignettes as a way of *summarising and revealing interesting points* concerning a *client population*. Most are based in the psychoanalytic tradition; e.g. Cath (1986) who provides vignettes of the experiences and particular concerns of grandparents in psychoanalysis; or Weiss (1972) who discusses how his clients reacted to his impending move away from the region where he had been practising. One non-psychoanalytic report was that by Lenzner & Aronson (1972) who used the vignette technique to outlined the psychological and psychiatric problems of recently admitted patients to a Coronary Care Unit.

There have been no reports to our knowledge of the use of vignettes in the way that we are going to describe in the remainder of this chapter: as a way of *summarising and revealing interesting points* concerning a *research* population. We in the DFRG decided to use vignettes of the interviews with family members as a way of summarising and revealing interesting points which we felt might get lost in more traditional quantitative of qualitative analyses. It should be stressed here, though, that the DFRG entered into this in a very exploratory way. Although the work cited above existed, we knew of no work which utilised vignettes in the way that we wished to; and as such we were attempting to define a new qualitative methodology.

The Study

The relatives who participated in the study were recruited from a variety of sources. Roughly half were recruited solely via identified problem drug users in treatment and hence were relatives who were not in contact with treatment agencies in their own right; the other half were obtained via services such as Families Anonymous or family support groups run within drug agencies with which they were themselves in contact.

Details of the participants are shown in Table 10.1. 28 partners (19 female, 9 male), 19 parents (11 mothers, 8 fathers), and 5 others (2 sisters, 2 brothers, and 1 daughter) were interviewed. In all, 33 women were interviewed and 19 men, making 52 respondents in all from 50 families due to 2 cases where both parents were seen together.

Of the fifty families, ten involved partners (5 male, 5 female) who were living with a user of prescribed minor tranquillisers, whereas all 40 other families involved relatives of users of a variety of illicit drugs, with opiates being the major drug in 14 cases, amphetamines in 19, and polydrug usage in 7). Parents had had, on average, 5.7 years of exposure to drug use by their sons and daughters, whose average age was 20.3 years; partners had had an average of 6.3 years of exposure to drug use by their partners, and had been with them for an average of 9.3 years.

TABLE 10.1
Participants in the Study

	Partners	Parents	Others [a]	Total
Females	19	11	3	33
Males	9	8	2	19
Total	28	19	5	52
Average years of exposure to problem drug use	6.3	5.7		
Average years drug user in relationship with relative	9.3	20.3		

(a) These comprised 2 sisters, 2 brothers, and 1 daughter.

MAJOR DRUG USED:

Prescribed minor tranquillizers	10
Opiates	14
Amphetamines	19
Poly-drug use	7
	50

Most of the relatives were interviewed singly and alone, using a semi-structured technique involving coverage of a detailed list of topics and sub-topics. These topics were developed from pilot work, and included the history and development of the problem, the effects on the family and how they had coped, whether or not they had been offered help, and the amount of social support they had received. The interviews lasted around two hours: detailed rough notes were taken during the interviews and very full notes were written in detail and were typed up into a written Interview Report as soon as possible after the interview. Each Interview Report was then reduced to a simple vignette by the interviewer and at least one other person, which aimed to distil the main points of the interview, as described above. In all, the DFRG have around 300 pages of typescript representing the interviews, as well as up to four different vignettes of each interview.

The Development of Vignettes

We developed guidelines for the writing of vignettes. They were to be limited to roughly two hundred words, which might include themes and patterns of behaviour from within the interview. If vignettists observed similarities between two interview reports (e.g. in themes or patterns of behaviour) the vignette could draw attention to these as well. We also gave ourselves the freedom when writing the vignettes to engage in creative speculation as to the dynamics of each case. However, as will be seen later, the style of each vignettist varied, some choosing to hold closely to the facts, others predominantly recording the themes which they had detected in the interview reports, and others tending to venture into the realms of conjecture.

At least two vignettes were normally made of each interview, one by an interviewer and one by another member of the group, in order to control differences between the perceptions of those interviewers who had personal contact with the relative and those who had none. It also seemed important in at least some cases to compare the vignettes of two or more people who had merely studied the transcript of an interview without seeing the interviewee. The result was that in some cases three or even four vignettes were made of each interview, giving a final total for the fifty cases of one hundred and seventeen vignettes compiled by the six then current members of the DFRG.

These vignettes together formed the data for our analysis. In other words, as part of our overall study we chose to compare and contrast the transcript summaries which we had all made. In this sense we were operating at one remove from the data provided by the relatives themselves. Clearly, this is a completely different method from the discourse analysts (see Harré, Billig, Beloff and Sherrard, Chapters 2 to 5, this volume) with our "bottom-up" approach, and belongs to the "grounded" rather than the "theory-led" school (see Hayes, Stratton and Finn, Chapters 6, 7 and 8, this volume).

How the Vignette Analysis was Carried Out

The aim of the vignette analysis was to examine the nature and possible use of "vignettes" as tools for summarising and analysing case material contained in transcripts of research (or clinical) interviews. In this research, the term "vignette" was used to describe the researcher's account of the relevant or core elements and recurrent themes of a relative's experience, as recorded in the report of the original interview, including such insights, conjecture and comments on the material as the researcher/vignettist might wish to include.

When roughly half the vignettes had been completed, two members of the group conducted independent preliminary analyses of the vignette material. One analysed twenty-six of her own vignettes, looking at the negative themes reported by relatives, the positive themes and the themes which could be interpreted as either negative or positive. The result was a list of eleven negative themes which had occurred in at least two vignettes, e.g. loneliness, financial suffering, wanting to move house; ten positive themes, e.g. learning tolerance, feeling closer to the drug taker, getting support from a selfhelp group; and thirteen themes which could be interpreted as either negative or positive, e.g. spoiling/cushioning the drug taker, having to be careful and "on guard", and switching off/detachment. The vignettes of this researcher kept almost entirely to the facts reported in the transcript and refrained from conjecture and interpretation. Consequently the themes which she reported were picked up when the transcripts were coded and subjected to quantitative analysis.

Another researcher analysed his thirty-two comparatively conjectural vignettes, extracting a number of the relative's positive and negative qualities as well as some negative feelings. He also observed various themes and features. Examples of the positive qualities of some relatives (as viewed by himself as a vignettist) included loyalty, heroism, being positive for the future, etc. Negative qualities included overprotectiveness, unassertiveness, holding a rose-tinted view of the drug taker, etc. He found that the most commonly occurring negative qualities reported in his vignettes were the relative's unassertiveness and over-indulgence (in ten of the thirty-two vignettes) and the relative's dependency on the drug taker (in six). The negative feelings which this research noted were the relatives feeling rejected and lonely, isolated and not helped, and overburdened with family responsibilities. He also listed fourteen recurring themes or similar phenomena. Examples included "No diminution in the relative's love for the drug taker" (noted in eight of the thirty-two vignettes) and "role changes", where the drug taker became the "child" and the relative the "parent", which he judged had happened in the experience of five wives or partners and one sister. This vignettist tended to formulate hypotheses about the underlying dynamics of a case, which involved his taking a mental step back from the known facts contained in the transcript and superimposing his own view of the situation. For example, in the case of one jealous partner he saw the drug as having attained the status of the "other woman". This interpretation could have been included in the quantitative analysis but only under the general heading of jealousy on the part of the relative.

These two ventures in analysis show the kind of material which can be gleaned from scrutinising vignettes. Some may be factual, firmly grounded in the accounts of the relatives themselves; others may be hypothetical, emanating more from the ideas of the vignettists.

Following these two preliminary attempts at examining the vignettes, the main analysis was performed. One of us (TM) analysed all 117 vignettes. His purpose was to pick out the essential elements of each vignette, classify them and compare them with each other, especially with other vignettes of the same interview. He scanned the vignettes for significant features and themes, including all thoughts, ideas, and observations noted by the vignettist. He also looked for agreement and common ground between vignettists working on the same report. Following that, he sorted the elements of each vignette into categories which he entitled "facts", "deductions", "observations", "themes", etc. and named the style or model employed by the vignettist in accordance with the predominant categories employed in compiling the vignette.

What the Vignette Analysis Revealed

Fact and Fancy

To make a vignette one has to assimilate a large amount of material, sift through it and pick out the essence of the case. This is an interesting mental exercise which depends upon the vignettist's experience and insight. The resulting vignette can only be the subjective view of one person as to what needs recording. Thus, when commenting on the reality of the relative's world, the vignettist will also be revealing glimpses of his own internal models and personal constructs. Styles vary from concrete to abstract, from factual to fanciful, and if one is seeking a better understanding of a case history or a life situation, both the factual and the fanciful have a role in generating hypotheses for further investigation. Where the vignettist takes a narrower view of his role and keeps to the facts, the resulting content analysis of his work will produce a more limited but safer set of hypotheses whereas the more adventurous vignettist, who indulges in riskier speculation, is likely to produce ideas of greater richness and originality for testing, although many of these will, no doubt, eventually prove invalid. The value of the factual approach lies in avoiding too many wild goose chases; the value of the creative or fanciful approach lies in the possibility of finding a golden egg in the process.

The following examples illustrate first the factual approach and secondly the fanciful. They are vignettes of the same transcript.

(In all examples, "R" is the relative, and "D" is the drug user.)

1. R is the partner of D, a weekend amphetamine user. There are three children, one of which was from a previous relationship of R's. Her coping strategies have included using dope herself and becoming obsessional about housework. She has some element of control by looking after the family finances. She wants him to stop using drugs and has tried ignoring him as well as pressuring him to stop, both to no avail. He has been violent towards her, very paranoid and has disappeared from the home, which has affected her sleeping. However, she feels there is excitement in the relationship and feels more affection for D. R thinks unemployment and fear of rejection in employment have contributed to his continued drug use but she remains optimistic about the future.

2. The main theme to emerge from this interview is one of control with its counterpart of dependency. The other themes which I noted, excitement and self blame, are subsidiary to the control theme. The relationship is like a battle ground, with the male amphetamine user (D) gaining control of the emotional heights with his female partner (R) counter-attacking by unilaterally assuming control of the family finances. R has tried to control D's drug use but this has failed. She keeps trying different strategies but can't find one that works and feels she cannot win. By keeping her guessing and never complacent, D trades on her insecurity. On the one hand R loves D more because she cannot take him for granted but on the other hand she is over-dependent on him and she can never relax. Her failure to do so and her self-blame enable her to see that she is the one that really needs the help. (It does make me think of the drug as "the other woman".)

Commonality

Such a vignette is the view of one person as to the key issue in a case, the vignettist is forced to select certain elements for inclusion and exclude others, however objective he or she may wish to be. Subjectivity is unavoidable. However, where two or more vignettists select the same key issues, one might reasonably expect those issues to be more important or relevant to the case than features which are noted by only one. To illustrate, in one case in the DFRG's study both vignettists mentioned the relative's depression and powerlessness as well as the effects on the children. However, one (who was also the interviewer) included the relative's present cheerfulness but also her feeling unsupported, while the other listed the bad effects on the drug taker and the changes in the relative's feelings towards him, as well as the relative's apathetic and zombie-like feelings. Whether the relative's depression and powerlessness, and the effects on the children, are really more important or relevant to the case than the individually mentioned issues, remains open to question.

Lack of Commonality

Where there were three or more vignettes of a case there was often no commonality (apart from demographic factors). Some might take the view that in such cases vignettes have no real use but this would seem to miss the point of the exercise. Lack of commonality merely reveals that each vignettist holds a different set of priorities, which will depend on his or her particular model of the world. The model which anyone holds is a product of different theoretical backgrounds, training, experience and personality factors. Bearing in mind that members of the DFRG include university lecturers, research psychologists with no clinical training and clinical psychologists working within the National Health Service, it may not be too surprising that there was often no common ground among the vignettists regarding the central aspects of the case. Moreover, the plethora of traumatic experiences of so many of these relatives made agreement on priorities still less likely. A more positive way to view the different versions of the same material is to liken them to snapshots of the same objects taken from different angles. By putting all the snapshots together it is possible to generate a three dimensional picture of the whole.

Analytical Style

It seemed clear from the analysis both that there were different styles or models which were used in creating a vignette, and that different vignettists used these various styles in different proportions. The major styles identified are shown in Table 10.2. As will be further explained below, there was also a relationship between frequency of occurrence of the different styles and their level of abstraction, and this also is outlined in Table 10.2.

This table shows that there were four main styles to emerge from the analysis—Descriptive, Deductive, Thematic and Speculative. The following brief description of these styles contains actual examples from the vignettes for the purpose of the illustration:

DESCRIPTIVE This is the most basic style, devoid of abstraction. Vignettists adopting this style stick to the facts, which are selected for inclusion by the vignettist following his or her internal set of priorities.
Example 1. *"My husband and I have tried to be supportive of D."*
Example 2. *"There is a family history of drug abuse."*
Descriptive statements occurred more frequently than any other type of

TABLE 10.2
Vignette Styles Ranked in Order of Frequency of
Occurrence and Level of Abstraction

Lowest	Most	Style
	A	
F	B	Speculative
R	S	
E	T	
Q	R	Thematic
U	A	
E	C	
N	T	Deductive
C	I	
Y	O	
	N	Descriptive
Highest	Least	

statement and were used by all vignettists, although this was also the preferred style of some.

DEDUCTIVE (i.e. deducing Y from the given X, or drawing a conclusion from some of the material in the interview).
This style lies at the first level of abstraction.
Example 1. *"The relative comes across as somewhat over controlling."*
Example 2. *"The relative seems to offer reassurance and support to the drug taker."*
These kinds of statements were frequently found in the vignettes.

THEMATIC (i.e. standing back from the material in order to detect underlying themes occurring either within the interview or across several interviews).
The thematic style lies at the second level of abstraction.
Example 1. "Love is a theme running through the interview and anger is mentioned several times."
Example 2. "Another major theme of this and many other interviews was the complexity of relationships with other people, some of whom are on the relative's side and some who are against".
Thematic statements were found somewhat less frequently than deductive statements and much less frequently than descriptive statements.

SPECULATIVE (i.e. speculations about the dynamics of the case).
This style includes the use of hypotheses and interpretations and lies at the highest level of abstraction, sometimes verging on fantasy.

Example 1. "*There is a sense that the relative endorsed the drug taker's behaviour to give herself some degree of value in the relationship*".

Example 2. "*The wife is likely to end up the emotional as well as the physical invalid*".

Example 3. (Interpretive) "*Perhaps one reason for the relative's over involvement is the similarity which the relative sees between the drug taker and the relative's dead father, a drinker.*"

The speculative style appears less frequently than the other styles. However, when it does appear it contains some of the more thought-provoking ideas that can be found in the vignettes.

The style or model adopted by the vignettists in carrying out their work was analysed and the results are set out below in Table 10.3. With each vignettist, some vignettes were written with one style predominating, whereas others were written utilising a variety of styles in combination.

It can be seen from Table 10.3 that vignettist A (a clinical psychology practitioner) adopted a predominantly Thematic style, although Speculation was included in about one in three vignettes. With vignettist B (a research assistant), on the other hand, there was an overriding tendency to keep to a description of the facts of the case.

The style/model employed by C (a university lecturer and clinical psychology practitioner) was primarily Thematic and secondarily Deductive; whereas vignettist D (also a research assistant like B) again tended to describe the facts and avoid speculation. With vignettist E (another university lecturer and clinical psychology practitioner) the Deductive style predominated, followed by the Thematic; and finally, with vignettist F (another clinical psychology practitioner), the Thematic approach was marginally preferred over the Descriptive.

This analysis implies that, within the research group, there was a tendency for the non-clinically qualified members to stay mainly with the facts and to produce descriptive vignettes, while the clinicians seemed more inclined to focus on themes and, in some cases, to speculate or use analogies in an apparent attempt to explain the dynamics of the case. It is unlikely that the somewhat different approaches can be attributed to different understandings of the purposes of the vignette process since all were present when the subject was fully discussed. A more likely explanation is that the research assistants were relatively inexperienced in conducting research and in thinking thematically and speculatively, whereas the clinicians and academics were more experienced. It is likely that this meant that the more experienced members of the group were both more confident at moving beyond the simple description of facts and events and had alternative (or more elaborate) theories available to them, which might explain these facts and events.

TABLE 10.3
Analysis of the Styles/Models of the Six Vignettists

Vignettist A: 32 Vignettes completed

Primary styles

  6 primarily Thematic
  5 primarily Deductive
  2 primarily Explanatory
13

Other styles used in combination

14 Thematic
10 Speculative
  6 Descriptive
  4 Explanatory via Analogy
  2 Deductive
  1 Observational
  1 Hypothetical
  1 Interpretative
39

Vignettist B: 26 Vignettes completed

Primary styles

17 primarily Descriptive
  3 primarily Deductive
  1 primarily Thematic
21

Other styles used in combination

  3 Descriptive
  2 Deductive
  2 Impressionistic
  1 Interpretative
  1 Thematic
  1 Speculative
10

Vignettist C: 24 Vignettes completed

Primary styles

  6 primarily Thematic
  4 primarily Deductive
  2 primarily Descriptive
  1 primarily Speculative
13

Other styles used in combination

  7 Thematic
  5 Deductive
  4 Speculative

  2 Descriptive
  1 Psychodynamic
  1 Explanatory
  1 Issue focused
  1 Observational
22

Vignettist D: 18 Vignettes completed

Primary styles

14 primarily Descriptive
  1 primarily Deductive
15

Other styles used in combination

  2 Descriptive
  1 Deductive
  1 Speculative
  1 Metaphorical
  1 Observational
6

Vignettist E: 12 Vignettes completed

Primary styles

  3 primarily Deductive
  2 primarily Thematic
  2 primarily Descriptive
  1 primarily Issue focused
8

Other styles used in combination

  4 Deductive
  2 Thematic
  1 Speculative
  1 Descriptive
8

Vignettist F: 5 Vignettes completed

Primary styles

  1 primarily Thematic
  1 primarily Descriptive
2

Other styles used in combination

  3 Thematic
  2 Descriptive
  1 Deductive
6

Because the Thematic and Speculative styles appeared to be the most interesting for developing new ideas, it was decided to examine these in more depth.

The Thematic Vignette Style: The Use of Themes in the Vignettes

Approximately 120 themes were identified in the 117 vignettes. (A discussion of the issues relating to the definition of a "theme" follows.) These themes were not evenly distributed either between vignettes or, as indicated in Table 10.3 above, between vignettes. Themes were either "within-interview", i.e. features of events recurring within the interview, or "across-interviews", i.e. features or events which, if not themes on account of their recurrence within one interview, became themes due to their common occurrence in other interviews. Some were both "within interview" and "across-interviews" themes.

Within-interview Themes

Not surprisingly, the majority of the themes highlighted one or other of the relative (R), the drug user (D), or the relationship between R and D, featuring aspects of their personalities, behaviour or feelings recurring within or across interviews. A minority of the themes focused on the behaviour of people other than R and D.

Themes relating to aspects of R's situation (including R's depiction of D) are shown in Table 10.4. Themes depicting negative issues relating to R are shown in parts (a) to (c). R's strengths also stood out as themes in some vignettes, and these are shown in (d). Other characteristics which were not necessarily classifiable as either positive or negative are shown in (e). A significant cluster of themes related to conflict and uncertainty: these are set out in (f). Finally, in (g) there is a short list of themes highlighting aspects of D's personality/behaviour.

In addition to the themes listed in Table 10.4, eleven others concerned the relationship between R and D. These themes highlighted serious communication difficulties, mutual interdependency, the theme of control and its counterpart of dependency, and sadomasochism, among others. A few miscellaneous themes included "the absentee father", "a strong negative view of the GP's part", "the way in which different family members take different positions", "time passing by with no real progress" and "the influence of other drug-using boyfriends and other drug users lurking in the background".

TABLE 10.4

(a) R as weak or fearful

— "A soft touch"
— Lack of firmness
— Fear of D's behaviour
— Fear of losing D
— Feelings of helplessness

— Needing to be needed
— Passivity
— Self-blaming
— Secretive

Other apparently negative aspects of R

— Indulgent mother
— Immature
— Jealous
— Confused
— Fascinated by seediness and villainy

— Overconcerned and overinvolved
— Regret
— Embarrassment
— Failure

(c) Negative aspects of R's situation

— Overburdened with family responsibilities
— Feeling of being forced into the role of the responsible person

(d) R's strengths

— being both kind but firm and controlling
— Stronger and more resolute (as a result of the experience of living with a drug taker)
— R's affection for D unaltered
— R as a survivor
— R's dogged determination in neither accepting D's drug use nor rejecting him
— "(R's) love is a theme running through this interview: earning love by looking after people, finding out what love really means, getting down to the nitty-gritty of loving and loving enough so that her partner would stay clean"
— Sticking by D despite everything

(e) Other aspects of R's behaviour

— Ambivalence towards D
— Preoccupation with D
— Rationalisation
— R's admiration for his wife, who "carried the whole cross"
— Denial, shock and attempts at reparation

— Excitement
— Control
— Anger

(f) Themes highlighting conflict and uncertainty

— R's increasing uncertainty about whether she had a future with D
— Uncertainty regarding the respective contribution to her (D's) behaviour of his (R's) addiction and his behaviour
— R's sometimes hard, sometimes soft approach
— Ambivalence and uncertainty
— The theme of right management (reiterating the conflict—sympathy vs. firmness)

(g) Themes highlighting D's personality/behaviour

— D the spoilt child
— D's secretiveness
— D's violence towards R
— D's keeping R guessing, and its consequences
— Again, the parents had been given a bad time by D
— D perceives R as weak and, as in [another case], takes advantage of it

Across-interviews Themes

Among the 120 themes identified, 35 were "across-interviews" themes. These themes tended to be introduced by the vignettist's showing signs of recognising the issue as one that had appeared in a previously examined interview. This recognition would often be signalled by the use of the word "again". For example, "Again the involved parent is too weak and unassertive, almost inviting further abuse." The word "again" occurred in 14 of the 35 examples. "Another", "usual" and "typical" were also common indices of recognition.

Some further illustrations are given below:

(Relating to coping behaviour): *"Again this tells a fairly typical story of parents who have been affected in various ways and have now had enough of the lies, deceit, etc. and have decided that their son should not come back to live with them after he comes out of prison"*
"There are the usual conflicts of trying to distance herself but worrying"
(Relating to aspects of R): *"Here again R has taken on both parental roles"*
(Relating to R and D's relationship): *"Again there is the special relationship between parent and child"*
(Relating to general issues): *"As in most cases, the longer the period of drug-taking the more the problem permeates the whole relationship and attracts attention upon itself"*
"Sibling jealousy towards the drug taker is another theme which is frequently seen in other interviews"
"Again there is the criticism of the doctor, in this case for prescribing repeat prescriptions"

The 35 "across-interviews" themes can be classified into 6 categories:

1. Aspects of R's personality, behaviour or situation (excluding coping);
2. R's coping behaviour (including conflicts about coping methods);
3. R's and D's relationship—positive and negative aspects;
4. R's relationship with others;
5. Aspects of D's behaviour;
6. General (including speculation about causation and other miscellaneous items).

The Speculative Vignette Style: The use of Speculation in the Vignettes

At the highest level of abstraction, where the vignettist allows his or her imagination (guided by experience) considerable licence, we find speculations about case dynamics as well as the use of analogy, metaphor and analytical interpretation.

Over 40 examples of speculative comments were found in the 117 vignettes. Almost half were speculations about what might be maintaining certain behaviour patterns; another quarter related to R's coping behaviour. Nearly all the remaining speculations concerned the cause of the drugs problem, the factors maintaining the relationship between R and D, and the future.

The following examples illustrate five categories of speculations:

Speculations about the factors maintaining certain behaviour patterns (all relating to R);
(re the mother of a male amphetamine/alcohol user)
"This is a classic case of the overindulgent, overprotective, unassertive mother who needs to be needed. It is almost as if she has transferred her love for her alcoholic first husband to her youngest son."
(re the female partner of a male opiate user)
"I feel she (R) is desperately trying to reach him (D) because she feels she can offer him help"
(re the female partner of a male opiate user)
"She seems to be on the knife edge and perhaps she finds this stimulating."
(re the wife of a tranquilliser user)
"R seems trapped in an unsuitable relationship with a weak man. Perhaps this is a convenient way of avoiding a mature relationship."
(re the husband of a prescribed tranquilliser user and heavy drinker)
"I am left with the feeling that R would prefer his wife to be dependent on him, and feels a little resentment at D's new found independence. This may stem from a feeling of redundancy and a sense that he has failed where the self-help group has succeeded with D."

Speculations about R's coping behaviours:
(re the female partner of a male opiate user)
"I wonder whether she (R) hasn't just got the combination of firmness and kindness that can actually help him?"
(re the husband of a prescribed tranquilliser user)
"R himself has been a heavy drinker over the last few years (to help him with D?)"

Speculations about the cause of the drugs problem:
(re the husband of a prescribed tranquilliser user)
"He (R) seems more or less resigned to jogging along in a rut for the rest of his days. Perhaps this is part of her problem."

Speculations about the factors maintaining the relationship between R and D:
(re the female partner of a male opiate user)
"One wonders if D will seem quite as important to R without drugs"

Speculations about the future:
(re the female partner of a male opiate user)
"It would not be surprising if she (R) took to drugs for the excitement and to feel more part of D's world."

The main finding of this analysis of speculative comments within the vignettes was that R was often thought by at least one vignettist to be implicated for some reason in D's drug taking behaviour; in essence colluding, satisfying a need or gaining some personal benefit from it. There are speculations about possible sadomasochism and the need for martyrdom, a need for excitement, or enjoyment of the stimulation of being with a drug user, R's need for D to be dependent on him/her, R's guilt of inadequacy leading to over-indulgence towards D, etc. This is not to say that R's "innocence" was questioned by all the vignettists or in the majority of cases. Where these speculations did occur they were clearly simply triggered by the case material and were not a necessary deduction from it. However, they do suggest lines of enquiry in the case of that relative or any other relative in a similar situation.

The use of speculation does raise an interesting point concerning the theoretical paradigm within which the research as a whole was conducted. As described at the beginning, our interest was in the experiences of relatives, and in the gaining of an understanding of how they coped, as opposed to examining issues of responsibility and etiology. Yet the more conjectural one becomes in a vignette, the more easy it is to start to impute responsibility for the situation as opposed to simply reporting it (see, for example, some of the comments in the second vignette in the "Fact and Fancy" section, especially "she is the one who really needs help" and "she is over-dependent").

The Use of Metaphors and Analogies

Finally, metaphors and analogies were also used in the vignettes to generate a better understanding of cases. At least 27 were detected, a third of which related to a role change between the main parties, e.g. "*D rescued R from the role of 'little mother' in her motherless (and affectionless?) family,*" and "*Here again he has taken on both parental roles—the breadwinner and the mother.*" It was common for the relative to be envisaged as taking on a parental role in relation to the drug user or, conversely, for the drug user to seem like an extra child in the family.

This, of course, is a phenomenon which is by no means restricted to families of drug users.

The tension between R and D and the struggle with drugs was referred to as a 'battle' on four occasions, with the most elaborate reference (already referred to above in the section on Fact and Fancy, when describing the nature of vignettes) running as follows:

"The relationship is like a battle ground, with the male amphetamine user (D) gaining control of the emotional heights while his female partner (R) counterattacked by unilaterally assuming control of the family finances."

In three other cases the drug itself was perceived to be playing a role, mainly that of "the other woman" in the relationship between R and D. For example, the following appeared in one vignette:

> *"It is as though there are not two but three main characters in the drama, R, D and the drugs;"*

Another vignette contained the following comment:

> *"Again, the drug seems to take on the role of 'the other woman'."*

Lastly, R was variously likened to Brunnhilde on the mountain top, with her emotions buried under a protective shield; a character in a drama; a martyr; a motor car in overdrive; a climber hanging on by his fingertips; a rescuer; a fighter; and a person going through a grieving process. This last analogy was illustrated as follows:

> *"I was struck by the similarity between the reactions of the parents I have interviewed and the grief reaction following a loss—denial, shock, searching, feeling depressed, self-reproach, self-pity but no loss of love—if anything, an increase—for the lost object/person."*

Conducting Vignette Analysis

Standardising the Process

Earlier we suggested that the lack of commonality among vignettists shows that each holds a different model of the world which leads to a different set of priorities. This may result in a richer in-depth view of the subject matter when seen from different angles. If this is so, would it be useful, even if it were possible, to attempt to increase the concordance between vignettists? The answer to this must surely depend upon the purpose to which the vignettes are to be put. If the intention is to use them to facilitate an understanding of case material, to suggest directions for future research, or to stimulate clinical debate on the different views held, then there may be no need to increase concordance. But if it is deemed important, say, to present a sophisticated summary of case material for clinical purposes, then it will be necessary to reduce disagreement regarding salient features and increase concordance. Unfortunately, the more constraints and guidelines that are applied to the process of composing a vignette the higher the danger of giving birth to a poor and lifeless end-product. A middle way needs to be found where there is greater consensus regarding the process of creating vignettes with the least possible loss of individuality and colour.

Suggestions for Improvement

1. In the present study, differences in the training and experience of the vignettists seemed to affect the content and the style of the vignettes. This should be borne in mind when deciding which members of a team should be allotted the task of composing vignettes. The level of concordance between vignettes may depend on team selection. It has become clear from our analysis that the more experienced members of the research group were more likely to use a wider range of analytical styles in the development of their vignettes, probably because they were more confident and had available to them a wider range of alternative theories which they could draw upon. On the other hand, the value of multiple viewpoints, including those from less experienced individuals, needs to be recognised. It will be important to ensure that the selection of vignettists allows for this range to be represented.

2. It is essential that any groups proposing to compose vignettes should set clear objectives. Is the purpose of the vignettes to summarise lengthy case material, to generate a better understand of the dynamics of the case, to stimulate ideas for further research, or what? If the objective is to summarise material, historical and family details will probably have to be included, but this will be less important when the main objective is to understand case dynamics and when those involved have access to or are familiar with the original material.

3. The group should also define their terms. This may not be as simple as it looks. At the outset the DFRG agreed to highlight "themes" in their vignettes but they did not define the meaning of a theme. The Concise Oxford Dictionary defines a theme in five ways but the only definition relevant to the vignettist is the musical one "a prominent or frequently occurring melody or group of notes in a composition". The essential characteristic of a theme for vignette purposes would seem to be the prominence or frequent occurrence of an event or behaviour, the latter being analogous to a "melody or a group of notes". Thus, the drug taker's often storming out from the family Christmas dinner, or frequently going to prison would be themes. So, too, would the jealousy of the drug taker's sibling and the relative's apparent overinvolvement with the drug taker, if these continually occurred. The main difference between the two sets of examples is that the former are recorded events or facts while the latter are inferences or deductions made either by the interviewee or the vignettist. It is the deductions made by the vignettist which are probably the most valuable in that they introduce new material made up of more than one piece of the old. Therefore, especially when seeking to gain a better understanding of the dynamics of a case, vignettists should be encouraged to look for ways of relating patterns of behaviour. For example, where the mother of a drug

taking son constantly goes out of her way to "help" her son by time and again lending him money which he fails to repay, cleaning up his room for him and pleading with the police on his behalf, one may reasonably infer that she is "over-involved". This understanding may lead to more appropriate clinical involvement in the mother/son relationship, or to a development of research ideas, or theoretical constructs.

4. Conclusions need to be explained by reference to the text, but in the briefest terms, and themes should be illustrated and, where possible, observations added, as in the following example of a theme of "preoccupation".

"One of the themes that I would pick out of this interview is what the mother says about the level of preoccupation with her daughter's problem, and in particular the way that she describes how they were thinking about their daughter's problems morning, noon and night, even when they were not seeing so much of her. Strangely, I wonder whether that means that concerned relatives are sometimes a bit happier when the problem is actually right with them where they can see it and keep an eye on it. It's almost the opposite of 'out of sight out of mind'.

5. At the outset it should be understood that the vignettists will attempt to include an answer to the question "What is really going on in this case?" Their overall impressions may well turn out to be the most valuable contribution that they can make. Even if they are incorrect, at least they open up a debate and suggest lines for further investigation. Sometimes the essence of a case or part of it might best be captured by the use of a simile or an analogy. This might include likening the relationship between the interviewer and the drug taker, or between any significant others, to a different type of familial relationship. In other words, has there been a role change such that, for example, the husband appears to be acting like a protective mother to his drug taking wife, or a role reversal where, for example, the mother is playing the daughter and the daughter the mother?

6. Finally, for both clinical and research purposes, it might be helpful for vignettes to end with a sentence looking at the way in which matters are likely to develop in the future, i.e. prognosis. Follow-up studies will confirm or deny the validity of such prognostications, which itself may be a useful learning experience.

The above suggestions are made to facilitate the standardisation and usefulness of vignette composition. To impose too many constraints would defeat the object of the exercise which, essentially, is to retain individuality and creativity while summarising the central features of a case. Those planning to use vignettes in their work may decide to include some of the above suggestions, exclude others and add different ones. This will depend on what end product is sought and to what purpose it will be put. All these issues need to be addressed at the outset. However, a trial run will be sure to highlight some differences of approach and understanding, and it will be for the group to decide whether these are helpful or need to be reduced.

In summary, prior to and during the exercise of composing vignettes, the following questions might be asked:

1. What objectives do you have in mind?
2. Have you clearly defined the terms which you are using?
3. What are the facts of the case and what are the problems?
4. What can be deduced or concluded from the given information? Briefly explain by reference to the text.
5. Are there any detectable underlying themes? If so, support them with examples of frequently occurring events or behaviour. Do similar themes show up in other case material?
6. What is your overall impression of the case? How do you arrive at this conclusion?
7. What analogies would best capture the essence of the case, or any part of it?
8. Do there appear to be any role changes or reversals of role among the main characters in the drama?
9 In a sentence or two, how might matters turn out in the future?

CONCLUSION

For clinical work and case discussions, vignettes are highly practical, being short, easily readable accounts of core elements of a case and containing ideas which may generate a greater understanding of the situation. We know of no work which has utilised vignettes for research purposes in the way discussed in this chapter. The DFRG found that the vignettes were both a useful aide memoir and a rich source of ideas for deepening their understanding of the processes which occur within families, with implications for further lines of research. However, it can take a surprisingly long time to compose a satisfactory vignette. There is, as mentioned above, room for improving the quality and comparability of the vignettes by having, from the outset, clearly defined terms and complete agreement as to the nature of the final product required. These are practical details which require initial attention.

Vignettes can be used to highlight themes and features both within and across cases with clear potential for understanding client and family processes and needs. Vignettes may also have a useful part to play in staff training, where trainees can be shown either a variety of cases in a short space of time or a single case history with several contrasting views of it.

It is also important to stress the advantage of conducting this vignette development and analysis within a research group setting. This type of research would be difficult for one researcher working in isolation to carry out, in that much of the interest has emerged from the process of comparing the different vignettes. It is also the case that having different vignettists with different views and models available to them has resulted in far richer and more varied data.

Finally, the process of creating vignettes is itself a learning exercise which requires the vignettist to assimilate a large amount of material and sift out the essential ingredients. This helps to sharpen our critical minds and generate a greater awareness of our internal models of the world. It shows us what we, as clinicians, researchers, or teachers, hold to be salient or significant, and the extent to which our views match those of our colleagues.

How to do Vignette Analysis

1. We used vignettes to analyse an interview study, but one could potentially use this method on a variety of other types of research data: books or papers, video tapes or films, case material, and so on. The same basic methods, however, need to be followed.

2. There are two major processes in conducting a vignette analysis: the production of the vignettes and their subsequent analysis.

3. There are certain decisions that need to be taken by the research team before the vignettes can be produced:

   a. All potential vignettists need to agree on what a vignette is. Clear guidelines need to be drawn up so that like can be compared with like. A maximum length is important.

   b. Decide who will make the vignettes on which cases. Ideally, a similar number of vignettes should be made by each vignettist. This helps to avoid bias in the final analysis and balance any practice effect. Where the interviewer is also the vignettist his/her view of the material is likely to have been affected by the interview experience.

4. To produce the vignettes the members of the team selected to be vignettists (in our case we all produced vignettes) need to examine the source material (the interviews in our case). As a first step teams may prefer to look at a wide spread of examples, although this is not necessary. Then each vignettist needs to take a single example and examine it in detail, and then write the vignette, using the previously arranged guidelines and maximum length. This process is then repeated for other examples of the source material.

5. Again, there are certain decisions that need to be taken by the research team before the vignettes can be analysed:

   a. In order to make inter-rater comparisons, two or more vignettists will be needed. The more vignettes, the longer it takes to complete the analysis. On the other hand, there is more interest in seeing how two or more of the vignettists differ or agree in their views on the salient aspects of a case.

b. Decide how many researchers are needed to analyse the vignettes, bearing in mind that it can take a surprisingly long time to complete the analysis. If two people share the same load, it could speed up the process but internal consistency should be higher with the same analyst making all the decisions.

6. To analyse the vignettes once they have been written, the analyser(s) will need to read through a number of vignettes, ensuring that a variety of vignettists and cases are examined. They need to note down what appear to be salient themes or categories, and then check these out against other examples. The purpose of this analysis is to pick out the essential elements of each vignette, classify them and compare them with each other, especially with vignettes of the same interview. Vignette analysts could examine thoughts, ideas, observations, agreement or disagreement between vignettists, and so on.

7. Once decisions have been taken as to what the themes and categories are, the contents of each vignette need to be marked, using different coloured highlighters or pens to represent the various categories (in our case, themes, deductions, interpretations, facts, etc.) To improve consistency, it may be helpful to write down a dictionary definition, or an operational one, of each of the categories used.

8. These categories can be further sub-categorised. For example the vignettist may detect a theme which occurs across interviews, or within one interview, or both. Themes can also be categorised according to content as, for example, a repeated reference to the personal qualities of the respondent. Again, speculations may be sub-categorised into speculations about causation, about what maintains certain behaviour patterns, about the future, etc.

9. These sub-categories form the basis upon which a decision can be made as to the predominant style or model used by the vignettist. Make a frequency count of the models' styles for each vignettist.

10. Tabulate all categories relevant to the original objectives, with commentary.

11. Return to your original research questions. Be explicit about how the vignette analysis has enabled you to have a clearer picture. Draw explicit conclusions, reinforced by evidence from the vignette analysis. Use the themes, categories, quotes from vignettes or from the original source material, to flesh out any conclusions you may have also reached from any quantitative analyses. Be explicit as to where the qualitative and quantitative analyses overlap and reinforce each other; and also be explicit about where they seem to point in opposite directions. If this happens, try to understand why this might be the case, and do not be seduced into believing that the quantitative results must be more correct than the qualitative!

NB: The process of categorising and sorting information contained in texts can be made easier by the use of appropriate computer software, such as *Text-Based Alpha* (Tesch, 1989) or one of those listed in the appendix in Miles and Huberman's source book on *Qualitative Data Analysis* (1994).

ACKNOWLEDGEMENTS

The authors would like to thank warmly the relatives who gave time to talk to us about matters that were very personal and usually very painful. We would also like to thank the other members of the now enlarged ADFRG (alcohol, drugs and the family research group), and the Editor, Nicky Hayes, for their useful comments on earlier drafts of this chapter.

11 Caring in casualty: The phenomenology of nursing care

Nigel Lemon & Helen Taylor
School of Human & Health Sciences, University of Huddersfield

In some research projects, the investigator is confronted with the need to understand the meaning of a concept which is apparently well understood by lay people but whose theoretical implications are less well understood from a social scientific perspective. Under these circumstances, the researcher needs to identify the lay meanings which are given to a concept and to draw out the implications of these for scientific understanding.

The focus of attention in the study described here is the concept of nursing care as it is understood by patients through their experience in the Accident and Emergency Department of a large city hospital.

Because this concept has so many different connotations, a phenomenological approach has been adopted. This approach is one which causes the researcher to deliberately suspend all of her previous presuppositions and to adopt a "naive" approach to the understanding of patients experience of care. It therefore has implications for the manner in which the whole research process is conducted, from the way in which the research questions are formulated to the final interpretation of the data which are obtained.

BACKGROUND TO THE RESEARCH

Since the introduction of the Griffiths proposals for General Management in the Health Service the issue of quality has occupied a central place in Health Service Thinking. The more recent Government White Paper "Working for Patients" which describes the working of the New NHS makes quality of care the focal point of the new system. As with many large organisations the most common way of approaching measurement of quality is to choose some easily measurable performance indicators (e.g. bed occupancy) and use this as an index against which the performance of the service can be judged. Under these conditions there is a natural tendency to grab at accessible objective information, whereby the "measurable" gains in significance and by implication "that which is not measured" becomes of lesser significance. The problem with this approach in thinking about the quality of care is that the unmeasurable includes things like accessibility, interpersonal skills of nurses, empathy and attentive personal service, which many people would regard as the hallmark of a caring service.

The study described here is an attempt to apply a qualitative approach to the understanding of the components of nursing care as they are experienced by patients in an Accident and Emergency Department of a large city hospital. Common observation of nursing care suggests that the "technical" and "basic" components of a nurses role (for example the carrying out of medical prescriptions and providing physical care) often take precedence over their "affective" caring function. The importance of this affective caring component is often emphasised by nurses, in their advocacy of "holistic" models of nursing care which is either expected or evaluated highly by the general public. Peterson (1988), for example has, shown that while researchers are often critical of nurses' interpersonal skills, patients generally report satisfaction with their nursing care and appear to regard physical care as the major priority.

Within the literature about nursing "caring" has been variously described as "a philosophy and science", an "ethic", a "moral imperative or ideal", an "interactive set of client expectations and nursing behaviours", an "affect", "expert nursing practice", a "human trait", an "interpersonal relationship" and even "a synonym for nursing itself". Overall there is no consensus about how caring is defined, what the components of care are, and what the process of caring consists of.

Where writers have tried to encapsulate the nature of "caring", the results have shown that the idea is an extremely complicated one and has both behavioural and philosophical angles. For instance in Leininger (p. 84, p. 46) an example of the definition of "caring" describes it as:

> Those human acts or processes that provide assistance to another individual or group based on an interest in or concern for that human being or to meet an expressed, obvious or anticipated need.

An important aspect of this very general definition is the recognition that it reflects a range of different cultural values and practice, according to which some activities may be considered as an aspect of caring in one setting which are not thought of in this way in another.

Other writers have been more explicit in defining what they mean by care. For example Watson (1985) distinguishes between expressive and instrumental aspects of care. By expressive care she means two things: those which are to do with establishing relationships, including trust, faith, hope, sensitivity, acceptance of feelings, compassion, empathy, touch, warmth, and gentleness, and those which offer support such as nurturing, comfort, and protection. In a similar way instrumental aspects include on the one hand physical helping behaviours, that is, those which provide assistance in the gratification of the patients physical needs and in the maintenance of the physical environment; but also those that involve teaching, advising and instructing patients about how they can maintain or improve their health.

While models like that of Leininger help to demonstrate the range of activities which can serve a caring function, they do not help us to identify which behaviours are going to be seen as important in a particular setting. Conversely Watson has put particular emphasis on the psychological, emotional and spiritual aspects of care, but almost to the exclusion of the other characteristics of everyday physical or technical nursing tasks. While both models provide a framework within which it is possible to see how different activities can have a caring function, by themselves they do not tell us how patients actually perceive the care that they receive.

Methodological Background

In order to understand "care" from a patient's perspective, this study took an explicitly phenomenological approach. The approach is generally first attributed to the writings of Edmund Husserl, but has been developed by other writers since. Phenomenology is both a philosophical approach to our understanding of the world, and also a way of gathering information about it. The two aspects are inextricably linked to each other. Viewed from this perspective, truths and facts do not exist in some Platonic heaven waiting to be discovered—they emerge only within specific situations and at specific times. Knowledge is historically generated and historically rooted. Relationships between variables are socially constructed and exist only within the social context which has generated them. Truth is dynamic and exists only in the interactions between persons and socio-historical settings. From this perspective the subjectivity of the human response to a situation is acknowledged and value attributed to it. Patients' responses to the care they receive can thus be interpreted only in terms of their own personal characteristics and the context in which they encounter it, and their potentially differing interpretations are equally valid within this context.

A concrete example of this approach offered by Spinelli (1989) will help to clarify the issue. Imagine that you are in an art gallery walking past a series of paintings, and your eye lights upon one which immediately catches your imagination. You may look carefully at certain features of it. You may recognise it as a well known painting which you have seen previously in books on art, and you are suddenly struck by the luminescence of the colour or by some aspect of composition. Eventually you move away to look at other paintings in the exhibition.

What happens to the painting? Does it continue to exist as you initially perceived it? Or is that particular perceived painting no longer in existence?

A phenomenologist would begin to answer this question by admitting that the painting did have physical substance. There is certainly some form of raw matter which causes us to have the physical reaction to the painting that we do. The painting is composed on a canvas on which pigments have been applied, the whole is encased in a frame. This is its raw material.

However the point that the phenomenologist would make is that the painting that you perceived, indeed the painting that anyone perceives and walks away from, can never be perceived in exactly the same way as it was initially. Even though the painting in its raw state continues to exist because the materials which make it up continue to exist, the "perceived painting" only exists in the way it does at the moment of perception.

Our experience of the world, therefore, is always made up of an interaction between the material substance of what we perceive, and our individual mental faculties. We never perceive only raw matter, nor do we perceive only mental phenomena. We always experience the interaction between the two.

The phenomenological approach to research involves four basic steps: *bracketing, analysing, intuiting,* and *describing.* The first three of these describe the general approach to problem formulation and describe how accounts of people's experience are gathered and selected. The final step, "describing", is concerned with the processes involved in analysing the accounts of the experience which have been obtained.

Bracketing

This describes the fundamental process of the phenomenological method. It describes the on-going concerted attempt by the researcher to "suspend" previous knowledge about a phenomenon in order to appreciate how it exhibits itself every time it is encountered. It is based upon Oiler's (1982, p. 179) observation

> that in reflecting back on experience what is uncovered is not pure experience, rather it is remembered experience

For this reason it is impossible to be totally free of bias in reflection on past experience, but it is possible to try to control it. From this position, in order to see lived experience, an individual must suspend or lay aside any pre-conceptions or biases regarding that experience. This suspension of judge-ment is called "phenomenological reduction". By attempting it, however, it becomes clear that complete reduction is an impossibility, and that it is not possible to approach a phenomenon without any presuppositions whatso-ever. Rather the conscious attempt to suspend these presuppositions makes us more aware of what they are and the influence that they have upon our interpretations.

The implications of these statements are that prior to any data gathering operation, researchers must engage in a process of preparatory self reflec-tion which enables them to identify their presuppositions and biases, as well as suggesting questions that may clarify the dimensions of the experience to be investigated.

This process may be best illustrated by describing the way in which the form of the study described here took shape. The study was originally conceived as a study of the caring behaviours of the Accident and Emer-gency Nurse as perceived by the patient. The underlying assumption of this study, as it is also reflected in the literature on caring touched on above, is that caring involves a series of activities performed by the nurse which are intended to assist patients' recovery. But caring can involve a feeling as well as a set of overt behaviours, and it may be that from the patient's per-spective it is not only what a nurse does which is seen by a patient as caring or not caring, but also the way in which this is done. The possibility exists that patients might make the distinction between two sets of apparently equivalent behaviours, on the basis that one demonstrated some "quality of care" for the patient in their performance which the other one lacked. Such a realisation led to a change to the title of the project and sensitised us to an important potential dimension of meaning which could repay further analysis later on. From this point on, our sensitivities were opened up to include the possibility that there may be a distinction between "caring for" a patient which would be based predominantly upon instrumental activities, and "caring about" which would involve more expressive behaviours.

A further presupposition also emerged as a consequence of this first stage in the phenomenological approach, which gave us further cause to examine the direction on which we had embarked. In addition to the possible dis-tinction between "caring for" and "caring about", is the possible idea of caring as having more than ordinary feeling for somebody. Nurses are encouraged to foster a degree of clinical detachment from their patients for both professional and personal reasons, but the possibility exists that nurses may also differ in the degree to which they cared for or cared about their patients. Within a professional relationship it became clear that there are clear expectations of the limits within which nurses are expected to care for or about their patients, which do not necessarily apply to relationships outside this professional context. From a professional point of view this particular component of caring is specifically de-emphasised, but this is in sharp contrast to the extensive discussion of this issue in more theoretical and philosophical treatments of the nature of caring (e.g. Fromm, 1962, Ray, 1981). The appreciation of the possibility of this component within a professional nursing relationship potentially opened up a different line of inquiry in the later stages of the study.

Analysing

The analysing stage of the phenomenological method is the term which is applied to the process whereby the experience itself is gathered together. When this is done introspectively by an individual, it involves a process of memory and self reflection which brings particular experiences to mind. When it is applied to the experiences of others it involves a series of choices about the form of experience which is to be gathered, and this in its turn involves decisions about whose experiences should be included in the study and the methods which are to be used to gather and record them. These decisions will necessarily follow from understanding of the presuppositions which are uncovered in the previous bracketing stage. In this particular instance, it was important to ensure that we chose people who had the sort of experience which was appropriate and who were motivated and able to articulate it. For similar reasons it was also necessary to conduct the interviews in a manner which allowed the maximum amount of flexibility for the patient to articulate what they regarded as caring behaviours, and to allow the expression of any or all of the possible interpretations which are described in the previous section on "bracketing".

Intuiting

This is a concept which is particularly difficult to describe with precision. It describes an "attitude of mind" to the experience in question, in which the researcher brackets her own preconceptions about it and which enables her to "look at the experience with wide open eyes, with knowledge, facts and theories held at bay" (Oiler, 1982). In the same way, as the researcher needs to bracket her own presuppositions in formulating a definition of the research questions, so too does she need to do something similar when faced with evidence of the experience of informants. As Swanson (1990) describes it, it is important for the researcher to be able to feel what it would be like to live in the informants world.

Such an intuitive process involves the application of art rather than objectivity. The phenomenological approach is unashamed in its rejection of the traditional approach of the natural sciences to the understanding of human beings. The results of research using a natural science approach in which a subject is not asked to report an experience, but to perform a task, has not been felt to transfer readily to personal life experience. As Strauss (1966) describes it, many researchers in the social sciences began to realise that there was a difference between "things known and the human knowledge of things". What was deleted in the scientific experiment, the subjective experience, was beginning to be perceived as more basic and real in the understanding of human knowledge and behaviour than the codifications that the experimental researchers called data. In order to do justice to experience it is necessary for the researcher to seek to live this experience as if it were her own, and it is this process to which the term "intuiting" is applied.

Describing

This is the final stage of the research process, in which the researcher pulls together her insights and tests these against the descriptions of experience which are revealed in the informants' quotes. The process can be loosely described as one in which the researcher tries to "tell a story" which describes the experience of her informant(s) in terms of a reduced model, which can be tested against informant quotes, and whose adequacy is also assessed through its reception by those who have lived or witnessed the phenomenon which is being described. The validity of a particular interpretation is thus tested internally, through correspondence with the data which informants descriptions produce, and externally by its correspondence with the experience of others who were not included within the investigation but which the results of it would be expected to illuminate. A similar appeal to the "experience of the audience" of a research report, rather than to more orthodox canons of predictability characterises the prescriptions of those who advocate the development of an explicitly feminist research methodology in the social sciences (e.g. Wilkinson, 1986).

THE STUDY

Because it is so difficult to define caring analytically, this particular study tried to take a fresh approach to the issue. The NHS is particularly concerned about the quality of the service it provides, and thus about the quality of care which patients feel they receive. Such "a customer oriented approach to care" pushes the onus for defining what is caring and what is not onto the patient. From this perspective the research question thus turns into one of how patients experience the care which they receive and how they interpret this experience.

The study therefore tries to find out how patients understand "care". The aim of the phenomenological approach is to gather information about life experience from the perspective of the individuals being studied, allowing the researcher to examine what these individuals perceive their reality to be. Through the analysis of these descriptions the researcher investigates the phenomenon for its grounded structures and then describes it.

The aim of the study was to articulate the meanings which patients who had been treated within the A & E department ascribed to their experience of care. A fundamental axiom which follows from the phenomenological approach is that each patient's experience of treatment is unique and idiosyncratic, and can only be understood in terms of the contributions which both the nurse and the patient make to their encounter. No claim is made that the patients who spoke in this study are representative of all patients who visit A & E. Each speaks with their own voice of their own specific experience. However, from these interpretations the researcher can map out the "grounded structures" which underlie each patient's experience of care, and then go on to see whether there are common elements between them.

Data were gathered by the use of semi-structured interviews, based upon interview guidelines identifying the broad areas which the interviewer wished to examine. While a number of different methods are available which would enable patients to describe their experience, the face to face interview offers the greatest possibility for modifying a line of enquiry and following up responses in a way that other methods of gathering such data cannot do. Such lack of standardisation inevitably raises concerns about reliability, and about the potential biasing effects of an interviewer who approaches different patients experience in different ways. However the essential feature of the phenomenological approach is that this experience is idiosyncratic and unique. In order to explore it and interpret it a parallel idiosyncratic and unique approach to the patient, which recognises the distinctive nature of this experience and seeks to be sensitive to its nuances, is required. For these reasons there is no substitute for the face to face interview for gathering information of this kind.

The Conduct of the Study

The study was undertaken in the Accident and Emergency Department of a large teaching hospital in the North East of England. The method requires "that participants have experience of the topic of the study and an ability to articulate the experience" (Colaizzi, 1978), and therefore in this case informants had to be patients over 18 who claimed they could remember the interactions they had with the nurse. That meant that patients needed to be fully conscious, prior to and during their attendance at the hospital. For this reason patients who had sustained head injuries, suffered convulsions or taken drugs were excluded from the study.

The initial approaches to ask whether patients were willing to co-operate were made by the sister or charge nurse on duty at the time. This was done for two reasons: firstly because the nurse would know whether the patient fulfilled the necessary criteria for inclusion within the study without being directly involved in care giving, and secondly because it made it easier for the patient to decline to participate as the researcher was not present. Patients who agreed to take part were then approached, either immediately on discharge by the researcher, or were contacted later by phone. At this time patients were told what the study was about and what time commitment was involved, and asked again if they were still willing to participate. In accordance with Guidelines drawn up by the Royal College of Nursing patients were given an explanation of the study and given the right to withdraw at any time during or after the interview, and written consent was obtained for the interviews to be conducted and audio-taped.

In the interviews stress was placed upon conducting the interview as a conversation, which was designed to help the patients to focus their thoughts and to allow them the maximum opportunity to express things in their own way. The interviewer sought clarification by reflecting on patients' descriptions of their experience and encouraging them to provide further information or clarification. The aim of the interviews was to cover the areas described in the guidelines but without forcing patients down tracks which they did not wish to explore. The interviews were all conducted in patients' own homes and lasted between one and four hours. For this first phase of the study a sample of seven interviews were recorded and transcribed verbatim.

The Outcomes of the Study

In order to show how this approach works in practice it is necessary to look at the way in which the data analysis task was approached in this particular instance. Transcripts of interviews with patients were examined through the use of the procedures described by Colaizzi (1978) namely:

1. Gain familiarity with the transcripts by reading and rereading in order to acquire a feeling for them and to make sense of them. Willingness to be open to what is there calls for the investigator to suspend (or bracket) any preconceived beliefs or experiences she may have about the phenomena and to "intuit" an understanding of the informants reality for herself.
2. On the basis of this, extract significant statements that describe the phenomena, for analysis.
3. Formulate meanings by reflecting on the meanings of the significant statements for each transcript.

4. Group these in to themes of related meaning. Internal validation of themes can then be achieved by referring back to the original statements to judge their adequacy.

5. Formulate these themes into a description of the phenomenon (of caring) as perceived by the participants.

To see how this worked in practice, examples from the interview transcripts and their interpretation are described below.

The first stage involves the reading and rereading of the transcripts until the researcher has gained "a feel for them". There are no absolute rules about how often this needs to be done, but the process depends upon the researcher being able to put herself in the position of the informant and to try to see things through her eyes. In doing so the researcher needs to consistently suspend her own presuppositions and to allow the informants' words to speak for themselves. The process is an inductive one, in that the researcher allows potential interpretations of meaning to emerge from the transcripts, but where she also suppresses her natural desires to impose these interpretations upon the data at this stage.

The second stage involves the identification of meaningful statements or phrases which refer to caring. In this particular case, 7 interviews generated 154 significant statements. Each statement is entered on a separate file card which also identifies the code number of the informant and the position which this statement occupies in transcript sequence. In order to give some feel for the nature of the material which emerges from this analysis, four examples are given below, each drawn from a different transcript:

"They were in tune with what I wanted, as though they could read my mind and they anticipated my needs, like telling me what they were doing and why and what would happen" (Jean)

"I don't know how you define reassurance ... other than it gives you some confidence that is, at that moment, lacking. The fact that there is a nurse there makes it feel as though you matter. I'm sure there is something there ... you feel sure that they are really trying their best" (Eric)

"... I mean anybody can stick to a routine but it's the caring about you that matters ... they did what they had to do, like blood pressure and things, but they also made the effort ... doing more than they just had to, by talking to me." (Anna)

"Well caring is, I suppose, really being interested in what's the matter with people and trying to do something to help them. I think you could tell when people are interested in what you're saying because otherwise their eyes are wandering about instead of looking at you ... you can tell when a person's really interested in how you're feeling and one that's asking it just for the sake of asking. Some people do look at you when you're talking to 'em, and others are kind of looking at you and listening ... they're taking in what you are saying." (Gladys)

The third stage is concerned with the formulation of the meanings which emerge from the statements. In this process the cards are read and re-read and the meaning or meanings of each statement recorded. This process can also involve going back to the recording of the interview to contextualise the statement, and to use any non-linguistic cues such as stress and intonation in order to clarify the meaning of the statement.

In many cases statements have multiple meanings, and an effort has to be made to capture all of these. In order to illustrate how this process works out the meanings formulated for the four statements described above are listed for reference.

The nurses were sensitive to the unstated concerns and needs of the patient. They understood, respected and responded to those concerns and needs.

The patient needed reassurance and emotional support and to feel valued as an individual. The nurses presence gives him this and demonstrates to him that the nurse is genuinely concerned and wants to help.

Caring involves doing more than the basic instrumental or technical tasks. It means giving something extra—making an effort.

Caring involves demonstrating genuine interest in the patient and a willingness not only to intervene and to interact with the patient to alleviate a problem, but also involves demonstrating genuine interest. The patient perceives this feeling of interest by her interpretation of the non-verbal behaviour of the nurse.

The fourth stage involves grouping these statements into themes which represent the meanings which have emerged. In this study four separate themes appeared to emerge from the formulated meanings at this stage. These were:

INTEREST—the nurses show genuine interest in the patients;
ACCESSIBILITY—The nurses were approachable, available and understood what the patients were going through;
INFORMATION—Patients appreciate information and like to know what is going on;
INDIVIDUALITY—Patients appreciate being treated as individuals and human beings.

The value of these groupings and the way in which individual statements can touch on a number of themes can be illustrated by examining the instances which are included within the first and largest category "Interest". The frequency with which this theme was mentioned can be taken as an indication of its salience in patients perception of the nature of care.

Jean, for example, describes how nurses showed interest in her as an individual:

"People were interested in me as a person, not a case of difficult breathing."

"He wanted to know me as a person, not just another patient. I was an individual, not just another patient, he wasn't just doing his job".

Anna equated the genuine interest with being treated as a human being. Because she had experienced several negative contacts with hospitals over the past year, it validated her status as a patient:

"Well they didn't make me feel like they thought I was putting it on, or that I was just a hypochondriac, they believed me. Whereas I've been in hospitals where they made me feel that way, they made me feel that I shouldn't really be there and like I'm moaning and that I shouldn't complain, do you know what I mean? They weren't like that at all. They made me feel like if I had got a complaint they were interested. They had the sort of attitude that made me feel like if I did feel poorly or dizzy, I could have told them about it, do you know what I mean?"

Nurses were also approachable and willing to follow through by doing something to help:

"She asked me if I wanted my friend and daughter brought in, and I said yes, and she went and found them and brought them in" (Anna)

The fifth stage is one in which the themes which have been identified through grouping of the statements are elaborated and combined, through logical reflection on their relationships with each other and by bringing in wider theoretical issues from the literature and from the findings of other studies. It is at this point that the researcher moves away from the primary data and tries to mould it into an exhaustive description of the phenomenon which is being studied.

Earlier in this paper we pointed out that the definition of caring behaviour was problematical, but in gathering data and in its interpretation we have deliberately eschewed any fundamental examination of the nature of the concept until this stage. The theoretical approach to caring developed by Watson (1985) attempts to analyse the types of relationship and the nature of the transactions between the care giver and the care receiver which serve to promote and to protect the humanity of the patient, and thus enhance the patient's own healing potential. In describing the processes involved in caring as well as the outcomes of care, Watson analysed the psychological, emotional and spiritual aspects of care—almost to the exclusion of other nursing tasks. For this reason the theory has been criticised for not reflecting clinical reality. It has been argued that the depth of the caring relationship which it envisages is impossible to attain in many nursing situations in which the length of hospitalisation is short, the contact is brief or the patient is unable to interact with the nurse.

Findings from a range of empirical studies of nurses' own perceptions of the nature of the caring relationship using more structured techniques have revealed that nurses and patients have contrasting views of what caring is about. For example, Larson (1981) analysed the perceptions of fifty types of nursing behaviours from the nurse's and patient's perspectives, and found that patients' perceptions of important caring behaviours involved such things as giving injections, knowing how to manage equipment, knowing when to call the doctor, and giving medications on time. On the other hand nurses ranked behaviours like touching the patient when help was needed, allowing patients to express feelings about disease and treatment, treating information confidentially, and getting to know patients as individuals as the most important caring behaviours. Apparently patients saw instrumental activities as being more important than expressive activities in conveying caring, while nurses saw it the other way round. This finding is reflected in other studies in this area (e.g. Mayer 1985; Cronin & Harrison, 1988).

Phenomenological research seeks to ask two related questions: What is the phenomenon that is lived and how does it express itself? In this instance, when asked about the phenomenon of care, patients define it in terms of its manifestations. In this sense the study has addressed the two issues as one. However an important distinction in writings about the concept of care by philosophers as opposed to nurses or psychologists, is the emphasis they place upon its general defining characteristics. A particularly significant one amongst existential philosophers is the notion of 'presence'. Thus Marcel (1971, pp. 25–6) writes:

> It is an undeniable fact ... that there are some people who reveal themselves as "present" that is to say at our disposal—when we are in pain or when we need to confide in someone, while there are other people who do not give us this feeling, however great is their goodwill ... The most attentive listener may give me the impression of not being present, he gives me nothing, he cannot make room for me in himself whatever the material favours he is prepared to grant me. The truth is there is a way of listening which is a way of giving and another which is a way of refusing ... Presence is something which reveals itself immediately and unmistakably in a look, a smile, an intonation or a handshake.

In these terms care is a property of the carer, and not simply a consequence of actions which nurses perform on, or for patients. Emphasis needs to be placed upon understanding the phenomenon of caring as well as on identifying its manifestations. For example in the selection from the transcripts below, presence means more than being physically present. Eric demonstrates his awareness of the role that the physical presence of the nurse plays in affirming his individuality:

"Physical presence is one thing for me ... just having a nurse there ... I'm not just left like a lump of meat waiting my turn".

No reference is made to anything that the nurse does—her influence relies upon some quality which affirms his existence as a human being. In a similar way the presence of the nurse can also convey that she is receptive not only to the stated concerns and questions of a patient, but also to those which are unstated. For example, as another patient describes it:

"They were very aware of my feelings of being anxious at being up there" (Jean)

"They were in tune with what I wanted, as though they could read my mind and they anticipated my needs, like telling me what they were doing and why and what would happen" (Jean)

For Leslie this being "in tune" is more graphically illustrated:

"It was very busy so I said I could manage, but she stayed and helped me clean up. I was very embarrassed and was going on about the state of the bedclothes. She just said "Don't worry Les, you're going to be alright, its not unusual to be sick after what you've gone through"—she knew. Well I burst our blarting then apologised because I've never messed me 'sen like that before and was scared that it meant I'd started losing me faculties, like the wife did after her stroke ... She stayed with me and we chatted about things and in the end we were laughing about somat"

Here the nurse has realised the reasons for Leslie agitation, she has not only recognised his embarrassment, but also his fear and has responded appropriately.

Nurses may perform routine "caring for" activities without much thought because they become second nature, and in this sense the nurse may relate to the patient as an object. The patient may speak but the nurse does not listen closely, and although she may respond she may hear the words but miss the meaning. "Being present" means that the nurse takes time to listen, she gives her undivided attention to the patient and is able to focus on his needs. This component is recognised by other writers. For example Paterson & Zderad (1976) propose that the ability of the nurse "to be with the patient" is an essential component of the care experience, which they define as an experience lived between human beings that is more than a benevolent technically competent, one way, nurse–patient interaction. This existential mode of interaction according to Gadow (1980) produces a feeling of security, relaxation and a sense of value. For example:

"I remember the nurse coming in often, it seemed like she was always there, checking on me and telling me that I was doing OK. She helped me to know that I was OK" (Leslie)

"They keep coming in and out and checking on you and sometimes she'd come and sit—so I felt cared for and safe" (John)

Such extracts indicate that "presence" is an important component of the caring process which is manifested in a number of behaviours, or, significantly, in no overt actions at all. It is also associated with the behaviours which were identified as major themes in stage 4 of the analysis, namely interest, accessibility, access to information and individuality. The presence of the nurse can indicate interest, can demonstrate that she is always available and able to provide information and support, and that she cares for the patient as an individual. By themselves these behaviours do not personify the nature of care as perceived by the patients who served as the informants in this study, but they do serve as significant indicators of the phenomenon.

The literature is replete with accounts of the failings of the health care system and its lack of sensitivity and responsiveness to patients' concerns. In the light of government legislation advancing the notion of patients as consumers, health care professionals are necessarily needing to become more responsive to patients' needs and desires. American experience also indicates that patients' experience of caring also affects their decisions as to where to go for treatment (e.g. Buerhaus, 1986) and this is likely to have obvious influences upon the financial viability of the NHS units.

The important issue is: how can such patient opinions be assessed? More traditional qualitative approaches, which ask patients to choose a response from a prepared set of alternatives, or to complete rating scales, have already indicated that patients and nurses have different expectations about the meaning of care, and appear to imply that nurses should concentrate upon the more instrumental aspects of their role, for it is this which patients appear to value as the indication of the care they receive in hospital. The results of this study however demonstrate a very different perspective. When the researcher is able to suspend (or "bracket") her presuppositions about the nature of care and allow patients to express their own experience in naive phenomenological terms, a different conception of care emerges which has profound implications for training and for health care delivery.

Naive Phenomenology as a Research Tool

The phenomenological approach thus provides both a philosophy of patient care, and also a procedure for documenting and describing the lived experienced of patients. Quantitative methodologies with their requirement to control, manipulate and measure, may be considered to be a necessary tool for those whose role is to manage and control a complex and expensive system of health care delivery. Such methodologies, which exclude attention to the subjective and the intuitive, can however produce information which is misleading. A concept such as "care", because it is a human expression as well as an activity, includes elements of subjectivity and intuition and as such requires exploration with techniques which are sensitive to these facets. To ignore them is not only likely to lead to research which gives a partial and distorted view of such phenomena, but is also likely to have important practical and financial implications.

When this has been said, it is also important to appreciate the limitations of this type of approach. The application of the phenomenological approach encourages openness in our approach to data and a willingness to initially suspend (or "bracket") our presuppositions in the definition of the research issues. The need to allow informants' own interpretation of their experience to be expressed, discourages the researcher from defining categories of analysis and encourages her to allow these to emerge through an intuitive process. In doing so, this approach emphasises the importance of the researcher's personal sensitivity and creativity in the initial stages of an investigation, in which the research questions are articulated and the methods of data gathering and analysis defined.

The difficulty with this approach arises when an interpretation is questioned. Writers in the phenomenological tradition do not normally discuss how the reliability and validity of their findings can be measured in an orthodox sense, nor can they say how representative they are. Since each person's experience is unique these would seem to be nonsensical questions. Instead the validity of the findings of an investigation depend on the extent to which they are "in tune" with the experience of their readers, so that when they read them they will be lead to say "Yes—that's just how I felt about it!" The findings thus reflect, but also serve to systematise, common everyday experience so that it can be communicated to others.

But where the audience shares a different perspective the results may be disparaged as "subjective" and not "verifiable". The phenomenologist would be unmoved by such a critique and would point to the limitations of positivistic approaches in dealing with conscious experience which have been reiterated earlier in the chapter. In certain situations however a researcher may need to be more circumspect. The phenomenological approach has particular value in the initial stages of a project in which a researcher is seeking to develop and articulate a theoretical position. Strauss and Corbin (1990) have referred elsewhere to such an approach as the "grounded theory" approach to research, in which the definition of the research question and the processes involved in the coding of data "emerge" in a sequential way from the researchers involvement with research data. Phenomenologists do not claim that their approach is the only useful framework for understanding experience, but they do claim that it is useful and that it provides a perspective which cannot be achieved through other means. In practical terms it will often provide the starting point for further exploration which is designed to satisfy the canons of more traditional positivistic science. Without it, however, these more traditional approaches could prove to be the poorer.

How to do Phenomenological Analysis

1. Prior to any data gathering operation, "bracket" presuppositions about what the nature of the research question is, so as to identify biases and presuppositions, as well as to suggest questions which may clarify the experience to be investigated.
2. Make decisions based on this about what sort of data is to be gathered and from whom.
3. Adopt an "intuitive" approach to this experience, which will enable you to approach your informants' accounts of the experience by seeing it through their eyes.
4. Describe your findings through:
   a) Gaining familiarity with the transcripts by reading and rereading in order to acquire a feeling for them and to make sense of them.
   b) On the basis of this, extracting significant statements that describe the phenomena, for analysis.
   c) Formulating meanings by reflecting on the meanings of the significant statements for each transcript.
4. Group these into themes of related meaning. Internal validation of these themes can then be achieved by referring back to the original statements to judge their adequacy.
5. Formulate these themes into a description of the phenomenon as perceived by the participants.

12

Using grounded theory in psychological research

Nick Pidgeon and Karen Henwood
School of Psychology, University of Wales, Bangor

INTRODUCTION

This chapter considers the case for, and one particular approach to, qualitative research in psychology. We take the view that any discussion of qualitative methods must make reference to wider and changing understandings of science, and in particular to the view that knowledge is always a social production. The approach of generating grounded theory is considered since it offers a set of useful strategies for handling, organising and analysing unstructured qualitative material. However, we also explain why some of the assumptions upon which the approach was originally based have had to be considerably updated and revised.

The paper is divided into three main sections. The first includes an elementary discussion of three main theories of scientific knowledge (epistemologies), and relates these to some of the characteristics of qualitative research. It also explains the background to grounded theory. The second, on using a grounded theory approach, outlines the various data-analytic strategies that can be used. In the third, we break down the general qualitative research process into a number of more specific and manageable goals, and comment upon various criteria that can be used in the assessment of qualitative research, drawing also upon humanistic/collaborative, feminist and discourse analysis approaches to scholarship and inquiry.

GROUNDED THEORY IN ITS WIDER CONTEXT: SCIENCE, EPISTEMOLOGY AND QUALITATIVE METHODS

The Social Construction of Scientific Knowledge

For most of us the first step in learning how to conduct our own psychological research involves understanding a received-wisdom about the way in which progress in the natural and social sciences is made. This view is based around the so-called hypothetico-deductive (or experimental) method, which strives for scientific description and explanation of the predictable relationships (causes and effects) between objects and events in the empirical world. The term hypothetico-deductive refers to the way in which the experimental method involves testing hypotheses or predictions deduced from prior theory, in settings where all relevant variables can be isolated and controlled by the researcher.

Since the goal of scientific method is better theory, by this account the truth or not of any theory depends upon whether it can be supported (or falsified) by the empirical evidence, which typically takes the form of observations from some experiment. Of course, psychology, in common with other sciences (e.g. biology), has never restricted itself entirely to laboratory experiments. A wider range of methods can and are used—for example questionnaires or observational designs—when controlled experimentation is not practically possible or desirable. However, all of these methods tend to be based upon the common philosophy of the need for objective observation and measurement in order that the findings of research will be replicable and generalisable, and such that further predictions can be made. Quantification is crucial within this philosophical approach because it enables scientists to operationalise and measure the variables contained in their theories and predictions, and to compare observations in "objectively" standardised ways.

The high esteem in which science has been held is in part due to the way that it holds out the possibility of generating knowledge that is more valid and reliable than mere fantasy and superstition. That is, the trappings of scientific method are believed to ensure the rigour and "objectivity" of research, and to produce results held to be better founded than purely "subjective" understandings. Within this model of research practice the influence of the researcher over the research process, or researcher subjectivity, is treated as a potential source of "bias", which potentially threatens to undermine the validity and reliability of any results. Research procedures are therefore advocated to guard against this source of bias.

One example in psychology would be the experimenter using standardised instructions across experimental conditions. Another is the disguising of the hypotheses under investigation, in order to avoid participants simply complying with their perception of what the researcher wants to know (known as demand characteristics; see Rosenthal, 1966). A dispassionate style of scientific reporting is also used when communicating findings, to further reinforce the view that research is an entirely non-subjective process.

However, in recent times the idealised and actual practices of science, as well as our own understandings of what it is to do science, have come under increasing scrutiny. These inquiries have centred around the thorny philosophical question of *epistemology*—that is our fundamental theory of knowledge and the ways in which it can be produced. The effect of this scrutiny has been to bring to light the particular assumptions about knowledge made by the hypothetico-deductive (and related) approaches to research, and which make it susceptible to critique. The most radical challenge suggests that science in practice is a quite different enterprise from that assumed in the received-wisdom described above. In order to illustrate this point, we can identify three basic epistemologies (i.e. theories of knowledge), each of which are represented in Fig. 12.1 (see also Woolgar 1988).

The first epistemology (1a) represents the received view of science, and is sometimes called *positivism*. Here scientific knowledge is assumed to be a direct reflection of objects in an underlying empirical world. Hence there is a direct relationship, shown in the diagram by the unbroken arrow from Left to Right, between objects in the world and their description in scientific theories. For example, the idea of heat is held to be a property of the world, and its analogue therefore appears in the theories of physics.

The second epistemology (1b) shown in Fig. 12.1, admits that *in principle* it is possible to generate accurate scientific representations from objects in the world, shown by the dotted line linking object to (correct) scientific knowledge. However, *in practice* a whole host of individual and social biases are likely to deflect the process of knowledge generation, producing alternative (incorrect) representations of the object of study. Examples of individual biases in psychology would include the demand characteristics discussed earlier. Scholars from the so-called "weak programme" in the sociology of scientific knowledge, have pointed out that in addition bias can operate at an institutional level (i.e. across a discipline as a whole).

Hence, when psychology was gripped by the behaviourist school of thought between 1910 and 1950, the relevance of any form of mental process in the scientific explanation of behaviour was denied—so much so that this amounted to an institutional blindness to processes of cognition, such as reasoning and thinking, within much of North American and British psychology. Today we know that this view was far too narrow, and in fact a constraint upon the development of certain forms of psychological inquiry.

The third epistemology (1c), known as *constructivism*, is more radical in its implications in that the relationship between knowledge and objects in

1a) Positivism (Traditional View of Science)

OBJECT ━━━━━━━━━━━━➤ SCIENTIFIC KNOWLEDGE

1b) Social Biases Account

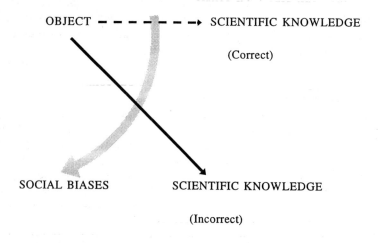

OBJECT ━ ━ ━ ━ ━ ━ ➤ SCIENTIFIC KNOWLEDGE

(Correct)

SOCIAL BIASES   SCIENTIFIC KNOWLEDGE

(Incorrect)

1c) Constructivism (Or Social Constructionism)

OBJECT ◄━━━━━━━━━━━ SCIENTIFIC KNOWLEDGE

FIG. 12.1.   Three Epistemologies (Theories of Knowledge).

248

the world is reversed (the arrow now goes from the right to the left). This signifies that it is knowledge which defines (i.e. constructs) how objects in the world are represented. That is, since objects cannot be apprehended directly they are rather constructed through the act of coming to know about the world. Hence the object which we label a kettle is not necessarily and intrinsically a kettle, but can be understood in any number of ways. For example, as a hot object or a device for making tea, depending upon the frame of reference of the observer (a small child or an adult wanting a cup of tea respectively).

What is more, radical constructivism argues that, among several accounts or representations of an object, there may not necessarily be any one accurate or "true" representation. Taken to the extreme, this leads to a rather unsatisfactory position known as *relativism* (all accounts or representations of an object are relative, and no one can be shown to be any better than any other). Of course, constructivism of whatever form seems particularly counter-intuitive (and has caused considerable controversy for this reason), given that our common-sense experience tells us that the whole world is organised as if the relationship goes from left to right, from object to knowledge (epistemology 1a).

However, psychology often shows us how our common sense experiences are not as simple as they might at first appear. To take one example, visual perception (of pattern, colour, and distance) is highly dependent upon the context of a scene and, while often useful, is only imperfectly correlated with actual physical measurements. So when driving along a road in fog, the car in front will appear further away than it does on a clear day (with possible fatal consequences for the driver). This is because a blurred edge is a learned cue to distance. Such a cue provides a rule (blurred edges are further away than clear ones) which serves us well in judging distance under most circumstances, but not when fog is present.

One quite central implication of radical constructivism (1c) therefore is to call into question the very notion of total objectivity, and the possibility of eradicating subjective biases, upon which the hypothetico-deductive ideal of science is based. This is because, as noted above, both scientific knowledge and its object of study are held to be in a mutually constitutive relationship—that is each depends upon the other for its definition. From the constructivist epistemological position all scientific knowing involves the (subjective) interpretation of meaning, and without this attempts to construct knowledge of the world could not proceed. Certain influential developments within contemporary social science and psychology follow the philosopher Michel Foucault (see Rabinow, 1984) in arguing that subjectivity is symbolic and not merely representational—and often bound up with the operation of social processes of domination/subordination or power. Accordingly, discourse analysts within psychology have stressed that subjectivity can usefully be studied as the practical accomplishment of language, text or discourse through which power relations are diffused (see Potter & Wetherell, 1987; also chapters in part 1, this volume). Some critical theorists also draw upon psychoanalytic theory to explain how emotions and relationships are necessarily part of the complex workings of unconscious subjectivity (Parker, 1992).

However, for the purposes of the present chapter we take a less fully theorised approach to the notion of subjectivity, and simply identify various dimensions that play a role in the way that knowledge is produced (see also Henwood & Pidgeon, 1995a). These are (1) participants' own understandings (2) researchers' interpretations (3) cultural meaning systems which inform both participants' and researchers' understandings and (4) acts of judging particular interpretations as valid by scientific communities. In the next section we consider the arguments which have been made for generating psychological accounts that are fully grounded in participants' own understandings and cultural knowledge.

Qualitative Research as an Alternative Paradigm of Inquiry

The radical constructivist formulation of scientific work is sometimes viewed as breaking totally from past perspectives on the research process and the generation of knowledge. However, many important precedents for it can be found in debates on the value of "interpretive", "contextual" or "qualitative" as opposed to "positivist", "hypothetico-deductive" or "quantitative" approaches and methods. In psychology these debates can be traced back to the writings of the 19th Century German historian and philosopher Wilhelm Dilthey, who argued that a clear distinction should be drawn between the disciplines of *Naturwissenschaften* (Natural science and *Geisteswissenschaften* (the moral or human sciences). In Dilthey's view (1894), whilst the former should be prosecuted by the external observation and explanation of physical events, the human sciences should be premised upon a concern for *Verstehen* (meaning or understanding). Dilthey directed his critique at the experimental psychology of the time, arguing unsuccessfully against its uncritical adherence to the natural science model and its reductionist approach to human consciousness.

Individual and small groupings of psychologists have launched similar criticism and appealed for changes since Dilthey, both in the way the "objects" of psychological inquiry are construed and the research methods that are used. Gordon Allport (1962), for example, proposed that the unique characteristics of individuals should be taken into account in personality psychology, in addition to the (still typical) strategy of locating people at points along general personality dimensions which account for the maximum variation in traits within a sample or population as a whole. Rom Harré and Paul Secord (1972) have been highly critical of social psychology's concern for overt behavioural sequences. They show how the intentionality and meaningfulness of human actions can be revealed by looking at the subtlety and range of categories which describe human conduct in everyday language.

Peter Reason and John Rowan (1981) have argued for the virtues of a more "human" mode of inquiry that analyses the flow of experience in the context of everyday life. And Jonathan Potter and Margaret Wetherell (1987) suggest that categories, attitudes and the self-concept are produced as versions of reality within everyday discourses and psychological texts. All of these arguments explicitly or implicitly propose that a shift is required away from methodological and substantive reliance upon the natural science model (or paradigm), and towards a more human and social approach to psychological inquiry.

The wider *quantity–quality* debate in the human sciences generally (see e.g. Bryman, 1988; Denzin and Lincoln, 1994; Lincoln and Guba, 1985) enables us to identify the main bulk of arguments that have been made for an alternative approach to research, together with the reasons why the term "qualitative" paradigm tends to be used. Within the qualitative literature, a quite fundamental observation is that multiple interpretations may be placed on human experience, thought and behaviour when viewed in context and in their full complexity. Put another way, human conduct is said to be always "pre-interpreted" by participants in the social world from a specific social location and their own frames of references. If researchers are to be able to understand people's participation in the social world, they must therefore engage in close inspection of how that world is perceived through the eyes of participants themselves—from their own social and phenomenological perspectives. Sometimes this is described as seeking participants' tacit, contextual "insider" knowledge.

A parallel argument is that researchers must, nevertheless, simultaneously maintain some degree of distance or "strangeness" from their participants. Without this they would live entirely within their participants' "natural attitude" and the tacit (that is, taken for granted) cultural assumptions and ways of life would not be revealed. Note that this does not amount to the stance of objectivity and non-involvement advocated within the natural science paradigm, since *understanding* the perspective of one's participants is an essential goal.

Taken together, the preceding points about the need for insider *and* outsider perspectives suggest that the researcher and the researched are interdependent, knowing subjects in the process of generating knowledge, rather than detached neutral observer and object of inquiry respectively, as suggested within the natural science paradigm. Humanistic (Reason &

Rowan, 1981) and feminist (Bowles & Duelli-Klein, 1983) researchers have in addition to this described the way that the researcher and the researcher are necessarily mutually involved in the conduct of human relationships. Some of these researchers then go on to advocate a collaborative model of research for ethical reasons, arguing that researchers should avoid treating research "subjects" as if they were mere objects of the experimenter's gaze (see Henwood & Pidgeon, 1995b).

The term "qualitative" tends to be used to describe research that is guided by the above principles. In particular it signifies that initially open or unstructured observation and/or involvement is necessary, together with a commitment to generating a deep and textured understanding, if we are to gain access to participants' own worlds and taken for granted cultural knowledge. Research which relies on quantification to operationalise pre-existing concepts, and to test theory defined rigidly in advance (and from a position outside the context of participants' lived worlds) is unlikely to be suited to this task. This is because it fixes meaning rather than allowing its emergence through the interplay between researcher and researched. A defining feature of much qualitative research is that it seeks to avoid overwriting internally structured subjectivities by imposing external "objective" systems of meaning.[1]

Linked to the above, qualitative research can also serve the important function of discovering or generating new ideas or theory. Hypothetico-deductive research is concerned with the verification or testing of theory that already exists, but neglects the equally important phase of discovery—probably because this necessitates a concern for researcher creativity and hence subjectivity. However, breaking out of the old to generate new ways of seeing is vital, even within the natural science model, in order to ensure the continuity and development of new scientific knowledge. The reason for this is explained by the work of Thomas Kuhn (1962), which has shown that "false" theories can sometimes become entrenched in a discipline's thinking. In such cases contrary evidence gained through the routine procedures of the hypothetico-deductive method is not enough to lead to rejection. Rather, theories are replaced only by fundamental shifts in thinking.

Breaking out is also essential for forms of scholarship, such as feminist research, which exist to challenge bodies of knowledge that have been generated from one particular and powerful social standpoint (in this case a masculinist viewpoint), and to replace them with less partial and less distorted interpretations and theories (see e.g. Harding 1987). Conducting close, detailed qualitative analyses which are grounded in participants' understandings and local contextual knowledges, and which seek to make explicit what is otherwise taken for granted, is an invaluable resource for the generation of new ideas.

So far we have seen that the distinction between qualitative and quantitative paradigms of research draws attention to the very different assumptions that researchers make about the relationship between subjectivity and objectivity in research. We need to be cautious, however, of some of the claims of simple difference that have been made. A first point is that discussions of the qualitative "paradigm" often group rather diverse lines of methodology and theoretical views regarding the epistemological question (Henwood and Pidgeon, 1994). A second point is that it would be misleading to view quantitative and qualitative research as mutually exclusive—with quantitative always signifying positivism and qualitative a constructivist epistemology. Quantification (number) and qualitative representations (word) may both be seen as ways of ordering or organising otherwise complex, unstructured material, and in this sense either could be consistent with constructivism (see e.g. Latour, 1987).

Others would argue that any decision to chose either a qualitative or a quantitative approach to data gathering and analysis could be seen merely as a matter of practical choice. Alan Bryman (1988) calls this view the *technical version* of the quantity–quality debate, since it assumes that quantity and quality do not represent separate and incommensurable paradigms at all, but merely methods that are chosen because they are most suited to the problem under investigation. Nevertheless, an equally compelling case can be made for retaining the view that at least two approaches to knowledge generation can be distinguished which, for want of better labels, may be called qualitative and quantitative paradigms of inquiry. By so doing, a much wider range of concerns and practices may be preserved as legitimate facets of psychological, human inquiry.

Grounded Theory Past and Present

Grounded theory is one particular approach to qualitative research and analysis that emerged as part of the 1960s debates about the relative merits of quantity and quality. As a specific term grounded theory was first introduced by the sociologists Barney Glaser and Anselm Strauss (1967). At that time sociological researchers were preoccupied with testing a few highly abstract and "grand" theories, to the neglect of generating more local, contextual theory of relevance to those being studied. Glaser and Strauss chose the term grounded theory to express the idea of theory that is generated by (or grounded in) a close inspection of qualitative data gathered from concrete settings; for example, unstructured data from interviews, participant observation and archival research. In particular, the approach seeks to counteract the preoccupation within positivism with testing prior theories (an argument relevant not just to sociology but, as we have seen, to psychology too) which may have little relevance to the particular content domain studied, and to take account of how reality is viewed by participants themselves. Glaser and Strauss' text *The Discovery of Grounded Theory* has served a useful purpose, therefore, in highlighting the value of systematic (but also highly creative) qualitative research, and in challenging the view that research proceeds solely by the quantitative testing of theory.

The term grounded theory has come, over time, to mean a number of different things. Today, not only is it used to refer to *theory* grounded in qualitative data, but also to describe Glaser and Strauss' methodology for the systematic analysis of unstructured qualitative data. The latter includes a range of qualitative data handling techniques, some of which we outline in the following section. This means that we can speak of the *method* of grounded theory in its own right. To further complicate matters the claim that a piece of research is *well-grounded* occurs frequently within qualitative social science, often as a rhetorical statement to signify the "goodness" of a piece of work.

The approach of grounded theory is clearly qualitative in relation to Bryman's technical numeric/non-numeric distinction. It also resonates with many of the features (outlined previously) of qualitative research as a distinctive research paradigm; in its commitment to local contextual theory, exploration of meanings in their full complexity and context, and a concern with reflecting participants' constructions of the world. However the approach as originally conceived (and in certain subsequent explications of the method such as by Strauss and Corbin, 1990) rests squarely upon a positivist epistemology. This is most obviously seen when Glaser and Strauss talk of the way in which theory is *discovered from* data (essentially assuming an unproblematic Observation→Theory relationship, as illustrated by 1a in Fig. 12.1). That is, they imply that a set of social or psychological relationships exist objectively in the world, are reflected in qualitative data, and are therefore there to be "captured" by any researcher who chances to pass by! Essentially, as originally described, this approach appears to rely upon classical induction—that is, the derivation, or discovery, of general principles from a set of observations.

The idea of discovery (and with it induction) has traditionally been held to play a central role in science since its inception, but we should not take a naïve view of it or of its role in inquiry. Consider the problem of understanding a foreign language which we have not learned previously. As a first language speaker of English, one can use what one knows to discover some sense in most other European languages. This of course is due to the historical independencies, and therefore shared concepts, between such language traditions. However, initially no sense at all can be made of less connected languages such as Chinese.

A similar situation exists when conducting research. We are inevitably faced with the problem of making sense of and organising our data. For this the researcher needs at least *some* theoretical resources to begin the process of interpretation and representation (Riessman, 1993). Such resources may come from formal theories, a related group of concepts, or a basic set of linguistic descriptors. They could also be more explicit: coming from a researcher's substantive interests which guide the questions asked; a philosophical stance or school of thought which provides a store of sensitizing concepts; and from one's own personal experiences, priorities and values (see Charmaz, 1990). Without the orientation provided by such frameworks no sense at all can be made of a data corpus (whether qualitative or quantitative). Accordingly, Glaser and Strauss themselves note that "the researcher does not approach reality as a tabula rasa" (or *blank sheet*; 1967, p. 3). If legitimate data are necessarily defined through theory, then this in turn raises the important question of what grounds grounded theory?

The resolution of this conundrum is to recognise that it makes no sense to claim that research can proceed *either* from testing theory alone, *or* from a pure, inductive analysis of data. Indeed, in our view, doing qualitative research brings this issue squarely to the fore. With grounded theory in particular, what appears to be "discovery" or "emergence" of theory is really the result of a constant interplay between data and the researcher's developing conceptualisations, a "flip flop" between ideas and research experience. For this reason, we prefer the notion of theory *generation* to describe the key aspects both of the social practice of science, as well as our own use of the grounded theory technique. The idea of theory generation highlights the "flip flop", the active and constitutive analytic process of inserting new discourses within old systems of meaning. This may be called a 'constructivist' revision of grounded theory (Charmaz, 1990).

This being the case, the value of the grounded theory approach is that it suggests a set of procedures which facilitate the operation of subjectivity (and in particular the researcher's interpretation and creativity) in the process of qualitative data analysis. It is important to recognise here that these should not be understood as standard procedures or rules for guaranteeing truth. Rather they are ways of putting into practice the requirement to actively engage in close and detailed analysis of your research materials, so that they can both stimulate and discipline the theoretical imagination (Henwood and Pidgeon, 1992). As we will see, a particularly important part of grounded theory is the requirement to fully document the analytic process. This not only serves as a trace, but also as a prompt to further analysis—an important part of which is to force the tacit, implicit or subliminal to the surface of awareness (Turner, 1981).

This process is not an easy one and it is therefore helpful to think of grounded theory strategies as ways into the maze of fractured and multi-seamed reality, which is infused with multiple and often conflicting interpretations and meanings. Grounded theory is less helpful on ways out of this maze (Pidgeon, Turner and Blockley, 1991), which rely upon the research-er's commitment to generating a focused understanding of the research problem and an (ultimately) coherent account addressing it. In our view the message from doing grounded theory work is that breaking out of prior conceptualisations should leave neither theory, data or the researcher unchanged.

DOING QUALITATIVE RESEARCH USING A GROUNDED APPROACH

One reason why grounded theory is useful for psychologists starting out in qualitative work is that it provides techniques (and fosters a range of explicit skills) to aid in qualitative data analysis, and in particular the generation of theory. This statement conveys more than the idea of using open-ended pilot studies merely to prepare the ground for subsequent quantitative research (a useful, if restricted, role that qualitative methods have played in the past in psychology). Rather, qualitative methodology can be seen as playing a central role in the quest for psychological knowledge, and can be reported on in its own right (see also Rennie, Phillips and Quartaro, 1988).

In approaching research, very often without strong or specific hypotheses to be tested, qualitative researchers are faced with the problem of dealing with large amounts of unstructured data. In their account of grounded theory, Glaser and Strauss advocate that researchers begin by building an array of concepts and categories from systematic inspection of the data corpus. Typically, this involves the development of an open-ended indexing system, where the researcher works systematically through the basic data transcripts, generating labels to describe both low-level features and more abstract concepts deemed relevant. This may be characterised as a means of moving towards a data description language.

The exercise of generating grounded theory is, in this respect, very dif-ferent from traditional content analysis (as described for example by Weber, 1985) where the researcher's task is to allocate instances to a set of *pre-defined*, mutually exclusive and exhaustive categories. In the early phases of grounded work the researcher must adopt a stance of maximum flexibility in generating new categories from the data. This is a creative process which taxes fully the interpretative powers of the researcher, who is nevertheless disciplined by the requirement that the categories generated should, in Glaser and Strauss' terms, *fit* (provide a recognisable description of) the data. Success in generating good grounded theory, which is well-grounded in data, depends upon maintaining a balance between full use of the researcher's own subjective understandings and this requirement of fit. In this section we develop the discussion with reference to specific strategies that we have used for grounded theory work.

The core steps in conducting any grounded theory with qualitative data are illustrated in Fig. 12.2. The aim here is to move from a set of unstructured materials, to a collection of theoretical codes, concepts and interpretations. The examples we shall give to illustrate the steps are drawn from two of our

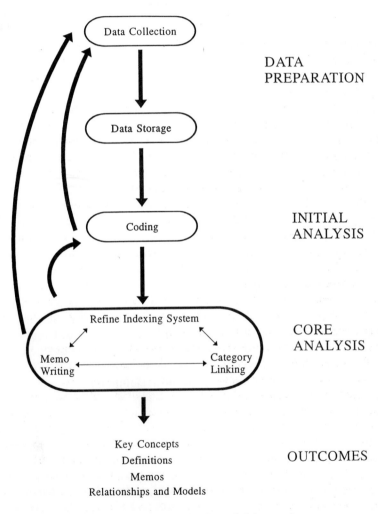

FIG. 12.2   Steps in the Grounded Approach.

own, rather different, studies—of engineering decision making (Pidgeon, Blockley & Turner, 1988) and of women's understandings and accounts of relationships between mothers and their adult daughters (Henwood, 1993). In each case the material to be analysed was obtained from tape-recorded interviews with participants. However, the strategies are equally suited for handling qualitative material obtained from fieldwork notes or other sources.

The discussion will handle the stages illustrated in Fig. 12.2. as if they are discrete steps, but it is important to stress that analysis proceeds from data to outcomes in only a loosely linear fashion. Grounded theory is an iterative process, and the researcher will often move between earlier and later steps as the analysis proceeds. For example, unlike in many accounts of social science methodology, which imply that data collection and analysis are separate phases, Glaser and Strauss emphasise the importance of combining the two. In particular, one can use early analyses to prompt further data collection; perhaps from new sources suggested by the analysis (known as *theoretical sampling*), or by returning to original participants to explore further aspects of the emerging interpretations. This iterative process is one facet of the flip-flop discussed earlier.

DATA PREPARATION

Collection

The gathering of interview data holds its own pitfalls for the unwary. Basic problems include: the failure to establish rapport with participants; inadvertently dominating sessions; asking "leading" questions; and becoming constrained by pre-formulated questions rather than adopting a more open-ended conversational style. A number of methodological texts in social science provide guidance on strategies to be adopted here (e.g. Burgess, 1984; Robson, 1993), with some including timely comparisons of different models of interviewing (Banister et al., 1994). The aim with initial data gathering is to generate a rich set of materials, although subsequent data collection may be more focused (using, for example, theoretical sampling).

The Permanent Record

The corpus of data must subsequently be assembled in some form of permanent record that allows ready access during analysis. Assuming that it has been desirable and possible to make tape-recordings, some researchers prefer to treat these as their record, and analyse directly from them. Others transcribe the data from interviews and protocols. Transcription from tape is highly labour intensive. As a rule of thumb, it takes some eight to ten hours to transcribe a one hour interview tape, depending upon the level of detail required (for example just content of speech, or this plus significant paralinguistic features). Another strategy is to transcribe only those aspects of the tape which feed into the developing analysis.

A useful next step in handling each discrete data set, say that from a single interview session, is to provide it with a label (for example date, interviewee and topic). The second is to allocate a numerical reference to segments of the text. Typically, this involves numbering pages, paragraphs or lines in the transcription. Table 12.1 (Part A) shows an example of how data is transcribed in this way, and is from an interview with an architect. He had been involved, with other members of a design team, in failing to

TABLE 12.1
Examples of Data and Coded Concepts (Engineering Project)

A. Paragraphs from an interview relating to Hazardous Waste case-study

Interview S, 27 April

Paragraph 8
I don't think there is any doubt that on this job I readily accepted the advice of the civil engineering consultant, L, and didn't have the experience to question that advice adequately. I was not aware of the appropriate site investigation procedure, and was more than willing to be seduced by the idea that we could cut corners to save time and money.

Paragraph 9
But L's motives were entirely honourable in this respect. He had done a bit of prior work on a site nearby. And his whole approach was based upon the expectation that there would be fairly massive gravel beds lying over the clay valley bottom, and the fundamental question in that area was to establish what depth of piling was required for the factory foundations. He was assuming all along that piling was the problem. And he was not (and he knew he was not) experienced in looking for trouble for roads. His experience said that we merely needed a flight auger test to establish the pile depths.

Source: Architect S, a member of the design team involved in the incident, describing the decision of the civil engineering consultant, L, restricting the scope of the initial site investigation to the question of the need for piled foundations for warehouse units.

B. Significant concepts identified within paragraphs

Paragraph 8
ACCEPTING PROFESSIONAL ADVICE
CRITICISING OTHER'S WORK
CUTTING CORNERS
EXPERIENCE

Paragraph 9
KNOWLEDGE OF LOCAL CONDITIONS
SELECTIVE PROBLEM REPRESENTATION OBSCURES WIDER VIEW
EXPERIENCE

predict the presence of hazardous chemical waste on an old industrial site that was being developed. The focus of the research had been the individual and organisational reasons behind the failure.

Initial Analysis: Coding

Having collected, transcribed (where appropriate) and labelled a sufficient quantity of material, the next task is to begin to build an indexing system for the data. The indexing system will subsequently allow the researcher to re-order the data collected, as interpretations of the material develop. A rule of thumb is that this initial indexing, referred to as coding, should proceed as soon as possible after data collection has commenced. One practical implication of this is that the researcher should plan interviews or other data collection allowing sufficient time between sessions for transcription and analysis.

Coding proceeds by means of the tentative development and labelling of concepts from the text, which the researcher considers to be of potential relevance to the problem being studied. That this process is not a simple one—and, as we have argued, involves a constitutive relationship between researcher and text—is clear from the fact that judgement is always asso-ciated with this labelling process. The facets of the data coded will vary depending upon how the aims of the study have been presented to partici-pants, the subsequent accounts offered by participants, as well as the interpretations of the investigator.

Seminar training and group discussions are particularly beneficial here for beginners to help to resolve questions of the most appropriate level of coding for a particular research question (see Turner, 1981; Strauss, 1987). The aim is to arrive at a form of labelling which will identify important aspects of the data corpus, as a first step towards characterising these in the degree of detail necessary for a clear understanding.

Grounded theory is most typically well-suited to the analysis of the broad "themes" and content of participants' accounts. Other approaches, which are premised on a theoretical understanding of the way language works (such as discourse or conversation analysis) are better able to orient the researcher to attend to *how* utterances are presented rather than solely *what* the content of an utterance is. However, a grounded theory orientation may still be useful for researchers with a background in discourse theory if their research focus has some interest int he more thematic aspects of a text. So it can be useful if a researcher is interested in language function but also wishes to engage in further, substantive, theory building (see Henwood & Pidgeon, 1994, also Billig, this volume).

The method used in the engineering project to construct an indexing system was to start with the first paragraph of the transcript or notes, asking

"What categories, concepts or labels do we need in order to account for what is of importance to use in this paragraph?". When we think of a label, this is recorded as the header on a 5″ by 8″ file card (although it is now quite possible to use computers for such indexing; see Fielding and Lee, 1991; Weitzman and Miles, 1995). A short précis of the precise instance in the paragraph, together with a reference to the specific transcript and paragraph (or line number) is noted on the card, which is then filed away in a central record box. The initial entry serves as the first *indicator* for the concept described by the card header. The process of coding then continues by checking whether further potentially significant aspects of the paragraph suggest new concept cards. This is then repeated with subsequent paragraphs.

The labels used in categorisation may be long-winded, ungainly or fanciful at this stage, but they may be formulated at any conceptual level which seems appropriate. What is crucial is that they should, to use Glaser and Strauss' term, *fit* the data well, so that the terms chosen provide a recognisable *description* of the item, activity or discourse under consideration. In our terms "flip-flop" requires a process of changing, re-changing and adjustment of the terms used until fit is improved. The value of the whole approach depends upon the search for goodness of fit as the stimulus to (but also discipline on) interpretation and understanding of participants' discourse.

As coding proceeds not only will the list of concepts (and hence file of cards) rapidly expand, but also concepts will begin to recur in subsequent paragraphs or transcripts. Table 12.1 (Part B) lists the concepts coded from the two paragraphs in Part A. Note that the concept *experience* occurs in both paragraph 8 and 9. It is important, for the purposes of subsequent analysis, to recognise that the aim here is not to record *all* of the instances of the recurrence of "experience". In this respect the grounded approach is again distinct from classical protocol (Ericsson & Simon, 1993) or content analysis (Weber, 1985) where the aim is primarily a counting exercise, recording how often a *pre-defined* concept is observed in the data set. Rather, the aim with grounded theory is to seek out *diversity*, collecting on each 5″ × 8″ card a set of *different* indicators pointing to the multiple and qualitative facets of a potentially significant concept.

Hence, experience in Paragraph 8 of Table 12.1 was suggested by the architect's belief that this is related to the ability to evaluate expert advice received.In contrast, in Paragraph 9 it refers to the level of local knowledge held (in this case regarding geological conditions). Taking both together allows a wider view of what the architect means when he talks of "experience". And in this way categories emerge as a product of both the researcher's interpretation and variation across the data corpus. A key orienting theme in all of this is the method of *constant comparative analysis*. Here the researcher is urged to be constantly alert to the similarities and differences which exist between instances, cases and concepts, to ensure that the full diversity and complexity of the data is explored.

The success of the initial coding will depend in part upon choosing an appropriate level of abstraction for the concepts used. The use of highly particular terms (e.g. *Cutting Corners*) will tie the analysis to the specific cases mentioned in the data, whereas if the concepts can be referred to in broader terms (e.g. *Selective Problem Representation Obscures Wider View*), it will be easier to move to a more general level of analysis. It is worth noting that some cards will eventually contain few instances. Non-recurrence does not necessarily mean that a concept is unimportant, but it does provide the researcher with one means of sifting for potentially irrelevant material.

Fig. 12.3 illustrates the file card for the concept *Selective Problem Representation Obscures Wider View*, showing a number of the entries made. The notion of a selective problem representation was an important one for this study, and emerged in a number of guises which the five entries illustrate. Once again, this highlights the importance of coding qualitative variety for a concept, in order to explore multiple facets. As well as card number, concept title, and entries with references to the transcribed data, it is useful to include potential links with other concepts on the card. In this case, a link with Card 19, *Perception of Simplicity/Complexity of Task*, is suggested by the researcher's hypothesis that a problem representation would need to be appropriately matched to task complexity. At an early stage of coding such links are likely to be highly tentative. However, they provide an important resource for later analysis, particularly if specifying relationships between significant concepts becomes necessary.

Core Analysis

The process of coding can be interrupted at any time by the collection of more data. However, as the number of cards increases, some with many entries on, some with few, the analysis shifts to other operations. For the indexing to be of any use, the coded concepts must be refined, extended and related to each other as further material is explored. Glaser and Strauss suggest that activities such as *refining the indexing system, memo writing*, and *category integration* (see Fig. 12.2) can provide useful resources for taking the analytic process forward.

In the case of the adult mother–daughter relationships study, initial coding of approximately 60 (1 to 1.5 hour) interviews with mothers (aged 50 to 80+), and daughters (aged between 18 and 49) about relationships with their own mothers and/or daughters led to the development of a long and varied, but highly unwieldy list of instances under the initial label *Relational Closeness*.[2] Analysis therefore proceeded by refining this core category, initially by means of a simple splitting into two cards roughly along the lines

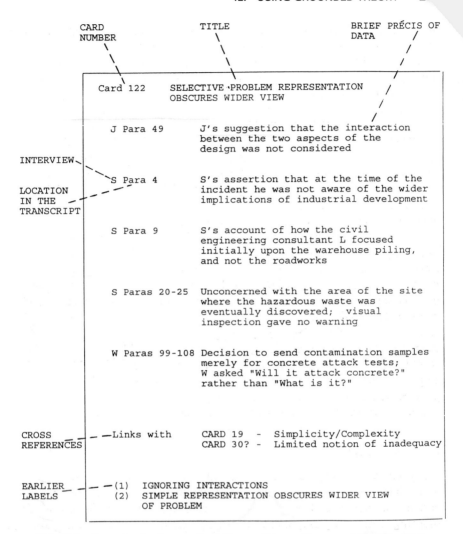

FIG. 12.3.   Example of a Concept Card (Source: Pidgeon, Turner and Blockley, 1988).

of positive and negative evaluative themes. The majority of attributes first coded on the original card were glossed as attaching global value to the relationship: e.g. feelings of fondness and affection; ability to confide about personal matters; feeling comfortable/lacking self-consciousness in one another's company. Subsequently coded features indicated a more mixed view of the emotional intensity of the relationship, ranging from a welcome but painful sense of gratitude and debt, to a state of hypersensitivity (where for example a mother's remarks could "pierce into" her daughter), and to a e from a relationship which involved confinement or smothering. s, the inextricable link between the two cards resulting from the ___ ᴅᴵⱽᴵꜱᴵᴼᴺ was retained, and coded through their respective labels *closeness* and *overcloseness*. This link then became a key stimulus for, and focus of, conceptual integration and theoretical development and reflection, mediated by the writing of analytic memos. An example of a memo, concerning the splitting of the concept of closeness is presented in Table 12.2.

Operations such as sub-dividing categories, or perhaps converting two cards into one, are likely to happen repeatedly, especially at the early stages of analysis, accompanied by re-labelling. One's record of previous labels used for a concept can therefore be useful for keeping track of the progression of conceptual analysis. Referring to the example file card shown in Fig. 12.3, the first entry shown on the card had suggested the label *Ignoring Interactions*

TABLE 12.2
Example Memo (Mother–daughter Project)

Memorandum: On Splitting of Relational Closeness
(July 1992 by Karen Henwood)

Splitting of this category (Relational Closeness) became necessary initially in order to make it more manageable. The splitting also provides a fruitful starting point for reflecting upon the relationship between certain categories: (1) closeness and the "gender marking" of the mother–daughter bond; and (2) closeness/overcloseness and representations of the good/bad mother. Not uncommonly, ascriptions of valued mother–daughter closeness are also associated with the assumption that women share a special feminine gender identity, including among other attributes those of selfless cooperation, and nurturance and empathy (see e.g. interview with RM, 21 August 91, p26 lines 401–435). In identifying the special qualities in mother–daughter relationships which follow from the presumed sharing of a feminine identity and gender roles, the women interviewed in this study may be pointing to a view of mother–daughter relationships as uniquely, and perhaps even universally, close. This has been a key element in social science thinking for many years (Young and Wilmott, 1957).

However, the emergence of the other side of the coin—overcloseness—suggests that such closeness may be an idealised view of mother–daughter relationships which is complicit with cultural definitions of femininity; tentatively therefore we could say that it is part of a wider "femininity discourse". My reasoning here is derived from research on cultural representations of motherhood, which suggest that dichotomous images of the "good and bad" mother simultaneously idealise and devalue women. This was first brought to mind by use in some of the interviews (with CN and DP) of powerful metaphors of demon-like mothers who clutch onto their children or keep them on an apron string. These are coded on both "overcloseness" and the "good/bad mother" cards.

Following the lines of such reasoning the source of at least one interviewee's (VV) sadness and hurt in her relationship with her daughter could only be understood by inferring that the daughter has contravened some extra-locally organised standard of conduct for adult daughters, which obliges them to be closely involved with their mothers over matters such as the care of the daughter's children.

(shown at the bottom). As further entries were added a more general label was deemed appropriate, *Simple Representation Obscures Wider View of Problem*. finally, this was refined to the working title at the head of the card.

There comes a time when the recollection and coding of additional data no longer contributes further, significantly varied, entries on a card. At this point a category is said to become *saturated*, to use Glaser & Strauss' (1967) term. The task for the researcher is then to try to make the analysis more explicit by summarising why all of these entries have been included under this label. One way of doing this is to write a definition for the concept, to state explicitly the qualities which have already been recognised in some implicit manner when a new entry has been classified into the category concerned (Turner, 1981). This is a demanding task, but can nevertheless be crucial to the analysis. It can lead to the development of a deeper and more precise understanding of the nature of the category and the analyst's interpretations of it. Table 12.3 illustrates a provisional definition, produced on the engineering project, for the concept *Selective Problem Representation Obscures Wider View*.

Later stages of analysis are also likely to involve attempts to *integrate the emerging categories* by creating links between them. As well as exploring the links suggested in the course of coding and memo-writing, it is often of use to sort and group sets of related concepts. This may involve drawing up diagrammatic representations (see e.g. Miles and Huberman, 1994) to illustrate salient links.

Outcomes

Although each analysis will be different (in part depending upon the goals of the project—see below) the outcomes of the process of analysis are likely to include: fully saturated core concepts (together with definitions); theoretical memos; propositions linking categories and providing central relationships;

TABLE 12.3
Provisional Definition (Engineering Project)

Provisional definition produced for concept card 122:
Selective Problem Representation Obscures Wider View.

A problem arises in structural engineering when uncertainty exists over the appropriate action(s) required to meet the engineer's goal or goals. In order to solve any problem an individual must first construct an appropriate problem representation. A complete problem representation includes the goal(s), elements modelling features of the environment, a set of relationships between the features, and possibly a set of potential solutions. A selective representation occurs when the total set of components included does not contain all of those necessary to solve the problem. As a consequence, however hard the individual tries to solve the problem, this will not be achieved without a restructuring of the problem that adds the missing (necessary) components.

and possibly diagrammatic models describing the ways in which certain concepts relate to one another. A particular strength of utilising the strategies outlined above is that a documented record of the progress of the analysis is generated. Hence, it will always be possible to trace the derivation of any interpretation by checking back through the cards, memos and definitions. Such detailed documentation, as we discuss later, can be an important resource for checking the trustworthiness of the analysis.

REFLECTIONS: OBJECTIVES AND EVALUATION

Possible Goals of Grounded Theory Work

One reading of the proposals and strategies suggested in the previous section is that the goal of qualitative analysis is always one of building complex and comprehensive theoretical systems from a suitably large corpus of data, much of which was sampled (theoretically) as the analysis progressed. This goal may be quite feasible for large-scale projects, where resources are available for both comprehensive data gathering and analysis. However, qualitative research is always highly labour intensive (and hence not for the faint hearted), and therefore for many projects there will always be the risk of the individual researcher becoming over-extended if such an ambitious goal is attempted. We feel that this is an important issue to raise for researchers starting out on qualitative research for the first time, and particularly at undergraduate or postgraduate level, where time and resources present particular constraints. The typical project goal in these latter cases will need to be both well-focused, and capable of resolution and write-up in a relatively short time-frame. We believe that it is therefore useful to specify a range of research goals which might be achieved through grounded theory work, and these are discussed under the three headings of taxonomy development, local theoretical reflection, and "fully-fledged" grounded theory.

Taxonomy Development

One basic practical outcome of the initial indexing operations of coding, saturation (where possible) and category definition will be a taxonomy of the concepts identified from the data corpus, together with some indication of their relative importance to the research question under study. Taxonomy development is likely to be particularly suitable for an undergraduate-level project, where often only a small corpus of interview or other textual data can be collected (and where the chances for theoretical sampling are limited). The basic taxonomy, as a research goal in its own right, might also be coupled with some initial reflection upon how key concepts might be related (e.g. by clustering related concepts). It is also worthwhile noting that the production of a taxonomy is a useful first goal in larger projects, as a means of communicating how the initial analysis is progressing (perhaps to a colleague or supervisor). Furthermore, snapshots of the way in which the taxonomy changes with time provide a permanent "trace" of the otherwise dynamic *process* of the analysis.

Local Theoretical Reflection (and Stimulating Creativity)

Of course, the aim of all grounded work is theory development through the reflective use of specific data-handling strategies *and* the researcher's creative interpretive skills. However, such an ideal does not resolve the very real problem of defining a theoretical focus when faced with a large body of ill-structured data, possibly drawn from multiple participant perspectives, and for which very many possible lines of interpretation are available. Therefore, at an intermediate stage of analysis (that is, following initial coding) several paths can be followed in order to focus and localise theoretical reflection.

One of these is to stimulate *conceptual development* with only a limited sub-set of related categories. Such development would focus upon questions of fit (through reflection upon category definitions), the depth of interpretation (i.e. the level of abstraction of the categories), as well as possible first relationships between categories. A second path would be to concentrate upon particular *cycles of interpretation* in the analysis. For example, by taking one or two core categories, using their definitions to suggest new interpretations and samples of data needed to explore those implications.

A third path for subsequent analysis is to focus upon *specific cases*, such as the data from a single participant, or alternatively a few contrastive interviews. Here the value of a constructivist view of grounded theory is that we should not expect participants' accounts to be internally consistent, and that comparative analysis *within* an account should focus upon possible fragmentary and contradictory aspects. In this respect the constructivist version of grounded theory shares some common ground with the approach of discourse analysis. Focusing upon individual cases in depth is also useful for the ultimate write-up of a study, where such cases might be presented as exemplars of the wider themes emerging from the analysis.

A fourth and final path for local reflection would be to attempt *theoretical comparison* between the emerging analysis and existing theoretical accounts of the problem domain (where these are available). Although this might at first seem incompatible with the philosophy of the grounded approach, there is no reason why the researcher should not engage in such reflection (and most writers explicitly encourage this). Indeed such theoretical comparison is often vital during the later stages of analysis, not only to enrich the analysis, but also to provide the researcher with at least some distance from the research material. Questions that might be posed as part

of this process would be: do the key concepts of the existi
current data; do the supposed existing relationships hold
present in the current set of concepts but missing in
Resolving such questions would provide satisfactory ou
focused (e.g. postgraduate) projects, as well as conclusio
presented within the standard journal report format.

"Fully-fledged" Grounded Theory

It is, of course, a matter of some debate as to what precisely constitutes a "fully-fledged" theory. This is especially so within the psychological and social sciences, where the terms model, conceptual framework and theory are so often used interchangeably. At one level a constructivist reading cautions us against seeking the final one, true and valid account. All readings of data must consequently be regarded as tentative and mutable, rather than in any sense closed. On the other hand, there will clearly be readings, by virtue of their scope, which go beyond mere taxonomy development or local theoretical reflection—perhaps because they combine several of these aspects, or are based upon samples that can in some sense be justified as theoretically complete.

Unfortunately, many of the writings on grounded theory are less than helpful in this respect, and it is perhaps a flaw of the method that the critical step between generating individual components and the generation of full theory systems remains relatively unexplained. In rather more abstract terms, Cathy Charmaz defines a theory as something which "explicates phenomena, specifies concepts which categorise the relevant phenomena, explains relationships between the concepts, and provides a framework for making predictions" (1990, p. 1164). We would also add that good grounded theory should be clear in indicating what it does not cover.

Criteria for Evaluating Grounded Theory Projects

Traditional discussions of criteria for judging psychological research are generally limited to questions about specific aspects of methodology, such as reliability (that is, replicability) and validity (correspondence between descriptors and what is intended to be described); and characteristics of theory including parsimony, empirical content, internal consistency, and generality. In our view, however, merely applying the above to evaluate grounded qualitative research risks undermining the very benefits that the approach brings. We would argue for the need for radically different means of evaluating such research in its own (rather than in positivisms') terms. The classical criteria rest on the norm of objectivity which assumes the independence of the knower and the known. As we have argued earlier, the constructivist view challenges the dualistic distinction between knower and known, leading to the realisation that personal and social forms of subjectivity are always present in research. Therefore criteria for judging the quality of grounded qualitative research must explicitly recognise this in the search for theory that is relevant and good.

On this view, it follows that there are no methodological criteria for guaranteeing the *absolute* accuracy of research (whether quantitative or qualitative). Notwithstanding this, a number of good practices have been suggested by qualitative researchers which can be used to guide both the progress of a study and its ultimate evaluation by researchers and their peers. We have chosen to focus upon practices that illustrate the rigour of qualitative research, thus challenging the traditional dichotomy between "hard" quantitative and "soft" qualitative research. On the other hand, and to use Catherine Marshall's phrase (1985), they do not overly "sanitise" the research process, and for this reason do not stifle the researcher's theoretical imagination.

Keeping Close to the Data: The Importance of Fit

A basic requirement of grounded theory work is that the categories constituting the building blocks of emergent theory should fit the data well, and that one way of working towards this is to write comprehensive definitions of key concepts summarising why phenomena have been labelled in a certain way. This exercise produces a public product which makes explicit the initially tacit conceptual classifications construed by the individual researcher, and allows both researcher and peers to evaluate fit.

Theory Integrated at Diverse Levels of Abstraction

Many qualitative researchers are seeking for theory that is rich, complex and dense, and integrated at diverse levels of generality. The analyst's memos are a key resource here, for explicating the synthesized structure of the emergent theory. Glaser and Strauss argue that "the synthesis provides readily apparent connections between data and lower and higher level conceptual abstractions of categories and properties" (1967, p. 37). The goal here is to ensure that the theory at all levels of abstraction is meaningfully related, providing a "thick" description (Geertz, 1973) of the problem domain.

Reflexivity

The constructivist view of research acknowledges the ways in which research activity inevitably shapes and constitutes the object of inquiry; the researcher and researched are characterised as interdependent in the social process of research. This is sometimes termed the reflexive character of research. The term reflexivity is, of course, a complex one and has, over the years, acquired many and varied usages. However, one practical implication of accepting the inevitable role of the researcher in the research process is that this should be highlighted and revealed in the documentation of qualitative studies. For example, the feminist researcher Shulamit Reinharz contrasts the conventional approach to conducting and reporting science, where researchers' attitudes are not revealed, recognised or analysed (in the attempt to be "objective" and "value free"), with the alternative or feminist view that researchers' attitudes should be fully described and discussed and their values "acknowledged, revealed and labelled" (1983, p. 172).

In a similar vein, Yvonna Lincoln & Egon Guba (1985) advise the keeping of a "reflexive journal". They suggest that such a journal should include the daily schedule and logistics of the study, a personal diary where reflections are noted on the role of one's own values and interests, and a log of methodological decisions and accompanying rationales. The keeping of a reflexive journal is but one facet of the important process of building up documentation in qualitative research. It can be argued here that reflexivity, in the sense of bringing to public light researcher subjectivities, tells a more complete account of the research process than is to be found in the customary sanitised versions of scientific report-writing, and is a move therefore towards "strong objectivity" (see Harding, 1991).

Documentation

For grounded theory and many other qualitative projects, it is useful to provide an account of what is done, and why it is done, at each phase in the research process. As well as reflecting upon values and assumptions, and writing memos and definitions for categories, researchers can also document such things as initial concerns and how these may change, sampling decisions, hunches about the quality of the data gathered, and observations about the context of data generation. In building up such a set of documents the researcher is laying a "paper-trail", open to external audit (Lincoln & Guba, 1985, Chapter 13) by immediate colleagues and more distant peers. The exercise provides a means of tracking the progress of (and stimulating) creative thought, and acts as a useful vehicle for increasing researcher reflexivity.

Theoretical Sampling and Negative Case Analysis

We have noted that sampling is an important consideration in qualitative research, and that this is often explicitly driven by theoretical concerns. A link can be made here with the practice of so-called "negative case analysis" (Kidder, 1981; Smith, this volume). This parallels the well-known strategy in science of ingeniously seeking wherever possible to falsify working hypotheses derived from an emergent model (see Magee, 1973). As analysis of initial cases proceeds, further cases would be selected for this disconfirming potential. Exploring cases which do not fit an emerging conceptual system can be invaluable because this serves as a device both for challenging initial assumptions and categories (hence guarding against premature closure of theorising), and for modifying and elaborating theory where necessary.

Sensitivity to Participant Realities (Respondent Validation)

One frequently cited, but hotly contested, approach to validating theory in qualitative studies is the suggestion that, as a consequence of good fit, the derived account should be readily recognisable to participants in the study who have provided data. Whilst there is a good case for this under some circumstances, there are also many reasons to be cautious of taking respondents' accounts wholly at face value; for example, people may not always be fully aware of reasons for their actions, and accounts may be offered to perform a variety of non-obvious and context-specific functions (e.g. allocating blame to others, warranting particular claims to truth) which go beyond the mere provision of information. Beyond this, there will be occasions where the researcher cannot accept the stricture to interpret participants' reality fully in their own terms.

Transferability

The question of the extent to which findings from a particular study can be said to have more general significance is an important one. In qualitative research, where sampling decisions have not been made on statistical grounds, one suggestion is that researchers talk in terms of the transferability, rather than generalisability, of findings (Lincoln & Guba, 1985). Most narrowly, this term refers to applying the findings of a study in contexts similar to the context in which they were first derived. This places a special onus on the qualitative researcher to report fully on the contextual features of a study, and is one reason why detailed reporting of case-studies is important. However, it is also necessary to guard against naïve empiricism here, and also not to treat context as just an adjunct to theory. In our view, rich and dense grounded theory, which is contextually sensitive to diverse levels of abstraction, will in itself suggest its own sphere of relevance and application.

Persuasiveness

If we are no longer able to rely upon correspondence with the empirical world as the ultimate arbiter of truth, a more pragmatic argument can be made that the outcome of research will tend to be evaluated in terms of their persuasiveness and power to inspire an audience. Following some of the considerations listed above should help to increase the persuasiveness of findings of qualitative research. Theory that is represented at diverse levels of abstraction, but which nevertheless fits the data well, should be challenging, stimulating, and yet highly plausible in the sense of clearly reflecting substantive aspects of the problem domain.

As a final comment, it is clear that the precise criteria to be applied for establishing the trustworthiness of a particular qualitative research project must be applied flexibly. In particular, the criteria adopted must reflect the goals of the project being addressed. With this in mind Table 12.4 illustrates one view of how the criteria above might be applied to the separate goals of grounded theory work discussed in the preceding section. For example, looking at Table 12.4, some criteria (documentation, fit and reflexivity) apply equally to the evaluation process for all goals, while others are particularly relevant to more specific goals. On the other hand for a project that aims for a full-fledged grounded theory, one might want to apply most or all of the criteria.

TABLE 12.4
Criteria of Evaluation for Specific Goals

All goals	*Relevant Criteria*
A) All goals	Documentation Reflexivity Fit
B) Taxonomy Development	(Documentation/Reflexivity) but above all Fit
C) Local theoretical development (Documentation/reflexivity/fit)	
	plus
— Conceptual development — Cycles of interpretation — Specific cases — Theoretical comparisons	Theory at diverse levels Sampling and Negative case analysis Respondent validation Transferability
D) Fully-fledged grounded theory (Documentation/reflexivity/fit)	
	plus
	Transferability Theory at diverse levels Sampling Negative case analysis plus (where appropriate) Respondent validation

CONCLUSION

In writing this chapter, we have had two main concerns. The first is to provide a broad and integrative account, linking the project of qualitative work to issues in scientific epistemology and to the history of discussions of quantity and quality in the human sciences. The second has been to focus on the particular approach of grounded theory, in order to make it more readily usable by psychologists at various stages of their research careers. In choosing to consider grounded theory work in detail, we do not wish to imply that it has a greater validity or that it necessarily has a wider applicability than other qualitative approaches and methods. However, it has considerable appeal, for many reasons, and is being used increasingly in growing areas of psychology (e.g. health psychology). Hence, it is both timely and necessary to flag up the pitfalls as well as the promises of the approach.

In many traditional psychology texts, method is often discussed in a vacuum, as if it is in some way separated from other issues. One overarching lesson to be drawn from debates about qualitative research is that researchers need to consider questions of epistemology, goals of research, and *appropriate* assessment criteria in order to make sensible methodological choices. Taking into account all of these could be seen as a daunting task. This, however, is not the only view which can be taken. Rather, we could see it as enabling psychologists to develop an informed and critical perspective on the research that they do. This is necessary if we are to guard against excessive insularity, and if we wish to be more open, trustworthy, and accountable to those communities which ultimately bear the consequences of our scientific work.

NOTES

1. From the point of view of research ethics, research within the qualitative paradigm is often said to have a special advantage in that participants are regarded as playing a more active, and a more completely self-expressive role in the research process. This advantage is not absolute or always present, however, since the researcher is ultimately responsible for presenting the outcomes of her research and in this respect is in a position of greater power over research participants. Also, although a participant's views are accepted as valid in their own terms, interpretation of their wider significance will often depend on an analysis of the researcher/researched relationship and relevant socio-political contexts.
2. The permanent record of interviews in this study took the form of more detailed transcription using conventions derived from discourse analysis. This form of representation carries with it dual possibilities for understanding language as representation or action in use. This in turn can play a role in framing analysis.

Final note

As the reader will have seen, this book spans a range of qualitative research methods, and, we hope, covers them in a way which will help psychology students—and other researchers—to understand how they have been derived, and how they can be applied in new research projects. The step-by-step guides produced by the authors will, we hope, be some help in this: at least in so far as giving the would-be qualitative researcher a way of getting started. For all of us, though, conducting qualitative research is a voyage of discovery, rather than a pre-set analytical process.

The value of qualitative research in enriching psychological knowledge is increasingly recognised. What may be less well recognised is the diversity of forms of qualitative research, and the range of choices available to the student or researcher wishing to use qualitative methods. We have tried here to make some of those choices and options apparent to the reader. Our chapters reflect a range of approaches to qualitative research, and in writing them, we hope we have managed to convey some of its richness and complexity. Above all, we hope that a student or researcher will carry away with them an awareness that qualitative research can be just as valuable, and no less rigorous, than quantitative treatments of psychological data. There is room in the psychologist's methodological pantheon for both quantitative and qualitative analysis, and more than enough scope for both.

Nicky Hayes (Editor)

REFERENCES

Abrams, D. & Hogg, M.A. (Eds.), (1990). *Social identity theory: Constructive critical advances.* Hemel Hempstead: Harvester Wheatsheaf.

Abramson, L.Y., Garber, J., & Seligman, M.E.P. (1980). Learned helplessness in humans: an attributional analysis. In J. Garber & M.E.P. Seligman (Eds.), *Human helplessness: Theory and applications.* New York: Academic Press.

Alexander, C. & Becker, H. (1978). The use of vignettes in survey research. *Public Opinion Quarterly, 42*, 93–104.

Allaire, Y. & Firsirotu, M.E. (1984). Theories of organisational culture. *Organisational Studies, 5(3)*, 193–226.

Allport, G.W. (1962). The general and the unique in psychological science. *Journal of Personality, 30*, 405–422.

Anderson, H. & Goolishian, H. (1988). Human systems as linguistic systems: preliminary and evolving ideas about the implications for clinical theory. *Family Process, 27*, 371–393.

Anderson, R.D. (1992). *Universities and elites in Britain since 1800.* London: Macmillan.

Antaki, C. (1994). *Arguing and explaining.* London: Sage.

Atkinson, J.M. & Heritage, J. (Eds.), (1984). *Structure of social action.* Cambridge: Cambridge University Press.

Baird, J. (1991). Looking at the man in Sherman and cutting the cloth to fit. *Alba, 1(4)*, 18–23.

Banister, P., Burman, E., Parker, I., Taylor, M., & Tindall, C. (1994). *Qualitative methods in psychology: A research guide.* Buckingham: Open University Press.

Bannister, D. & Fransella, F. (1986). *Inquiring man: The psychology of personal constructs. (3rd Ed.).* London: Croom Helm.

Barker, R.G. & Wright, H.F. (1951). *One Boy's Day.* New York: Harper.

Barley, S.R. (1983). Semiotics and the study of occupational and organisational cultures. *Administrative Science Quarterly, 28*, 393–413.

Beattie, G. (1992). *We are the people: Journeys through the heart of Protestant Ulster.* London: Heinemann.

Beloff, H. (1980). A place not so far apart: Conclusions of an outsider. In J. Harbison & J. Harbison (Eds.), *A society under stress. Children and Young people in Northern Ireland.* Shepton Mallet, Somerset: Open Books.

Beloff, H. (1985). *Camera culture.* Oxford: Basil Blackwell.

Beloff, H. (1988). The eye and me: Self-portraits of eminent photographers, *Philosophical Psychology, 1,* 295–311.

Beloff, H. (1989). A tradition of threatened identities. In J. Harbison (Ed.), *Growing up in Northern Ireland.* Belfast: Stranmillis College, Learning Resources Unit.

Beloff, H. (1990). Rembrandt's impression management. In *Rembrandt by himself.* Glasgow Museums & Art Galleries.

Beloff, H. (1994a). Reading visual rhetoric, *The Psychologist: Bulletin of the British Psychological Society, 7,* 495–499.

Beloff, H. (1994b). Reading visual rhetoric: A reply, *The Psychologist: Bulletin of the British Psychological Society, 7,* 510.

Berger, J. (1972). *Ways of seeing.* Harmondsworth: Penguin.

Billig, M. (1987). *Arguing and thinking: A rhetorical approach to social psychology.* Cambridge: Cambridge University Press.

Billig, M. (1989). The argumentative nature of holding strong views: A case study. *European Journal of Social Psychology, 19,* 203–222.

Billig, M. (1990). Collective memory, ideology and the British Royal Family. In D. Middleton and D. Edwards (Ed.), *Collective remembering.* Sage: London.

Billig, M. (1991). *Ideology & Opinions. Studies in rhetorical psychology.* London: Sage.

Billig, M. (1992). *Talking of the royal family.* London: Routledge.

Billig, M. (1994). Reading art and corrupted pleasures: Commentary on H. Beloff "Reading visual rhetoric". *The Psychologist: Bulletin of the British Psychological Society, 7,* 500–501.

Billig, M., Condor, S., Edwards, D., Gane, M., Middleton, D., & Radley, A.R. (1988). *Ideological dilemmas: A social psychology of everyday thinking.* Sage: London.

Blechman, E. (1982). Conventional wisdom about familiar contributions to substance abuse. *American Journal of Drug and Alcohol Abuse, 9,* 35–53.

Bourdieu, P. (1984). *Distinction: A social critique of the judgment of taste.* London: Routledge & Kegan Paul.

Bowlby, J. (1988). *A secure base.* London: Tavistock.

Bowles, G. & Duelli Klein, R. (Eds.), (1983). *Theories of women's studies.* London: Routledge & Kegan Paul.

Bradley, U. (Ed.), (1987). *Applied marketing and social research 2nd ed.* Chichester: Wiley.

Brewer, J.D. (1992). The Public and the Police. In P. Stringer & G. Robinson (Eds.), *Social attitudes in Northern Ireland. The second report, 1991–1992.* Belfast: Blackstaff Press.

British Psychological Society (1993). Ethical principles. *The Psychologist, 6(1),* 33–35.

Bromley, D.B. (1986). *The case-study method in psychology and related disciplines.* Chichester: Wiley.

Brown, G. & Yule, G. (1983). *Discourse analysis.* Cambridge: Cambridge University Press.

Bruce, S. (1992). *The red hand. Protestant paramilitaries in Northern Ireland.* Oxford: Oxford University Press.

Bryman, A. (1988). *Quantity and quality in social research.* London: Unwin Hyman.

Buerhaus, P. (1986). The economics of caring; challenges and new opportunities for nursing. *Topics in Clinical Nursing, 8(2),* 13–21.

Burgess, R.G. (1984). *In the field: An introduction to field research.* London: Allen and Unwin.

Cairns, E. (1987). *Caught in crossfire. Children and the Northern Ireland conflict.* Belfast: Appletree Press.

Canter, D. (1988). Review of camera culture. *Journal of Environmental Psychology, 8,* 339–342.

Canter, D. (1994). Ways of seeing: Comments on Halla Beloff's "Reading visual rhetoric", *The Psychologist: Bulletin of the British Psychological Society, 11*, 502–503.

Cath, S. (1986). Clinical vignettes: A range of grandparental experiences. *Journal of Geriatric Psychiatry, 19*, 57–68.

Cecchin, G. (1987). Hypothesizing, circularity and neutrality revisited: An invitation to curiosity. *Family Process, 26*, 405–413.

Cermak, T. (1986). *Diagnosing and treating co-dependence.* Minneapolis: Johnson Institute Books.

Charmaz, C. (1990). Discovering chronic illness: Using grounded theory, *Social Science and Medicine, 30(11)*, 1161–1172.

Colaizzi, P. (1978). Psychological research as the phenomenologist views it. In R. Valle & M. King (Eds.), *Existential phenomenological alternatives for psychology.* New York: Oxford University Press.

Colley, L. (1992). *Britons: Forging the Nation 1707–1837.* New Haven: Yale University Press.

Conway, M. & Ross, M. (1984). Getting what you want by revising what you had. *Journal of Personality and Social Psychology, 47*, 738–748.

Costain-Schou, K. & Hewison, J. (1994). Issues of interpretive methodology. *Human Systems, 5*, 45–68.

Coulter, J. (1992). Bilmes on internal states: A critical commentary. *Journal for the theory of social behaviour, 22(3)*, 239–251.

Cronin, S.N. & Harrison, B. (1988). Importance of nurse caring behaviours as perceived by patients after myocardial infarction. *Heart and Lung, 17(4)*, 374–380.

De Waele, J.P. (1986). Individual psychology: Methodology. In R. Harré and R. Lamb (Eds.), *Dictionary of personality and social psychology.* Oxford: Blackwell.

Denzin, N.K., & Lincoln, Y.S. (Eds.), (1994). *Handbook of qualitative research.* London: Sage.

Dilthey, W. (1894). *Descriptive psychology and historical understanding.* English translation. The Hague: Martinus Nijhoff, 1977.

Doise, W. (1986). *Levels of explanation in social psychology.* Cambridge: Cambridge University Press.

Doise, W., Clemence, A., & Lorenzi-Coldi, F. (1993). *The quantitative analysis of social representations.* London: Harvester Wheatsheaf.

Dorment, R. (1992). Will the real Ms Sherman stand up? *Daily Telegraph,* 14 August.

Edwards, D. & Middleton, D. (1988). Conversational remembering and family relationships: how children learn to remember. *Journal of Social and Personal Relationships, 5*, 3–25.

Edwards, D. & Potter, J. (1993a). *Discursive Psychology.* Sage: London.

Edwards, D. & Potter, J. (1993b). Language and causation: A discursive action model of description and attribution. *Psychological Review, 100*, 23–41.

Edwards, D., Middleton, D., & Potter, J. (1992). Towards a discursive psychology of remembering. *The Psychologist, 15*, 441–446.

Ericsson, K.A. & Simon, H.A. (1993). *Protocol analysis: verbal reports as data (2nd Ed).* Cambridge, Massachusetts: MIT Press.

Farr, R. (1990). Social representations as widespread beliefs. In C. Fraser & G. Gaskell (Eds.), *The social psychological study of widespread beliefs.* Oxford: Clarendon Press.

Farr, R.M. (1996). *The roots of modern social psychology.* Oxford: Blackwell.

Farrow, J. (1987). The use of vignette analysis of dangerous driving situations involving alcohol to differentiate adolescent DWI offenders and high school drivers. *American Journal of Drug and Alcohol Abuse, 13*, 157–174.

Fielding, N.G. & Lee, R.M. (1991). *Using computers in qualitative research.* London: Sage.

Finn, G.P.T. (1990a). *"The writing on the wall": Ideology and the Northern Irish conflict.* Paper to the annual conference of the British Psychological Society, Swansea, April, 1990.

Finn, G.P.T. (1990b). *The role of conspiracy theory in the ideology of Paisleyism*. Paper presented to the London Conference of the British Psychological Society, December, 1990.

Finn, G.P.T. (1992). *Societal psychology: Some approaches*. Paper to the annual conference of the Scottish Branch of the British Psychological Society.

Finn, G.P.T. (1994). Sporting symbols, sporting identities: Soccer and intergroup conflict in Scotland and Northern Ireland. In I.S. Wood (Ed.), *Scotland and Ulster*. Edinburgh, Mercat Press.

Finn, G.P.T. (1996). *Visual images as social representations of the Northern Ireland conflict*. Paper to the XXV International Congress of Psychology, Montreal, Canada.

Finn, G.P.T. (1997). Portraying group identities in the Northern Irish Conflict. Manuscript submitted for publication.

Fowler, F.J. & Mangione, T.W. (1990). *Standardised survey interviewing: minimising interviewer related error*. London: Sage.

Fowler, R. (1986). *Linguistic criticism*. Oxford: Oxford University Press.

Fransella, F. & Bannister, D. (1977). *A manual of repertory grid technique*. London: Academic Press.

Fromm, E. (1962). *The art of loving*. New York: Bantam Books.

Gadow, S. (1980). Existential advocacy. In S.F. Spicker & S. Gadow (Eds.), *Nursing: Ideas and images, opening dialogue with the humanities*. New York: Springer-Verlag.

Gallagher, A.M. (1987). Psychological approaches to the Northern Ireland conflict, *Canadian Journal of Irish Studies, 12*, 21–32.

Gallagher, A.M. (1992). Civil liberties and the state. In P. Stringer & G. Robinson (Eds.), *Social attitudes in Northern Ireland. The second report, 1991–1992*. Belfast: Blackstaff Press.

Gallagher, A.M. *Identity and ideology in social conflict: The case of Northern Ireland*. (Unpublished doctoral thesis, Queen's University: Belfast, 1986).

Gallagher, C. & Hanratty, A. (1989). The war on the walls, *Ulster Folklife, 35*, 100–108.

Garber, M. (1993). *Vested interests*. Harmondsworth: Penguin.

Gaskell, G. & Fraser, C. (1990). The social psychological study of widespread beliefs. In C. Fraser & G. Gaskell (Eds.), *The social psychological study of widespread beliefs*. Oxford: Clarendon Press.

Geertz, C. (1973). Thick description: toward an interpretive theory of culture. In C. Geertz, *The interpretation of cultures: Selected essays*. New York: Basic Books.

Gilbert, G.N. & Mulkay, M. (1984). *Opening Pandora's box: A sociological analysis of scientists' discourse*. Cambridge: Cambridge University Press.

Glaser, B.G. & Strauss, A.L. (1967). *The discovery of grounded theory: Strategies for qualitative research*. New York: Aldine.

Goffman, E. (1964). *Stigma: The management of spoiled identity*. Harmondsworth: Penguin.

Goffman, E. (1967). *Interaction ritual*. Harmondsworth: Allen Lane/The Penguin Press.

Goffman, E. (1979). *Gender advertisements*. Basingstoke: Macmillan.

Goodwin, B. (1982). *Using political ideas*. Chichester: Wiley.

Gossop, M. & Grant, M. (1991). A six country survey of the content and structure of heroin treatment programmes using methadone. *British Journal of Addiction, 86*, 1151–1160.

Guelke, A. & Wright, F. (1992). On a 'British' withdrawal from Northern Ireland. In P. Stringer & G. Robinson (Eds.), *Social attitudes in Northern Ireland. The second report, 1991–1992*. Belfast: Blackstaff Press.

Hammersley, M. (1992). *What's wrong with ethnography?* London: Routledge.

Harbinson, J. (1989). (Ed.), *Growing up in Northern Ireland*. Belfast: Stranmillis College Learning Resources Unit.

Harding, S. (1991). *Whose science: Whose knowledge? Thinking from women's lives*. Milton Keynes: Open University Press.

Harding, S. (Ed.), (1987). *Feminism and methodology*. Milton Keynes: Open University Press.

Harré, R. (1979). *Social being*. Oxford: Blackwell.

Harré, R. (1986). *The social construction of emotions*. Oxford: Blackwell.

Harré, R. (1979). *Social being*. Oxford: Basil Blackwell.

Harré, R. & Secord, P.F. (1972). *The explanation of social behaviour*. Oxford: Blackwell.

Harrison, R. (1972). Understanding your organisation's culture. *Harvard Business Review*, May– June, 1972.

Hayes, N.J. (1991). *Social identity, social representations and organisational cultures*. PhD thesis, CNAA/Huddersfield.

Hayes, N.J. (1995). *Psychology in perspective*. Basingstoke: Macmillan.

Heider, F. (1958). *The psychology of interpersonal relations*. Wiley, New York.

Henwood, K.L. (1993). Women and later life: The discursive construction of identities within family relationships. *Journal of Ageing Studies*, *7(3)*, 303–319.

Henwood, K.L. & Pidgeon, N.F. (1992). Qualitative research and psychological theorizing. *British Journal of Psychology*, *83*, 97–111.

Henwood, K.L. & Pidgeon, N.F. (1994). Beyond the qualitative paradigm: a framework for introducing diversity in qualitative psychology. *Journal of Community and Applied Social Psychology*, *4(4)*, 225–238.

Henwood, K.L. & Pidgeon, N.F. (1995a). Grounded theory and psychological research. *The psychologist: Bulletin of the British Psychological Society*, *8(3)*, 115–118.

Henwood, K.L. & Pidgeon, N.F. (1995b). Remaking the link: qualitative research and feminist standpoint theory. *Feminism and Psychology*, *5(1)*, 7–30.

Heritage, J. (1984). *Garfunkel and ethnomethodology*. Polity Press: Cambridge.

Heverly, M., Fitt, D., & Newman, F. (1984). Constructing case vignettes for evaluating clinical judgement: An empirical model. *Evaluation and Proram Planning*, *7*, 45–55.

Hjortso, Butler, B., Clemmesen, L., Jepsen, P., Kastrup, M., Vilmar, T., & Bech, P. (1989). The use of case vignettes in studies of inter-rater reliability of psychiatric target syndromes and diagnoses. *Acta Psychiatrica Scandinavia*, *80*, 632–638.

Hollway, W. (1984). Gender difference and the production of subjectivity. In J. Henriques et al. (Eds.), *Changing the subject*. London: Methuen.

Home Office (1990). *Statistics on the misuse of drugs*. London: HMSO.

Keenan, B. (1992). *An evil cradling*. London: Vintage.

Kelly, G.A. (1955). *The psychology of personal constructs*. New York: Norton.

Kelly, G.A. (1963). *A theory of personality: The psychology of personal constructs*. New York: Norton.

Kidder, L.H. (1981). Qualitative research and quasi-experimental frameworks. In M.B. Brewer & B.E. Collins (Eds.), *Scientific inquiry and the social sciences*. San Francisco: Jossey Bass.

Kuhn, T.S. (1962). *The structure of scientific revolutions*. Chicago: University of Chicago Press.

Lakoff, G. & Johnson, M. (1980). *Metaphors we live by*. Chicago: University of Chicago Press.

Larson, P.J. (1981). Oncology patients and professional nurses perceptions of important nursing care behaviours (Doctoral dissertation University of California). *Dissertation Abstracts*, *12*, 42.

Latour, B. (1987). *Science in Action*. Milton Keynes: Open University Press.

Leininger, M. (1984). Care; the essence of nursing and health. In M. Leininger (Ed.), *Care; the essence of nursing and health*. Thorofare, New Jersey: Charles B. Slack.

Lenzner, A., & Aronson, A. (1972). Psychiatric vignettes from a coronary care unit. *Psychosomatics*, *13*, 179–184.

Lewin, K. (1947). Feedback problems of social diagnosis and action. *Human Relations*, *1*, 147–153.

Lincoln, Y.S. & Guba, E.G. (1985). *Naturalistic inquiry*. Beverly Hills: Sage.

Loftus, B. (1990). *Mirrors. William III & Mother Ireland*. Dundrum, Co Down: Picture Press.

Loftus, B. (1994). *Mirrors: Orange & green*. Dundrum, Co Down: Picture Press.

Lowenthal, M.F., Thurner, M., Chiriboga, D. et al. (1976). *Four stages of life*. San Francisco: Jossey-Bass.

Lundberg, C.C. (1990). Surfacing organisational culture. *Journal of Managerial Psychology, 5,* 19–26.

Lutz, C.A. (1988). *Unnatural emotions.* Chicago and London: Chicago University Press.

Magee, B. (1973). *Popper.* London: Fontana.

Marcel, G. (1971). *The philosophy of existence* (translated R.F. Grabow). Philadelphia: University of Pennsylvania Press.

Marsh, P., Rosser, E., & Harré, R. (1977). *The rules of disorder.* London: Routledge and Kegan Paul.

Marshall, C. (1985). Appropriate criteria of trustworthiness and goodness for qualitative research on education organisations. *Quality and Quantity, 19,* 353–373.

Massarik, F. (1981). The interviewing process re-examined. In P. Reason and J. Rowan (Eds.), *Human inquiry: A source book of new paradigm research.* Chichester: Wiley.

Mayer, D. (1985). *Oncology nurses versus cancer patients perceptions of nurse caring behaviours: a replication study.* M.S.N. thesis, Yale School of Nursing.

McCulloch, A.W. (1992). Adjustment to old age in a changing society. Ph.D. Thesis, University of Southampton; cited in G. Stokes. *On being old: The psychology of later life.* Brighton: Falmer Press.

Mead, G.H. (1934). *Mind, Self and Society.* Chicago: University of Chicago.

Middleton, D. & Edwards, D. (1990). *Collective remembering.* London: Sage.

Miles, M.B. & Huberman, A.M. (1994). *Qualitative data analysis: A sourcebook of new methods (2nd ed).* Beverly Hills: Sage.

Misener, T. (1986). Towards a nursing definition of child maltreatment using seriousness vignettes. *Advances in Nursing Science, 8,* 1–14.

Mishler, E.G. (1986). *Research Interviewing.* Cambridge: Harvard University Press.

Moscovici, S. (1984). The phenomenon of social representations. In R. Farr & S. Moscovici (Eds.), *Social representations.* Cambridge/Paris: Cambridge University Press/Editions de la Maison des Sciences de l'Homme.

Moscovici, S. & Hewstone, M. (1983). Social representations and social expectations: From the "naïve" to the "amateur" scientist. In M. Hewstone (ed) Attribution theory & functional extensions. Oxford: Blackwell.

Nairn, T. (1988). *The enchanted glass: Britain and its monarchy.* London: Hutchinson Radius.

National Graves Association (1985). *The Last Post (3rd ed.).* Dublin: National Graves Association.

Neisser, U. (1981). John Dean's memory: A case study. *Cognition, 9,* 1–22.

Nelson, S. (1984). *Ulster's uncertain defenders. Loyalists and the Northern Ireland conflict.* Belfast: Blackstaff Press.

Nicolson, P. (1986). Developing a feminist approach to depression following childbirth. In S. Wilkinson (Ed.), *Feminist social psychology: Developing theory and practice.* Milton Keynes: Open University.

Nicolson, P. (1990). Understanding postnatal depression: A mother-centred approach. *Journal of Advanced Nursing, 15,* 689–695.

O Connor, F. (1993). *In search of a state. Catholics in Northern Ireland.* Belfast: Blackstaff Press.

Oakley, A. (1979). *Becoming a mother.* Oxford: Martin Robertson.

Oiler, C. (1982). The phenomenological approach in nursing research. *Nursing Research, 31,* 178–181.

Orford, J., Rigby, K., Miller, A., Tod, A., Bennett, G., & Velleman, R. (1992). Ways of coping with excessive drug use in the family: A provisional typology. *Journal of Community and Applied Social Psychology, 2(3),* 163–183.

Osborne, R.D. (1991). Discrimination and fair employment. In P. Stringer & G. Robinson (Eds.), *Social attitudes in Northern Ireland, 1990–1991 Edition* Belfast: Blackstaff Press.

Osgood, C.E., Saporta, S., & Nunnally, J. (1956). Evaluative assertion analysis. *Litera 3*, 47–102.

Paolino, T. & McGrady, B. (1977). *The alcoholic marriage: Alternative processes*. New York: Grune and Stratton.

Parker, I. (1992). *Discourse dynamics: Critical analysis for social and individual psychology*. London: Routledge.

Parker, T. (1993). *May the Lord in his mercy be kind to Belfast*. London: Jonathan Cape.

Parrott, J. & Harré, R. (1992). Smedslundian suburbs in Wittengenstein's city. *Psychological Inquiry, 2*, 358–361.

Paterson, J. & Zderad, L. (1976). *Humanistic nursing*. New York: John Wiley & Sons.

Penfield, W. & Rasmussen, T. (1950). *The cerebral cortex of man: A clinical study of localisation*. Boston, MA: Little, Brown.

Peterson, C., Semmel, A., von Baeyer, C., Abramson, L.Y., Metalsky, G.I., & Seligman, M.E.P. (1982). the attributional style questionnaire. *Cognitive Therapy and Research, 6*, 287–300.

Peterson, M. (1988). The norms and values held by three groups of nurses concerning psychosocial nursing practice. *International Journal of Nursing Studies, 25(2)*, 85–103.

Pidgeon, N.F., Blockley, D.I., & Turner, B.A. (1988). Site investigations: lessons from a late discovery of hazardous waste. *The Structural Engineer, 66(19)*, 311–315.

Pidgeon, N.F., Turner, B.A., & Blockley, D.I. (1991). The use of grounded theory for conceptual analysis in knowledge elicitation. *International Journal of Man–Machine Studies, 35*, 151–173.

Pointon, M. (1990). *Naked authority: The body in western painting 1830–1908*. Cambridge: Cambridge University Press.

Potter, J. & Edwards, D. (1990). Nigel Lawson's tent: discourse analysis, attribution theory and the social psychology of fact. *European Journal of Social Psychology, 20*, 24–40.

Potter, J. & Wetherell, M. (1987). *Discourse and social psychology: Beyond attitudes and beliefs*. London: Sage.

Potter, J. & Reicher, S. (1987). Discourses of community and conflict: the organization of social categories in accounts of a "riot". *British Journal of Social Psychology, 26*, 25–40.

Potter, J. & Wetherell, M. (1987). *Discourse and social psychology*. London: Sage.

Potter, J. & Wetherell, M. (1995). Discourse analysis. In J.A. Smith, R. Harré & L. Van Langenhove (Eds.), *Rethinking Methods in Psychology*. London: Sage.

Rabinow, P. (Ed) (1984). *The Foucault reader*. Harmondsworth: Penguin.

Ray, M. (1981). A philosophical analysis of caring within nursing. In M. Leininger (Ed.), *Care; the essence of nursing and health*. Thorofare, New Jersey: Charles B. Slack.

Reason, P. & Rowan, J. (Eds), (1981). *Human inquiry: A sourcebook of new paradigm research*. Chichester: Wiley.

Reinharz, S. (1983). Experiential analysis: a contribution to feminist research. In G. Bowles & R. Duelli Klein (Eds.), *Theories of women's studies*. London: Routledge and Kegan Paul.

Rennie, D.L., Phillips, J.R., & Quartaro, G.K. (1988). Grounded theory: A promising approach to conceptualization in psychology? *Canadian Psychology, 29(2)*, 139–150.

Ribordy, S., Camras, L., Stefani, R., & Spaccarelli, S. (1988). Vignettes for emotional recognition research and affective therapy with children. *Journal of Clinical Child Psychology, 17*, 322–325.

Riessman, C.K. (1993). *Narrative analysis*. Newbury Park, CA: Sage.

Robinson, W.P. (1994). Writing Verbal Sense: A commentary on Halla Beloff's "Reading Visual Rhetoric", *The Psychologist: Bulletin of the British Psychological Society, 11*, 504–505.

Robson, C. (1993). *Real world research*. Oxford: Blackwell.

Robson, S. & Foster A. (1989). *Qualitative research in action*. London: Arnold.

Rolston, B. (1987). Politics, paintings and popular culture: the political wall murals of Northern Ireland. *Media, Culture and Society, 9,* 5–28.

Rolston, B. (1988). Contemporary political wall murals in the North of Ireland: "Drawing Support". *Éire-Ireland, 23,* 3–18.

Rolston, B. (1992). *Drawing support. Murals in the North of Ireland.* Belfast: Beyond the Pale Publications.

Rosenthal, R. (1996). *Experimenter effects in behavioural research.* New York: Appleton, Century Crofts.

Ross, M. (1989). Relation of implicit theories to the construction of personal histories. *Psychological Review, 96,* 341–357.

Routh, D. & King, K. (1972). Social class bias in clinical judgement. *Journal of Consulting and Clinical Psychology, 38,* 202–207.

Saunders, G. (1989). *The nude: A new perspective.* The Herbert Press.

Sayers, J. (1994). Reading visual rhetoric from a psychoanalytic and feminist viewpoint. *The Psychologist: Bulletin of the British Psychological Society, 11,* 506–507.

Scarbrough, E. (1990). Attitudes, social representations, and ideology. In C. Fraser & G. Gaskell (Eds.), *The social psychological study of widespread beliefs.* Oxford: Clarendon Press.

Schein, E.H. (1990). Organisational culture. *American Psychologist, 45,* 109–119.

Schofield, L. & Oakes, J. (1975). Social class bias in clinical judgement and recommendation for treatment using the biographical vignette techniques. *Psychological Reports, 37,* 75–82.

Segal, L. (1986). *The dream of reality: Heinz Von Foerster's constructivism.* New York: Norton.

Sherman, C. (1987). *Catalogue.* Whitney Museum of American Art.

Sherrard, C. (1988). Rhetorical weapons: Chomsky's attack on Skinner. *Educational Psychology, 8,* 197–205.

Sherrard, C. (1995). Social identity and aesthetic taste. *Philosophical Psychology, 8,* 139–153.

Sherrard, C. & Bousfield, C. (1991). Aesthetic taste and group identity. *British Psychological Society Abstracts.* (p. 2).

Shotter, J. (1993a). *Cultural politics of everyday life.* Milton Keynes: Open University.

Shotter, J. (1993b). *Conversational realities.* London: Sage.

Silverman, D. (1993). *Interpreting qualitative data: Methods for analysing talk, text and interaction.* London: Sage.

Silverman, I. (1977). *The human subject in the psychological laboratory.* New York: Pergamon.

Smith, J.A. (1990). Transforming identities: A repertory grid case-study of the transition to motherhood. *British Journal of Medical Psychology, 63,* 239–253.

Smith, J.A. (1991). Conceiving selves: A case study of changing identities during the transition to motherhood. *Journal of Language and Social Psychology, 10,* 225–243.

Smith, J.A. (1992). Pregnancy and the transition to motherhood. In P. Nicolson & J. Usher (Eds.), *The psychology of women's health and health care.* London: Macmillan.

Smith, J.A. (1994). Reconstructing selves: An analysis of discrepancies between women's contemporaneous & retrospective accounts of the transition to motherhood. *British Journal of Psychology, 85,* 371–392.

Smith, J.A., Harré, R., & Van Langenhove, L. (1995). Idiography and the case-study. In J.A. Smith, R. Harré, & L. Van Langenhove (Eds.), *Rethinking Psychology,* London: Sage.

Smith, J.K. (1989). *The nature of social and educational inquiry: Empiricism versus interpretation.* Norwood, NJ: Ablex.

Spence, J. (1995). *Cultural Sniping.* London: Routledge.

Spinelli, E. (1989). *The interpreted world: An introduction to phenomenological psychology.* London: Sage.

Spurling, F. (1988). *Stevie Smith: A critical biography.* London: Faber & Faber.

Sriram, T., Chandrashekar, C., Issac, M., Srinivasa Murthy, R., Kishore Kumar, K., Moily, S., & Shanmughem, V. (1990). Development of case vignettes to assess the mental health training of primary care medical officer. *Acta Psychiatrica Scandinavia, 82,* 174–177.

Stearns, C.Z., & Stearns, P.N. (1987). *Emotions and social change.* New York: Holmes and Meier.

Stelmachers, Z., & Sherman, R. (1990). Use of case vignettes in suicide risk assessment. *Suicide and life-threatening behaviour, 20,* 65–84.

Stone, W., & Klein, L. (1989). The clinical vignette: Use in teaching and evaluation of group therapists. *Group, 13,* 3–9.

Stratton, P. (1991). Attributions, baseball and consumer behaviour. *Journal of the Market Research Society, 33,* 163–178.

Stratton, P. (1992). Selling constructionism to market research. *Human Systems, 3,* 253–273.

Stratton, P.M., Heard, D.H., Hanks, H.G., Munton, A.G., Brewin, C.R., & Davidson, C. (1986). Coding causal beliefs in natural discourse. *British Journal of Social Psychology, 25,* 299–313.

Stratton, P.M., Munton, A.G., Hanks, H.G.I., Heard, D.H., & Davidson, C. (1988). *Leeds Attributional Coding System (LACS) Manual.* Leeds, LFTRC.

Strauss, A.L. (1987). *Qualitative analysis for social scientists.* Cambridge: CUP.

Strauss, A.L. & Corbin, J. (1990). *Basics of qualitative research: Grounded theory procedures and techniques.* Newbury Park: Sage.

Strauss, E. (1966). *Phenomenological psychology.* New York: Basic Books.

Sundberg, S., Barbaree, H., & Marshall, W. (1991). Victim blame and the disinhibition of sexual arousal to rape vignettes. *Violence and Victims, 6,* 103–120.

Swanson, K.M. (1990). Providing care in the NICU: sometimes an act of love. *Advances in Nursing Science, 13, 1,* 60–73.

Tajfel, H. (1982). *Social identity and intergroup relations.* Cambridge: Cambridge University Press.

Tannen, D. (1986). *Conversational style.* Norwood, NJ: Ablex.

Tesch, R. (1989). *Textbase alpha user's manual.* Desert Hot Springs: Qualitative Research Management.

Thayer, L. (1977). Variables for developing simulated counselling vignettes. *Counsellor Education and Supervision, 17,* 65–68.

Tseelon, E. (1992). What is beautiful is bad: Physical attraction as stigma. *The Journal for the theory of Social Behaviour, 22,* 295–309.

Turner, B.A. (1981). Some practical aspects of qualitative data analysis: One way of organising some of the cognitive processes associated with the generation of grounded theory. *Quality and Quantity, 15,* 225–247.

Turner, J.C., Hogg, M.A., Oakes, P.J., Reicher, S.D., & Wetherell, M.S. (1987). *Rediscovering the social group. A self-categorisation theory.* Oxford: Basil Blackwell.

Urban, M. (1992). *Big boys' rules. The SAS and the secret struggle against the IRA.* London: Faber & Faber.

Van Maanen, J. & Barley, S.R. (1985). Cultural organisation: fragments of a theory. In P.J. Frost et al. (Eds), *Organisational culture.* London: Saga.

Velleman, R. (1992). *Alcohol and the family.* London: Institute of Alcohol Studies Occasional Paper.

Velleman, R., Bennett, G., Miller, R., Orford, J., Rigby, K., & Tod, A. (1993). The families of problem drug users: the accounts of fifty close relatives. *Addiction, 88,* 1275–1283.

von Cranach, M. (1981). The psychological study of goal-directed action: basic issues. In M. von Cranach and R. Harré (eds), *The analysis of action.* Cambridge: Cambridge University Press.

Watson, J. (1985). *Nursing: Human science and human care. A theory of nursing.* Norwalk: Appleton Century Crofts.

Weber, R.P. (1985). *Basic content analysis.* London: Sage.

Weiers, R.M. (1988). *Marketing research* (2nd ed.). Prentice Hall: New Jersey.

Weiss, S. (1972). Some thoughts and clinical vignettes on translocation of an analytic practice. *International Journal of Psycho-analysis, 53,* 503–513.

Weitzman, E.A. & Miles, M.B. (1995). *Computer programs for qualitative data analysis: A software sourcebook.* Newbury Park, CA: Sage.

Westman, M. & Etzion, D. (1990). The career success/personal failure phenomenon as perceived by others: Comparing vignettes of male and female managers. *Journal of Vocational Behaviour, 37,* 209–224.

Wetherell, M. (1994). Good art, bad art, social constructionism and humanism: A commentary on 'Reading visual rhetoric' by Halla Beloff. *The Psychologist: Bulletin of the British Psychological Society, 11,* 508–509.

Wetherell, M., Stiven, H., & Potter, J. (1987). Unequal egalitarianism: A preliminary study of discourses concerning gender and employment opportunities. *British Journal of Social Psychology, 26,* 59–71.

Wilkinson, D. (1986). *Feminist social psychology.* Milton Keynes: Open University Press.

Williams, M. (1976). Presenting oneself in talk: The disclosure of occupation. In R. Harré (Ed), *Life sentences.* Chichester: Wiley.

Williamson, J. (1978). *Decoding advertisements.* Boyars.

Wittgenstein, L. (1953). *Philosophical investigations.* Oxford: Blackwell.

Wooffitt, R. (1992). *Telling tales of the unexpected: The organization of factual discourse.* Hemel Hempstead: Harvester Wheatsheaf.

Woolgar, S. (1988). *Science: The very idea.* London: Tavistock.

Wyatt, F. (1964). The reconstruction of the individual and of the collective past. In R.W. White (Ed.), *The study of lives: Essays on personality in honor of Henry A. Murray.* New York: Atherton Press.

Yager, J., Linn, L., Lweake, B., Gastaldo, G., & Palkowski, C. (1986). Initial clinical judgements by internists, family physicians, and psychiatrists in response to patient vignettes: II Ordering of laboratory tests, consultations and treatments. *General Hospital Psychiatry, 8,* 152–158.

Zimmerman, D.H. (1992). The interactional organization of calls for emergency assistance. In P. Drew & J. Heritage (Eds.). *Talk at work: Interaction in institutional settings.* Cambridge: Cambridge University Press.

Author Index

Subject Index